# More Than Her Share

*A Real Conversation of Hope When the
Diagnosis is Too Much*

Janelle LaRae

*Illustrated by*
Abigail Grace George

Janelle LaRae Books

# Praise for Janelle LaRae

"This book isn't just for people dealing with cancer. It will resonate with anyone who has faced difficult challenges, all while juggling the demands of everyday life. It offers a quiet reminder that hope brings us peace and gives us the strength to endure."

— Sarah Van Dyken

"Janelle's words were so authentic that I often found myself in the room with her, witnessing her pain and feeling her struggle as though it were my own. My heart connected with her and all women who live life bravely and beautifully under times of suffocating distress."

— LeAnn Donohue

"I love the way it is written and the details. It's not just a book about [a] cancer journey, there's a lot of depth. Anyone who reads it, I feel, will find something they can relate to."

— Chanthy Birch

"It is a How To Survive guide for cancer. It normalizes the hard parts of the journey."

— Abigail George

"I heard your words in my head as I read them. I imagined I could see you . . . as your story unfolded. I cried with you at times and I learned so much!! . . . I applaud your stubborn strength and thank our precious God for you."

— Debra McDorman-Wilson

"I felt like you were talking to me. Just telling me your story, not writing in a way other than how you would have a personal conversation with a friend over coffee."

"I do think each person who reads this book will connect with parts of your story, and other people with other parts. This all comes through so real, I would not want less of your story."

"A mix of powerful and real and brave and vulnerable."

— Kari Taiclet

# Contents

*More Than Her Share*

*More Than Her Share is dedicated to my husband and daughters. You were with me through each journey. I couldn't have done it alone.*

# Preface

This is a story about a journey. It began with a phone call. They called to inform me I would carry cancer in my backpack on this journey. I would also carry other burdens that made cancer feel like a feather. Sometimes the pack was too heavy, sometimes I barely felt the weight, but it continued with me.

I thought I could say I finished the journey, but it isn't really over. I survived the trip with cancer, but it's not the ending that you came for. You want to know *how* I survived. How did I manage to get out of bed each morning knowing I had cancer and not knowing what it would do to me? How am I here? What did I tell myself each day to avoid simply giving up? How did I keep walking with that heavy pack?

Cancer touches most people in some way. Whether you have battled it within your own body or have watched someone you love fight each day, it is a challenge. It is a thief. It takes a strong body and mind to simply keep moving. I hope my story illustrates how I kept moving. I hope my raw emotions help you to accept your own. I hope my victories give you hope. This story reveals what is happening behind the brave face and the hopeful smile. Every person battling cancer is fighting two battles. One is the physical - the one most people can see and mark on their calendar. The second battle is the mental - it is the self-talk, the doubt, the fear and the fight for hope amidst the scary stories running on a loop. I fought both battles while simultaneously battling other health issues that snuck in between cancer diagnoses. I pray my story helps you with your own journey.

$\sim$

This is my story. This is how I saw my world during these seasons. If I were to go through all these experiences again, I would have a different story. I would see things differently. These journeys took over 8 years. I am a different person at the end than I was at the beginning. I handled the difficult days differently. I don't think the way I dealt with anything was right or wrong, it was the way I dealt with it. The difficult things come and we do the best we know how. We find hope and refuge wherever we can. Today, that place of hope may look different than tomorrow.

During these seasons, I felt many things. They were my feelings, my perceptions. I observed myself and my world. I'm confident the other people in this story have different versions than me. I wrote in my journals about everything I was experiencing during this time. I used those notes to write this book. There are some statements I made in the moment that I don't completely agree with today, but they were true then, so I didn't change them.

# Chapter 1

## *Missed Appointment*

I knew I should have tried to call before today, but I couldn't recall the phone number. I kept hoping they would mail a reminder or call to remind me. They usually remind me. They don't want you to miss your appointment. Why didn't they remind me? I have a good memory. I'm the champion at that game. I'm pretty sure it was supposed to be today. Maybe I'm remembering something else.

I finally called and spoke to someone at 2:00. My

appointment was 8:00 this morning. I rescheduled my second mammogram for September 14, 2012. It will be on a Friday, so I won't have to take a day off of work. I'm a teacher. It sure would have been nice to get it over with today, but that's what I get for procrastinating.

When my grandma Hazel on my mom's side was 64, she was diagnosed with breast cancer. I was 14, and only remember bits and pieces. She had surgery and chemotherapy. I remember going to the hospital once to see her after her negative reaction to the chemo. I visited her at least once a week growing up. She watched my brother and me when my mom had to go into town to do errands. During that time, she lived on a dairy farm. She always had a huge garden. We spent hours sitting on her porch, helping her snap beans for canning. During Christmas, we baked sugar cookies. There was no limit to the candies and frosting she let us pile on our cookies.

In my early visits to my doctors, the fact of my grandma's breast cancer didn't raise any red flags. Since my mom never had breast cancer, no one was worried about me. I fell into the classic category with most other women, I would get my first mammogram at 40. In 2011, during my yearly check-up, I told my gynecologist about Grandma Hazel's second bout with breast cancer at the age of 82. She completed her radiation treatment in 2009. The other news I told her was that my other grandmother, Grandma Martha on my dad's side, had also just been diagnosed with breast cancer. Grandma Martha was 84. She also had surgery and radiation.

Grandma Martha lived right next to railroad tracks and we probably played on or near them more than we should have. Her large yard wrapped around her house. There was no barrier to stop us from racing around her blue house like it was the center of a race track. I can still see the flowers framing the foundation and greeting each visitor.

After hearing this new information about both my grandmothers and breast cancer, my doctor decided to be cautious. Perhaps, it would be wise to get a baseline mammogram.

In September 2011, at the age of 34, I braved my first mammogram.

I heard all the horror stories from my mom and her friends. I heard about how they squish your breasts flat. It feels like they are forcing them to fit into an envelope, then they turn the machine the other way and squish the opposite direction. I heard my mother talking with her friends about the experience: the squeezing, the turning, the pain. Mothers might consider not telling their daughters all the bad things about getting older. They could let them decide for themselves which things are bad, then they can talk about the bad together after the discovery. They can tell them what will happen, but put some sort of positive light on it so the girl doesn't dread everything from her period to menopause. I read the jokes about what a man would do if he had to stick himself into that mammogram machine. It is an understatement to say I was nervous for my first mammogram.

I went without question, but with trepidation. I walked into that office because my doctor thought it was best for me. I filled out the questionnaire about my female history: When did I have my first period? When did I have the most recent one? Did I have any breast surgeries? Did I have a family member with breast cancer? How many pregnancies

did I have? How many children did I have? There weren't
too many questions. I filled it out quickly. The last two
questions are always a little painful. I have to record that I
have had 3 pregnancies and 2 children. Each time I answer
those questions I remember October 2000.

My husband, Jason, and I were married in November of
1996. After 3 years of apartment-living in 750 square feet
of cinder block walls and blue floral wallpaper, we felt it
was time to move out. I had already graduated with my
teaching degree and was teaching 3rd grade at a local
school. Jason had 2 years left of college. We built a little
house 7 miles away, and moved in December 1999. It had 3
bedrooms. Our entire cinder block apartment would have fit
into the living room and kitchen. While many were storing
up supplies to prepare for the new millennium, we
welcomed Y2K by putting together an entertainment center
in our new house, quietly watching the clock pass midnight.

Anxious to own a pet, we bought a 6-week old black lab
as soon as our grass took seed in our backyard. Kobie had
dump trucks of puppy energy, so we went to the Humane
Society to find him a friend. We brought the sweet
lab/border collie mix home after she settled her chin on our
knees and rolled over to reveal her soft belly. Kobie and
Eliza became fast friends. They were our babies for a year
and a half. They made messes, caused problems, hogged the
bed, and we loved every bit of them.

Jason was going to graduate in May 2001. Since we
were also anxious to begin a family with humans (not just
dogs), we began trying to get pregnant in the summer of
2000. If we timed it right, the baby would be born shortly
after graduation. Jason planned to begin teaching in the fall
and I planned to stay home.

I was pregnant in September 2000. The secretary of the

school where I taught third grade, during that time, was also pregnant. She was in her forties. She was confident I would have a much easier pregnancy than her. Yes, I remember that comment. I'm sure she does too. I had a miscarriage in October, shortly after our 8 week appointment, just after we called everyone to share the good news. We were devastated. We called everyone back. As difficult as this was, we were grateful for their comfort. If we hadn't just told them the good news, we would have missed out on receiving their comfort when we shared the sad news. My mom happened to be coming for a visit the weekend after my miscarriage. She lives in Spokane, about 400 miles from us. She distracted me with a sewing project while I healed. We made a tree skirt. I still put that skirt around my tree every Christmas.

We were thrilled to be pregnant again by Christmas. My excitement was coupled with some breath-holding. I didn't fully exhale until after my first ultrasound. The doctor pointed out the racing heartbeat of the baby: somewhere around 130 beats per minute. I remember the first baby's heart rate was only about 70 bpm. The realization hit me then. They knew. They knew I would miscarry that first baby. This one would be okay. I spent most of my pregnancy barely able to eat. I heard nausea was a sign of a healthy baby. This intense nausea became a comfort. I didn't worry. I was grateful and took one day at a time. I was 7 months pregnant and teaching 3rd grade when my husband graduated from college.

Hannah was born on a Monday at the end of August, 2001. While I was on my way to the doctor for her 2-week check-up, the Twin Towers collapsed. My daughter's life will always landmark the attack of 9/11. Hannah is kind, sweet, and sensitive. Her heart breaks for others. She has a gift for sensing and uniquely meeting the needs of others.

On a Thursday in June 2004, Abigail was born. She entered this world with passion. She is my "all in" girl. When she was younger, she was completely happy, completely mad, and rarely anything in between. As she has grown, she is still all-in, but not to the same extreme. She is intelligent, a gifted artist, a horse-enthusiast and an animal-loving young woman. Abby will always find the beauty and the amazing in the simplest moments.

How many pregnancies did I have? Three. How many children did I have? Two. I was ready for the next step. The lady walked me back to a little room where I changed into the giant pink hospital shirt that tied in the front. I placed my clothes in a locker and took the key with the purple plastic bungee bracelet. Because this was my first mammogram, they instructed me to watch a video explaining what they were going to do and why they were going to do it. I'm not sure how I knew, but I knew everything they were saying, and what I didn't know, I knew I would soon find out. It was more embarrassing sitting there watching that video while the next lady came by than just going ahead with the procedure. I decided to just get it over with and I clicked the television off.

In the first exam room, I encountered a lady with short brown curly 50s-style hair. She asked me to sit on a table. She was kind enough to talk to me for a little while, explaining what she was looking for and how I could do my own breast exam. I removed my pink hospital-gown-style shirt, held my arms out to the side, raised them up, and stood still while she looked at my breasts. I knew this was medical. I knew it was no big deal, but for me, it was a little unnerving. I felt self-conscious. I knew what was happening, but that knowledge didn't automatically make me comfortable with sitting half naked in a cold room while a stranger stared at me. Finally, I laid down on the table and she conducted a physical breast exam, explaining why she was moving in circles and exactly what she was looking for. The best part about this exam is that I knew the results immediately. I passed the first test.

I put on my stylish hospital shirt and waited for part two. I walked into a 12 by 8 room. The squishing machine was on the right. Straight ahead, a computer sat behind a big plastic screen, protecting the operator from the effects of the machine. A tall lady, with long brown hair who was probably 10 years my senior, welcomed me. She was very sweet, yet business-like. We didn't have much small talk. She asked me to take my arm out of the sleeve of my shirt. I laid my breast on the plastic tray and stood as close to it as possible. She turned the lever, bringing down the plastic plate, making me as flat as possible. I imagined the goal was to turn a melon into a pancake. My large melons are apt to make this challenging for the pancake creator. She walked behind her plastic shield, pushed a button that made a beep, then she released me from the clamp.

"You can relax now."

I relaxed my breast. I backed away from the machine, but the rest of me was anything but relaxed. I awkwardly stood half naked, not knowing what to do with myself. Do I keep my back turned? Do I put my shirt back on? What do I have to do next? Are we moving to the other side or are you going to make another pancake out of this breast? Perhaps you would like to make waffles instead? She turned the machine sideways and re-clamped me from the side. I became a ball of dough. First, you flatten it one way, then you flip it and flatten it the other way. She repeated her steps, I repeated mine. Finally, she told me I could put my arm back into my sleeve and take the other arm out, so she could make bread from my other breast.

The video might have been more helpful if it had informed me what to do with my arms, eyes, feet and thoughts during this procedure. What was I supposed to do with my floppy breast while she adjusted the machine or looked at the pictures? I wanted to wrap right up in that fashionable shirt, but I thought that was a little prudish. These people do this all day. Breasts are not sexual, they are biological. They are no different to them than our elbows. This experience isn't something they are concerned about. Perhaps their training should include telling people what they can do with their arms. What does "you can relax now" really mean? Does it mean I can put my clothes on and put my feet up while I wait for you, or does it mean my boob can relax to its full length, attempting to reach my belly button while the rest of my body stands at attention, waiting for the next set of instructions.

"You can relax now," she said, finally followed by, "you can put your shirt on, we are finished!" I added the exclamation.

I used my key with the purple bracelet to unlock my clothes, got dressed and left.

My first mammogram was behind me.

.  .  .

I was scheduled to repeat this experience on Friday, September 14th, 2012. I figured it would be much the same because I hadn't gotten any more comfortable showing my breasts to strangers than I was a year ago, and I hadn't heard they were doing mammograms any differently. Why do we willingly allow people to torture us? We reason: It's good for me, my insurance pays for preventative procedures, I might as well take advantage of it.

September 14th came quickly. The secretary asked if I took the day off of school. "We have 4-day school weeks, we don't have school on Fridays." Her jealousy was evident. Everyone dreams of 4-day work weeks, 3-day work weeks. . . She saw my address of Notus and confidently asked why I didn't go to Fruitland for my mammogram rather than Meridian. It took me a moment to realize what she was saying because I'd never asked myself why I didn't go to Fruitland. Then I realized this was another person who had never heard of the tiny town of Notus. They think it is the same as Nyssa which is 15 miles west of Notus, and in the state of Oregon rather than Idaho. Notus is a town of about 450 people. The saying is, "Don't blink or you won't notice Notus." I need to remember I didn't know a thing about Notus until I moved there. I didn't even know it existed. So, I gently explained that Fruitland was farther away from where I lived than this hospital located in Meridian. Meridian wasn't that long of a trip. I filled out my forms, answered my questions and waited my turn.

I was born in Deer Park, Washington. Deer Park was a tiny town you might miss if you weren't paying attention. I grew up in Chattaroy, Washington on a twenty-one acre farm. I graduated from Riverside High School in a class of

104 students in 1995. By the grace of God, I ended up at Northwest Nazarene College, working towards a bachelor's degree in Elementary Education. I met my husband in January of my freshman year. We married in the fall of our Sophomore year. Jason came from a small town outside of Reno: Fernley, Nevada. Nampa, Idaho was a relatively small town in 1996. The years have brought exponential growth to the area. Our lives took us to many places in the Treasure Valley, the name they give all these towns nestled in between the mountains in southwest Idaho. In an attempt to start fresh in 2006, we landed in the tiny town of Notus. Sometimes Notus can feel really far away from everything, you are in a small community, but you are still close enough to the big towns to always have what you need.

This mammogram was much like the first one except for a few things. They didn't make me watch the video and the ladies were much less personable than last time. The first lady, the one who did my physical exam, decided to point out that I was the same age as her daughter. I often add interpretation to things that people say when I can sense there is more, so even though she probably was only making an observation, I heard, "My daughter doesn't get mammograms, what the hell are YOU doing here?"

The second lady needed no interpretation. She informed me I was young to be getting a mammogram. She was surprised this was my second. She proudly exclaimed, "I haven't had a mammogram in 2 years. I have a friend who has never had one. She just *believes* she won't get cancer. This is a lot of radiation to put into your body if you start at this age."

WOW! Last year, I was so proud of myself for obeying my doctor. Thanks to these technicians, I was ready to call my doctor and ask, "Are you sure I should be doing this every year, perhaps it would be better if I went every other year?" After I got home, I realized I should have told that lady I was obeying my doctor (who knows infinitely more than her), and knows me and my specific situation. I don't ever think of those things in the moment. I felt miserable when I left and my misery had nothing to do with the pancake press. As I went home, relieved that it was over, I thought, "At least I don't have to do this again for another year."

On Tuesday, September 18th, 2012, the phone rang.

"We found an unidentified cluster on your breast that we want to look at again. It's not a big deal," they say. "Nothing to worry about," they say. "But could you come in for a follow up mammogram? We want to double check something."

All they said may be true: nothing to worry about, no big deal, but whatever the outcome, no one wants to hear there is something in their body that wasn't there before.

Initially, I wasn't going to tell my husband. He had been so stressed over school, the one he taught at, and the classes he was taking towards his master's degree. I didn't want to add to his stress. This unidentified object inside me might be no big deal. Lots of people are called in for a second mammo-gram. My mom has been called in many times, it is always nothing.

I told him anyway.

I know it added to his stress, but he needed to know.

I told my friend Patti.

She offered to go with me to the appointment if Jason wasn't able to go.

I asked him.

He hadn't thought about going along, maybe he could.

We both went into town on Saturday, September 22nd for a second mammogram. I couldn't believe I had to do this again.

They only needed to redo the left breast. That is where they saw something. They took a couple of pictures with a much fancier machine than I had the previous week. Then they took a blown up picture. They enlarged the image, so they could see every detail. The technician showed the doctor the images. As soon as the doctor approved them, I was permitted to get dressed again. The nurse went to get Jason from the waiting room and the two of us went into the "viewing room" with the doctor. The room was small, too small for such a big moment. The doctor sat in a chair facing multiple computer screens. We sat in two chairs facing him. There was another desk or table on the far wall with more screens. The room felt too full. The doctor with the funny name showed us the images. There were small white dots on my left breast. These dots were what they called calcifications. On the enlarged picture, the dots looked like grains of salt. On the regular sized picture, you can barely see them. "These calcifications could be nothing, but we are not sure. We recommend a biopsy to find out what they are. I have already spoken with your doctor, and she agrees with that recommendation. What would you like to do?"

This will be the only time we are asked this question.

I was in shock. I didn't really feel like I had a choice. Those calcifications were a sign of something. It was possible the "something" was nothing, but without a biopsy, I wouldn't know for sure. I would be continuously wondering if I was okay. What were those things? The wondering would be unbearable. I had to do the biopsy just to know what was going on.

# Chapter 2

## *Biopsy, of Course*

"We'll do the biopsy."
      They showed us the room where they would do it.
      They told us it wouldn't take very long, 90 minutes total, but the actual biopsy takes just a few minutes.

They explained how I would lie on the table on my stomach with my breast falling through the hole.

They explained how, after they raised the table to at least 4 feet in the air, they would insert a needle to take a piece of tissue out so they could examine it.

They asked if we had any questions.

It's difficult to have questions about something you know nothing about. True, I knew nothing, but I also didn't know what I didn't know.

I couldn't think of any questions.


We scheduled the biopsy for Friday, September 28th. Again, I wouldn't have to take the day off of work.

My brain knows this happens to women all the time.

My brain knows that much of the time it is nothing.

My mom had to have two biopsies, both times - nothing.

I know this.

I regularly remind myself of these facts.

It doesn't matter what my brain knows.

My mind is racing.

What is going to happen?

What if they find something bad?

Doctors tend to try to make things sound better than they are.

Do they know that this is something bad, but aren't telling me because they don't have proof yet?


I've never had surgery before.

I can't believe I have to have surgery!

It will probably be fine, but it might not be fine.

It's no big deal, nothing's wrong yet, but what if something is?


I had to reflect on what my life looked like at this point. What was before me? What was I going to do? How was I going to convince myself that I could do this, that I could survive anything that may or may not be coming? I envision our paths in life like highways and freeways with exits.

There are many different paths set before us in our lives. Some we choose to go down, some we are forced down. When I went into the doctor for my yearly mammogram, I was still on the freeway of my life. This is normal, nothing is unique about my actions. When I was called in for the second mammogram, I was forced off the freeway onto an exit that is sometimes used, but no one chooses that exit. My head was on a swivel as I was watching and waiting for a sign that would direct me back to the freeway. Yesterday, I lost hope of that sign for now, and was instead forced farther down the road no one chooses to travel. Today, the freeway is farther away, and I hold onto the hope there still may be a sign showing me how to get back. There is nothing wrong with this road right now, but if I remain on it too long, the pavement turns to gravel and makes the trip much more difficult. There is still hope of turning back. I cling to that hope.

∾

I went for a walk with my Daddy (my God) and Shelby (my dog). We talked. I told Him I couldn't pray for healing because I wasn't actually broken. I just kept telling Him that I trust Him. Whatever comes or doesn't come. I trust Him. I can fall backwards into His arms and know He'll catch me. I know how much He cares about me and loves me, and I trust Him fully. After all my rambling about how much I trust Him. He said, "I am trustworthy." Oh the peace and joy that washed over me! That's all I needed. Those words were whispered into my soul. I knew it wasn't my own voice. I could lean in and trust fully.

I believed everything about trusting my Daddy. I believed it would be ok. I believed that I would make it, but all that belief didn't change reality. All that belief didn't take away the concern and fear lurking beneath the surface. I felt like I was holding my breath. The weight of the unknown sat on me like an anvil. I felt pressed down by it. I felt like I needed to remember to breathe, breathe slowly to control the fast beating of my heart. I tried to keep my mind busy, but it kept going back to forbidden thoughts.

I had an unsettling dream about the biopsy surgery. I awoke feeling as though I had been in a wrestling match. My stomach was in complicated knots, it was difficult to want to eat. I could cry in a second, but I willed myself out of it. I had become stone. If I let go, I may not get myself back. What if I travel too far down this path and I can't find my way back? I was simply holding on.

I never had any kind of surgery before. My most extensive hospital visits consisted of stitches when I was 7 and the two times I stayed while having my babies. I was going to have surgery. I was terrified. I struggled to envision how they were going to do it and even though I knew it would be fine, I thought about and worried about it all the time. Of course, I didn't say anything about my thoughts and worries.

Sometimes speaking about them makes them more real. If I didn't say anything, I could pretend it would be okay.

Sunday arrived like an annoying neighbor. I didn't want to go to church. I didn't want to talk to anyone. I didn't want to pretend all was okay and I didn't want to make a big deal about the fact that it might not be. I held it together until the singing began. I attempted to sing. Then I cried. I cried and cried. I couldn't stop crying. I wasn't scared, I wasn't sad. I was just *feeling* the weight and had no choice but to let go.

Of course, my tears brought sincere questions from everyone who saw me and I answered honestly. I realized this place, this church, is a place where people cared about me. It's not pretend. I needed to learn to accept it. I needed to learn to let go and receive their compassion. I've seemingly held myself up for so long that I have to practice letting go and letting others hold me up. I stink at letting others help me. It could be because I think I'm strong enough. I made it through my parents' divorce, the miscarriage of my first baby, people attacking me with lies, financial struggles, sleepless nights . . . I had come to think I was unbreakable. And if something was breaking me, I needed to keep it to myself because other people don't really want to hear about it; they can't or don't want to help. They have their own problems, why would they want to take on mine as well? I had convinced myself that other people didn't want to hear about my problems, and that I was strong enough to handle them by myself. I didn't want to burden anyone else. What if they have their own problems and mine are too much? What if they don't care and are only pretending? What if one day they use this weakness against me? Unfortunately, I have not learned any new lessons, and I still do that. I don't speak my mind. I don't ask for help. I don't tell people when I don't feel well. I just put my head down and keep walking. On this day, in this instance, my tears gave me away, and I felt comforted by loved ones. If I could learn to let go more often and let others comfort me, I would probably feel much more free.

My husband and I held a leadership position in a former church and there were expectations of us. These expectations were meant to keep us in a position where people looked up to us and sought us out, but we weren't supposed to show our weaknesses. We were supposed to lead, but not reveal our struggles. The result was that we had few close relationships. We were close enough to people that we thoroughly enjoyed being with these people, but we didn't share everything with them. We never shared weakness or vulnerability. Today, I know how wrong this view was. It still affected my relationships in this healthy church.

My reluctance and fear to share with people and trust them with my weakness on this day stemmed from my past experiences in church. Jason was a youth pastor of a church for over 3 years in the early 2000s when Hannah was a baby. During those 3 years, we felt left out and separate. The other church leaders regularly gathered together without us. I remember one Thanksgiving in particular. Because we had no family in the area, Jason, Hannah and I spent it alone. There is nothing wrong with a quiet Thanksgiving, but we were young and poor and we felt rejected and confused when the other pastors didn't seek to include us or ask about our plans.

The church had 2 services each Sunday, a youth service on Wednesday and different prayer services and Bible Studies throughout the week. At this particular church, Jason was also the middle school and high school teacher of the church's school. He was busy. He was at all the church events because it was part of his job. He didn't want Hannah and me to be stressed or busy, so he often asked me to stay home with Hannah for most of the "required attendance" church events. He had to be there, but he didn't want to drag us around. Because I wasn't present at all these events, people talked about me behind my back. One of the leaders attempted to turn the young women of the youth group against me by lying to me about how the girls were upset with me. She said "Beth" was upset, but she handled it so I didn't need to talk to her about it. She told me that one girl was upset because of something I said to her in one of our small groups. Despite the leader's advice, I had the sense to meet with these young women and I asked them directly. The girls never had any sort of problem with me, or anything I did, and our relationships became stronger despite the efforts of the leader.

The church leaders expected us to be examples to the other people in the church and we were expected to keep our problems to ourselves because the church members might not respect us as leaders. Their actions and words convinced me I needed to keep any issues I had quiet. I beat myself up over having a messy house, or for watching television in the middle of the day. I thought I had to always have everything together. I had an internal list of "shoulds" that kept me under constant pressure.

This experience made me doubt if I could really trust people in a church with my vulnerabilities. If I told them how I struggled, would they judge me? What if I shared my doubts with them, would they tell me I was wrong? Could I really trust these people with my true thoughts and feelings?

All this baggage came with me into this church full of real, honest, and loving people which explains why I was surprised by their compassion, their non-judging comments, their willingness to do whatever was needed and to pray for me. I appreciated them remembering that people are fragile, especially the ones that look like they are made of granite, like me. They let me break and crack in front of them. They held me gently and didn't try to glue me back together. They let me be and accepted me, cracks and all.

I tried not to make too big of a deal of this biopsy. If it turned out to be nothing, I didn't want to have over-dramatized the situation. However, since I didn't know the future and only knew the present, I still had to deal with every thought and feeling in the meantime.

So far, I'd had a routine mammogram, a follow-up mammogram, and told I needed a biopsy. Nothing had really happened yet, nothing was really known yet, but I was a mess. I went to school the day after my loving encounter with people at church. I went through all the motions. I didn't tell anyone what was going on. I thought I was doing quite well until I got into my car to go home. I broke. I crumbled in my seat like an old cookie. I cried all the way home. The weight was back and it was getting heavier. I immediately called my mom when I got home and asked her if I was normal.

I thought...
      This shouldn't be a big deal.
      She had had biopsies.
      She had never told me about crying all the way home.
      I must be making a bigger deal out of this than it was.
      I must be worrying about nothing.

. . .

My mom assured me I was normal.

We talked for a while.

She let me know it was okay to cry, it was okay to be worried.

I was ok.

~

"The doctor is going out of town on Friday. Can we reschedule your biopsy for Wednesday?" asked the nurse on Tuesday afternoon.

"Tomorrow?" I confirmed.

I asked for Wednesday afternoon off.

I wouldn't have to wait until Friday.

I could get it over with!

I finally told the people I work with what was going on.

It's amazing how letting people know about your life and the secrets you are protecting them from actually relieves a lot of the weight. I was no longer walking around carrying this heavy secret. I stayed late Tuesday night preparing for a substitute. I made sure they had every bit of information I could give them. I went to school Wednesday morning. Right before lunch, I informed my students they would have a sub for the afternoon. Of course they asked where I was going, I told them I had an appointment. Then I remembered to breathe.

I walked into the special breast imaging center, the same one where I had my second mammogram. They took me to the room where I changed into my favorite pink shirt. I went to the back room where they did another mammogram. They needed to make sure they knew where everything was and that nothing had moved. After they were pleased with the picture, they took me into the room where the biopsy would transpire. I was terrified and cold. I tried to hide my terror behind a calm demeanor. The nurse got me a warm blanket. Oh, the pleasure of a heated blanket! I may start putting blankets in my oven at home just to have a warm blanket to sit under. She talked with me a little about what they were going to do. She had me sign a consent form. As we were waiting for the doctor and technician to join us we began talking about books. She had read some amazing books. Every good book I mentioned she had already read, and every good book she mentioned I hadn't heard of. I tried to place them somewhere in my head where I would remember their titles or authors, but in my current state of mind I couldn't even remember the nurse's name. We chatted for a while. I began to relax, then the doctor came in. He explained what would happen again. I had to tell them my name and birthday. They made a green mark with a marker on my left collar bone so they would be sure they were working on the correct side. Like an announcement at an airport, they officially stated what they would do, and just as loudly, then I signed again.

The next step was to get onto the table. I had to lie on my stomach. My left arm was out of my sleeve, my left breast literally fell through the hole in the table. They placed a pillow by my head. My left arm was straight down at my side. My right arm was curled up by my face. They tried to ease the pressure on my hips by putting a pillow under them. The person who created this table never had to lie on it. It was a table. There was no cushion. It was contoured only slightly, I might as well have been lying on a board. I was uncomfortable physically and emotionally with my body in a strange and vulnerable position. The nice nurse who told me about the books stood on the side of the table I was facing, which happened to be the side facing the wall. I'm sure she was uncomfortable squeezing between the board/table and the wall, but she stayed. She tried to talk to me and keep me somewhat distracted. I kept getting more tired and uncomfortable. I just wanted to close my eyes and wait for it to be over, but I would open my eyes when she came over and try to have a conversation with her. In the midst of this painful, uncomfortable, stressful ordeal, I was worried about this nurse and trying to be polite and awake for her.

Because of the location of the calcifications, it took them a long time to get my breast in position. The technician clamped my breast, took a picture to see if she was in the right spot, unclamped, readjusted, took another picture and repeated. She repeated this series at least 10 times. They had to find the correct spot for the needle to go in. They couldn't move the needle, but they thought they could move me. Finally, she got it in the right spot. It was time for the numbing needle. In order to be numb to pain that we know is coming we must have a little pain. The doctor stuck me with the local anesthetic many times. Fortunately, I only felt it the first time. Then it was time for the biopsy. The machine was set up so that the needle would enter my breast in a certain spot and take out a piece of tissue, then it would come out and go in another spot. It would move in a circle like a clock going in and out 12 times. I felt a slight vibration on the table, but felt no pain. The nurse kept chatting with me, the needle was doing its job and now my right arm was falling asleep. I couldn't move. They had me in the perfect place. If I moved they would have to redo what they had done, so I stayed still.

Finally, the biopsy was complete, but the poking wasn't. The anesthesia was wearing off, but they still needed to insert the clip that would mark the spot they biopsied for anyone who came along in the future. Because the biopsy often removes some or all of the calcifications and future doctors need to know the location where all this occurred, they insert this clip which will only show up on x-rays. The doctor had to inject me with more anesthesia, then one more needle would insert this clip. It was like a small flag saying "I have conquered." Not unlike what soldiers do when they take a territory. My breast had been taken, it had been conquered with 12 deadly sword attacks. I was defeated.

They took a few more pictures. Then I was released from the clamp. The nurse who had been talking to me had to put pressure on the hole they created for 5 minutes to stop the bleeding. She cleaned it up, taped on some gauze then sent me off for another set of pictures. I went back to the mammogram machine where I had begun earlier that day. The technician squeezed and took pictures. She needed to be sure the clip was there and in the right place. The squeezing restarted the blood flow. I was embarrassed when I realized I had gotten blood all over me and the machine. I wouldn't have gotten it on myself if someone had told me what to do with my arms. I folded them and squeezed the blood right onto my arms.

. . .

They encouraged me to get dressed.

They informed my husband I was finished.

I could go home and rest.

I needed to stay out of the shower for 24 hours.

I needed to refrain from lifting for 5 days.

I needed to leave the bandage on for 24 hours.

They gave me some pain medication and sent me home.

I quickly called the school and told them I wouldn't be in on Thursday.

The anesthesia made me a little queasy that evening. I ate very little. The next day I began getting a cold or some other bug. I was weak and tired. I was fairly confident the biopsy hadn't caused that. Perhaps it was brought on by 2 weeks of stress. I've learned over the years that stress will make me sick faster than any bug or germ. Unfortunately, the stress was only beginning. The results of the biopsy would come in 2-3 days. I rested and waited.

Historically, I'm not very good at being sick. Don't get me wrong. I love laying around and watching television, sleeping all day and having people wait on me, but that's not usually what happens. Usually, I get sick the day after I decided not to clean up the house, the day after I took a day off and the laundry has become a clothes volcano, the dishes look like skyscrapers on the counter, the dog hair is forming into new animals on the floor and Abigail has begun to draw pictures in the dust. I can't do anything about it, but I sure would like someone to do something. So I am sick and help-less. I stay away from the mess hoping that "out of sight, out of mind" really works, but it doesn't. I know the house is a mess. I can't solve that problem and my family has their own list of "to dos." They can't help. I close my eyes. I change the channel. I know it is more important for me to rest and be healthy. I know the housework isn't that big of a deal. I know that I'm the only person it bothers. All that knowledge does little good for the battle inside me. I change the channel and try not to think about it.

I'm the tough capable one, being sick doesn't suit me. It means that someone has to take up my tasks. It doesn't, but that's what I think it means. That's what I tend to expect or hope those around me might do. "Mom would have done laundry today, but she can't, let's do it for her." No one thinks like that. I suppose I should stop hoping. I've learned this is common. When I talk to other women, they experience the same thing. When they are sick, everyone takes the day off with mom, instead of helping mom. I dread it. When I feel better, all the chores I couldn't do will be waiting for me with open arms. It would be nice, just once, to feel better without a mound of tasks waiting for me. I would love to wake up one morning and think, "Wow, I feel so much better. Look at this nice house, I can do something with my family today." Instead, on the day of health, I must clean.

I stayed down most of the weekend. Later, I would find out that my need to rest because I didn't feel well had nothing to do with the biopsy. Most people bounce right back from those. Unfortunately, I wasn't most people, and I wouldn't do anything the way most people do.

# Chapter 3

## *Anvils and Phone Calls*

The call came on Friday afternoon, September 28, 2012. I was still in my classroom. I was preparing to go home. I was still recovering from the biopsy the week before. I don't remember his name or even his title. I thought I heard him say something about radiology. I don't think he was a doctor or a nurse.

He told me the biopsy results were in.

He told me it was a precursor to cancer.

If I left it alone it would probably turn into cancer, eventually.

"They will want to remove it." he said.


Amazingly, I felt relieved. I had had a sense this thing wasn't going to be nothing, but if it had to be something this precursor to cancer thing was the best "something" it could be. All they will need to do is remove it. Next week, I will hear from my doctor and get more information, but it was nice to have some information for now.

I shared with a friend that the unknown was the cause of my greatest emotions. Wondering about the future brought on doubt and fear. Speculating filled me with terror and dread. This new information was known. I now had a plan of attack. I was nervous about surgery and recovery, but not as scared as I was before.

The unknown is terrifying. It plays with your mind and it takes all your energy to keep your mind under control and focused on the present instead of catastrophizing the future.

I called everyone and told them what the mysterious person said. I told people at church. I texted family and friends who were waiting for a quick answer.


We all breathed easier.

It wasn't cancer.

It was something that happens before cancer, but it wasn't cancer.

I relaxed that weekend.

I felt a cartoon anvil drop from my shoulders.

It was going to be okay.

I finally started to breathe again. I hadn't noticed I was

even holding my breath until I was free to release it like the air out of a balloon.

October 1st fell on a Monday. I had a long day ahead. Parent/Teacher conferences were supposed to be held on October 2nd and 3rd, but the schedule only allowed for twenty-four 15 minute intervals to meet with parents during those 2 days. I had 30 students. I needed more time. In order to fit everyone in, I stayed at school until 6:00 on Monday night. I was beginning to lose my voice. My cold, after my biopsy, had escalated a little since I hadn't really taken a break. I kept moving, kept doing my job, and kept caring for my family, in part because I needed to keep moving, in part because these things were a distraction from my unknown, scary future. I knew I sounded awful to these parents. My disappearing voice made it sound like I was deathly ill, but I talked anyway. Parents probably wondered why I wasn't home in bed. I sounded like a lifetime smoker with pneumonia. I didn't *feel* horrible, but I definitely sounded like I was on the verge of death.

If only parents knew how often I teach when I feel crappy. I give 110% for their kids. They may look at me and think I'm not doing enough. They have no idea. I put the education of their children higher than my own health. I teach tired, I teach weak, I teach when I am using the last scraps of energy. I will go home and collapse, but first, I will give them my all.

I was in the middle of telling my 3rd grade parents how great their students were when I received a call on my cell phone. I ignored it. I calmly and hoarsely finished meeting with worried parents. They are all a bit worried. They wonder if this is the year they get the bad news about their kid or they are worried they will hear the same bad news again. Unless I actively need parents' help, I tend to tell them all the promising and wonderful things. These kids and parents are doing their best. Most of the time, they need my compassion and understanding. Then they will rise to my expectations and to their potential.

When the last parent left, I picked up my phone to return the missed phone call. I had no idea what I would hear on the other end of the line. Her name was Jill. She began telling me what I could expect over the next few months. Before she began detailing my timeline, she asked if I wanted to hear the pathology report from my biopsy. I told her that would be a good idea. The mystery man hadn't informed me of much that Friday. Jill explained that what I had was called "ductal carcinoma in situ," cancer of the ducts. The *in situ* was the most important part. It meant that this cancer was "non-invasive." I felt like someone I loved had slapped me in the face.

I was in shock and snapped into reality at the same time. "So it *is* cancer?" I asked. I had to quickly take in the fact I had cancer because she was still talking. I'm not sure how I did it, but I continued listening and writing all her words. I was sitting alone in my classroom. Except for the janitor, I was the only one in the building. It felt like a business meeting. I had my place at the table as if on an important business call. I had my pen in hand. Only I wasn't taking notes on a student, I wasn't recording the decisions of an important company. I was taking notes on what the next year of my life was going to look like because I had just been diagnosed with cancer.

Jill said she would be putting me in contact with a surgeon.

I would probably have genetic testing because I'm only 35.

After the surgery they will probably want me to go through radiation therapy.

It was unlikely that I would need chemotherapy.

I should write down everything, because even though I think I will remember all this and what day I did what, I won't.

I need to make a medical timeline.

I need to get my family history of cancer.

I need to write down all the medications I take.


Amidst this mountain of overwhelming news, Jill was wonderful. She answered all my questions. She gave me her cell phone number telling me I could call her anytime. She was my advocate and was ready to help me. I didn't contact her a lot over the next few months, but knowing I could, gave me peace. I had a person who would fight for me, or at the very least, answer my questions.

I drove the eight-tenths of a mile home in shock. I kept repeating the sentence, "I have cancer," over and over, trying to believe it because it didn't make sense. Periodically, I pretended this was all a mistake. It must have been someone else's mammogram they saw. There wasn't anything on my mammogram, they were just making this up so they could make more money. Sometimes I wondered if there was a conspiracy. I knew this wasn't true, but the unbelievability of reality stretched my mind to fantastical ideas. Because of my family history, I knew one day this might happen. One day I could get cancer, but I didn't expect it to happen at this age. I was going to have to call all those people I talked to on Friday and tell them what I originally said was all wrong.


It was worse.

    I didn't have accurate information before.

    I really did have cancer.

    I really did.


I walked into the house wearing the cartoon-anvil-heaviness again. I had to tell Jason. I was thankful I wrote it all down. I read off my notes. Sharing this information with him was more like sharing notes from a meeting than sharing I had *breast cancer*.


This news definitely didn't seem real. This type of thing doesn't happen to me. I am healthy. Of all of the people in my family, I am the one without health issues. I always mark "no" on the long list of medical problems listed on the paper they repeatedly ask you to fill out at the doctor's office. I never have questions or concerns for the doctor. This news felt wrong. I knew my amazing health wouldn't last forever, but I didn't expect it to vanish this early.

    I told people this came as a shock at my age. One relative actually pointed out it would be a shock no matter when it happened. She didn't understand. I expected at 60-something I might have a medical issue or two. Nothing was supposed to happen at 35.

I was okay.

In the early days, I was okay. In the early days, I moved forward like a determined horse leading its carriage. My master was kind enough to put blinders on so I only had to see what was in front of me. The carriage I pulled was heavy. I was certain it carried the weight of four "Biggest Loser" contestants ("Biggest Loser" was a popular weight loss show during this time. Contestants began the show at weights between two and four-hundred pounds and after weeks of hard work, they walked away lean and strong. The contestants in my cart were just beginning their journey). The only thing I could do was focus on my next step. I knew I might have a day when I broke and wanted to fling those people out of the carriage and let them walk on their own, God knows they needed the exercise. I also knew I wouldn't do that to them, but I might want to. Today was not that day. Today I was okay. Today I would put one foot in front of the other and finish the journey.

In case I forgot to tell you, I was sick. It started the day after the biopsy and, until the day I got the news, I thought I was getting better. October 2nd came and with it, another 13 hour day. I taught 3rd-graders for seven of those hours. I spent the other hours speaking with their parents. After the first hour of parent conferences, I was losing my voice again. Historically, the loss of one's voice is a sign of improvement. It's like the last straw. I didn't think anything of it. I conferenced with the parents of 28 students over the course of Tuesday and Wednesday. I shared all my observations of their children. I smiled. I gave advice. I never let them know I just found out I had cancer. I didn't give them a hint. I didn't even act like anything was wrong. You may think this is amazing. You may think you would have been screaming it from the rooftops. It is not that simple to give people that news. It feels really personal and it feels like you might be one of those "downer people."

An old friend sees you and smiles. They say "Hi, how are you?" with their great-to-see-you face. For a moment, in your head you want to say. "I'm good, I have breast cancer." Then you hear what that will sound like. You see their face fall into a frown. You see that your honesty has put a huge damper on their day and essentially placed duct tape over their mouth. They will probably ignore you for the rest of the day, feel sorry for you, and make you feel more alone than if you kept your secret. So, you keep your secret. At least, that is what I did. I rarely told people what I was facing unless I had an amazing daily relationship with them. It was the first time in my life I wished the gossip tree was working better. People weren't talking about me and they were forcing me to talk about myself. I failed them. I kept my secret. I kept teaching as if nothing was wrong. I smiled and greeted people as if it was still the beginning of September. I finished two 13 hour days of teaching and conferences, holding my breath and straining my voice. Thursday night came. The last parents went home and so did I.

Thankfully, my mom drove in on Thursday night. We were both tired from our long days: my conferences, her 400 mile drive. We went to bed at a decent hour, looking forward to our weekend together.

.  .  .

Friday morning, with my mom, was a treasure. Jason and the girls went to school and my mom and I had the day to spend together. Jason taught high school science, Abby went to 2nd grade, and Hannah went to 5th grade. I was still feeling less than whole, but I was determined to enjoy my mom. We sat and had coffee together that morning. We visited about the recent events. The timing of her trip had been perfect. She had planned this trip over a month ago. It was lucky timing that it fell the weekend after my diagnosis. My mom brought a few items she had been working on with her. She had re-finished an old dresser that my grandma Hazel purchased over 60 years ago and painted it Abby's favorite turquoise blue. That color now holds the name "Abby Blue." Unfortunately, in order to get the dresser into Abby's room we would have to clean it. Not the dresser, the room. Abby is a wonderful daughter full of energy and life, but she saves everything just in case she might need it. She treasures every piece of trash as future art. My mom understands, she does the same thing. With all that treasure, we were going to have to dig to find the floor. We spent at least 3 hours cleaning her room, hanging up clothes, throwing away 5 garbage bags of trash and preparing a space for her new dresser. Since I still didn't feel well, I gave about 30% and did all the sitting jobs. Abby had a pink bookshelf that Jason made Hannah years ago. My mom painted it Abby Blue to match the dresser. She also brought a mirror for Hannah. She had already painted the wooden frame pink. We rearranged a few items on her walls so we could hang it.

When our basement was finished, we intended to use the two rooms at the far end as rooms for our hobby things. Jason got one and I got one. It was a dream come true, a room for my sewing and a place to do bills and write without cluttering up the rest of the house. But I had no furniture in it. My mom brought me a chair, a desk, some pictures she painted, a cork board and a lamp. Everything was pink and sage green. The chair had a light pink cushion with dragonflies, sporting sage green wings, hanging out with dark pink ladybugs. All things I love. I love dragonflies. I'm not sure why. I think it's their name and their beauty. It's like they are trying to be a butterfly with their pretty colors, but they are ferocious like a dragon, yet ordinary like a fly. I know none of these things are scientific about drag-onflies, but it's how I think of them. The cork board and pictures were both bright pink. It was the pinkest room I have ever had. It was not "little girl pink," it was adult pink - if there is such a thing. I have bright colors mixed in, but most things have a pink hue to them. At the time, I didn't realize all these new pieces of furniture would become breast cancer reminders. They are not bad reminders, simply reminders of a season. It was wonderful to finally have furniture in my little room.

We almost had Abby's bookshelf painted when the girls got home from school. I shouldn't say we. My mom did all the painting. I watched. Both girls were thrilled with their new bedroom items. Abby was also excited about her clean room. We all hung out that evening, relaxing and visiting.

The next day, Saturday, October 6th, I had an MRI. They wanted to scan and make sure there wasn't something else the mammogram may have missed, and they wanted to check the location again. I never had an MRI before. I had no idea what to expect. My mom went with me and Jason and the girls stayed home. I checked in at the hospital where the MRI station was. They walked me back to another area where I checked in again. They guided me down the hall and into an area where I changed. I wore scrubs for the first time. I would have loved to take those blue scrubs home. They were the most comfortable clothes I have ever worn. They showed me to a small room filled with medical supplies. I sat in a chair in my soft, comfy scrubs and waited for yet another person. She came in and gave me an IV that they would use to inject me with dye later. I had some cough drops with me to reduce my incessant coughing, so I sucked on them and let my eyes wander around the room. There were different sized needles, gloves, plastic bins with labels, along with drawer upon drawer of miscellaneous supplies. I usually use these waiting sessions to check my vision. I try to read small things from across the room to see if I still have amazing eye sight. However, my phonics skills are so good that I can figure out a word from only a few letters so I'm not really testing my vision. I'm testing my ability to decode words in a sentence. I still do it. It's an interesting way to pass the time. I was very tired and would have loved to lie down and go to sleep. I waited in that room for a lifetime. When they finally finished with the person ahead of me, they rescued me from my boredom.

It was my turn. They took me to a large room where I removed my shoes. They showed me to the bed of the machine where I laid on my stomach with my head in a concave support, similar to what they have on massage tables. Sadly, I knew there would be no soft fingers on my tight muscles on this day. When I opened my eyes, there was a reflecting glass in front of me so I could see the technicians in the other room through the window that separated them from me. My breasts were nestled into concave grooves so the machine could get a good picture. I suppose if I had laid on my back with my breasts falling to the side, they wouldn't be as easy to photograph. The ladies explained I would hear a humming and ticking noise from the MRI machine while it worked. I needed to lie very still and breathe normally. Don't forget I have been sick. My lack of voice has resulted in the hacking cough that often concludes my illnesses. I had to lie there for 45 minutes and not cough. Fortunately, I was on my stomach. If I had been on my back, keeping my cough in would have been like stopping a hungry baby from crying. The lady informed me if I moved during the session, everything would be ruined and I would have to come back another day to do it again. My anxiety about keeping my cough in just leapt to the roof now that she added the terror of ruining this test.

The ladies left me to hide behind the safety of the thick door and the window while I laid on my stomach with my boobs hanging down, just like the biopsy. Fortunately, this bed wasn't as uncomfortable as the biopsy table. My bed slid back into the center of the machine. I've heard horror stories about MRIs and how people feel claustrophobic. I might have had that sense if I could have seen the small space I was inserted into. My eyes could only see the little mirror below me, so the knowledge of how much space was above my head remained a mystery. The machine made its noises. It was louder than I expected.

I laid very still.
    I didn't cough.

The machine worked its magic for about 30 minutes. Every once in a while there was a pause as the machine adjusted and the technician told me I could cough if I needed to. It was nice to know there were breaks, in case a cough wouldn't stay locked in my chest. It finally came time for the dye. They began injecting the dye into my body through the IV. The machine took pictures for another 15 minutes.

The machine watched the dye traveling through me, finding, and coloring the cancer. Then it was over. The bed moved out and away from the machine. The technician came to help me get up. I sat on the bed for a second to regain my balance. During the different photography sessions the ladies came in to adjust something, and I got very familiar with their shoes. I could see the ladies talking behind the glass. They could have been making small talk or talking about me. I didn't know. I didn't feel well and all these new experiences were not what I expected to be doing this fall. It never made me feel better or less anxious to know that many people experience these things. I had never experienced them before and I hadn't planned on it. Every new experience was mysterious and terrifying.

My mom spent the procedure in the waiting room. I imagine her nerves were wracked as she worried about what I was going through and how I was dealing with it. I didn't have the energy or thoughts to check in with her. I knew I could only manage my own steps, my own journey. I took off my comfy scrubs and went out to join her. I described the experience as weird. The medical community doesn't take into account what they are doing to a person. Medicine is looking for ways to see you and fix you: how it feels and looks to the patient seems to be irrelevant. It's like we don't even exist. We are objects with problems rather than people. It's good that even though the new-fangled machines treat us like objects, the people who run them still know how to treat us like people and make us feel at ease when we feel scared and uncomfortable. No one goes in for an MRI for the fun of it. A person gets an MRI because something is wrong. A good technician realizes that and puts the person at ease. I appreciated that compassion from the two ladies in charge of my MRI on this day. Their gentleness and kindness made my anxious self feel safe and cared for.

After the long morning, my mom and I were ready for a late breakfast. My grandma Hazel gave my mom a Starbucks card a while back, so Grandma bought us some breakfast sandwiches and some coffee. My mom had never eaten those sandwiches before, and she was pleasantly surprised. We had a little bit of shopping to do before going home, so we drove towards Nampa and stopped in at the local thrift store for some finishing touches on Halloween costumes for the girls.

Every year my girls' school has themed Halloween parties. The students dress up as a character from a book they are reading at school. This year it was *The Wizard of Oz*. Abby decided to be the lion, and Hannah chose to be the scarecrow. Fortunately, I remembered to tell my mom about these things before she came. If we need something, she usually has it. Over the years my mom has collected a number of items she thinks she might be able to use (this is likely where Abby gets her need to collect things). She can create anything out of what, to the untrained eye, appears to be nothing. Creating things, improving things, and repurposing them is a gift my mom has. She can see treasure in trash, potential in any project. My mom's gift was an asset growing up with little money. She makes gifts and practical items for everyone. She has enough supplies to open her own craft store. I appreciate this about her and am thankful for her resourcefulness. Some people don't understand how she thinks and what she does. I grew up with her gifts; they are some of what makes her my unique mom.

When I was young, I could depend on my mom to create things while we were off at school. Most of all, I could depend on her to create a home where we felt safe. She sewed our clothes. She was often awake long past midnight finishing an Easter dress or a special outfit for the first day of school. One time, I went to school with my skirt sewed onto me because she ran out of time to add buttons. When she was in high school she taught herself to make her own clothes. Making clothes was something she did because she was good at it and in those days, before the Walmarts and the Targets, she could make them for a fraction of the cost. She made meals for dinner each night. On summers and weekends, she made us lunches and snacks. When I was younger, it was rare that I fixed my own lunch. She painted new things and refurbished old ones. She took painting classes and created much of the art and decorations around our house. She was frugal and wise with money. I remember having a large brown couch for most of my young years. One day, we came home from school to find a new blue couch in the place of that old brown one. It was new to us, but definitely not new. My mom found it at a yard sale and probably used money from recycling cans to buy it. This gift of my hers has helped me fill my house with nice things and saved me more money than I can count.

On this trip, she brought material for a mane and tail for Abby. She brought straw and patches for Hannah's overalls. We just needed a straw hat and a plaid shirt for Hannah. We found both at a local thrift store for only a few dollars. Since we were there, I looked at some other clothes: I found 2 wonderful skirts for school. I love buying things at the thrift store. Because they are inexpensive, I don't have to worry about how much I love them in order to make the purchase. I also get to include vintage styles that are absent from the typical department store.

While we were out, my mom purchased a CD she had been wanting. She played a song for me on the way home filled with words she was having trouble speaking on her own. The song essentially said, "I will love you through it. I can't take it away, I can't make it better, I can't fix it, but I will love you through it." She was saying that to me. It was the first glimpse I had of what this cancer was doing to her. I wasn't thinking about what it would be like to have a young daughter get breast cancer and have to watch her battle it. She had just traversed this path with her own mom the year before. She never dreamed she would watch her daughter trudge through it. She couldn't do anything to take away my burden except be there. She had to imagine what I was going through. She had to watch me be tired and in pain. She had to hear how I kept going to work and didn't tell people what was going on. She had to wonder how I was getting up in the morning. She had to wonder if I would be okay. This is not a scenario a parent imagines, yet here she was. She did her best. She just loved me. That's all anyone can do when the person you love is embarking on a difficult journey. You can't take the journey for them, and you can rarely make it easier, but you can love them through it. I am thankful for my mom.

We kept working on all the projects on Sunday. We made the girls' costumes. We sewed the mane on and sewed the round bear ears into pinched lion ears. We sewed straw into the pants, sleeves, and hat of the scarecrow costume. Hannah got to sew on her own patches. After failing at dying a cord used for making baskets for the lion's tail, we used a hanger and some brown material and made a perfect tail for the lion. When we were finished, we had two wonderful costumes ready - 25 days early. I've never been that early for Halloween. Thank goodness my mom is so handy. My mom left the next morning. I was grateful she had come and thankful she stayed with us for 5 days.

When my mom revealed her heart to me, it helped me see that the people around me watching me were grieving differently than I was. I didn't feel the same grief because I had something to do. I had action I needed to take. They had to watch and wonder how I was managing, how I kept going. At this point the statement, "I have cancer," was still not real to me. It is difficult to say and even more difficult to believe. It's about as real as "I am married," the day after the wedding. Things don't necessarily feel different, but you feel like they should.

As the next week came and went, I felt peaceful. At least that is what my journal said at the time. I knew I needed to have surgery. I knew I would be meeting with the surgeon soon. I knew he would tell me what would happen next. I didn't know much more than that, so the "not knowing" made me feel peaceful. Looking back, I don't really think that was the case. I remember the heavy burden I carried. I remember there was a lot of not knowing. I remember, in a sense, holding my breath for fear that if I relaxed everything would burst. But that is not what my journal says. My journal says "I'm not scared right now, but I think it's because I can't see. I'm thankful for this peaceful time when I can process all that's going on." I'm surprised I felt that way. I wrote that many days in a row. I had time to think about what was happening and reflect and that made me peaceful. I'm so glad I wrote that down or I wouldn't have believed it. Looking back, it is also possible I was choosing that. It is possible I sought out what would give me peace because anything else would have broken me.

# Chapter 4

## *Strong Roots*

On Thursday, October 11, 2012, I went to see the surgeon. I was excited to finally know the next step. I sat in the surgeon's office waiting for answers and direction. Before he could tell me what he saw on the MRI, he heard the cough I had been dragging with me for the past 2 weeks. He was about to inform me I had a spot on my lung, but when he heard my hacking cough, he figured I probably had pneumonia. I was relieved. I had been sick since my biopsy on September 26th. I thought I just couldn't shake this cold. I had been trying to function as if all was well, when in reality I was walking around with pneumonia. I was so relieved to have a name for my struggles, I willingly went home and laid on the couch all weekend. I was actually *really* sick, no sense in trying to muscle through any longer. I wasn't going to get better if I kept pretending I wasn't sick. It was time to rest and heal.

In addition to discovering why I had been hacking up hairballs for the past 2 weeks, the surgeon explained that the biopsied area was *ductal carcinoma in situ* which means that biologically it can't spread. He confirmed what Jill told me. It doesn't have the skills or knowledge to be able to spread. They will remove it and do radiation in case there is more hiding in other ducts.

The doctor informed me there were some other unknowns we needed answers for. There was another spot near the biopsied location on my breast that showed up on the MRI. They will remove it, but they won't know what it is until after the surgery. If it turns out to be an invasive cancer, I may need chemotherapy.

Because of my age they wanted to do genetic testing to see if I have the gene that keeps my body from fighting off these cancer cells. If the test comes back negative, then all will stay the same. If it comes back positive, my chances of getting cancer again are 80% so they will suggest a bilateral mastectomy. Those were the facts. This was the list of information I got from my appointment. Just as things were becoming known, others were becoming unknown. Some answers and some more questions.

My prayers following that appointment were that the other spot was non-invasive and that the genetic test would come back negative. Jason was already envisioning a silver lining to the worst case scenario. He asked if he can pick out my new boobs if I have to get a mastectomy. Having smaller not so cumbersome breasts would be nice, but such a surgery also seemed like a lot of work. Jason called me his hero. I felt honored and humbled. I wasn't sure what I had done to earn that title, but I was grateful he saw that in me.

It's overwhelming to talk to people about all of this and keep them updated. They get confused when I try to explain the "what ifs." Looking back, I probably didn't need to tell people every detail. I could have just told them the next step or where I currently was in the treatment plan. I explained they would do a genetic test, and the results of that would determine what type of surgery I had. The results of the test on the mass in my breast after surgery would determine if I had radiation or radiation and chemo-therapy. There were too many "if this then that, if that then this." I think people got overwhelmed when I tried to explain all of it. Some people got confused and thought I was taking extreme measures. They didn't hear me explaining what the doctors were telling me. They didn't hear me sharing facts that birthed fear. They didn't hear me trying to be wise in every decision. They questioned if I should really be doing this next step. They questioned if it was real. Their responses made me feel discouraged and invisible. I was willing to share, I needed them to be willing to listen.

One particular person would regularly talk to other people who had had breast cancer then she would come back to me and say "well, so and so didn't have to do that" or "so and so said you should be fine if you do this." She never heard me explain what was happening and what my doctor recommended. According to her, these friends' stories should have been my guide for all health decisions. She spoke to me as though she knew more than anybody I was talking to about my own health. Fortunately, that only happened with that one person. It wasn't going to help me to know what "Sally's" doctor said about her breast cancer. It wasn't going to help me to know about anyone else's case. I didn't know it at the time, but the most helpful thing to hear was the simple fact that others have gone through this and they understood. I needed empathy, not examples of sixty-year old women's stories that didn't quite fit.

I continued to be torn like Dr. Jekyll and Mr. Hyde. I wanted people to know what was going on so they understood why I might act a little funny, but I also didn't want to be the one to bring up the topic. I didn't mind talking about things, but I didn't want to begin the conversation. I preferred answering questions and offering information that was sought out. I guess that was my way of checking to see if they really wanted to know. There is no worse feeling than sharing something important and finding out the person you are speaking to didn't hear a word you said.

The teachers I worked with knew. I didn't tell parents or students. How do you say that? How do you announce to a room of 3rd graders or even to their parents, I have cancer? Perhaps someone else can. Most of the families in my class heard about it from others at this point. Eventually, they would all be told, but not by me. One day when I had to leave early, the school counselor told my class for me. There was no measure to my gratitude. I think this also gave people an opportunity to have whichever reaction they needed without me there.

Since my husband and my daughters went to a different school than me, their situation was more open. My girls talked about my cancer with their friends. Their teachers knew. Jason talked about it. It was much simpler to say my wife or my mom has cancer than to say *I* have cancer. I thought about this fact a lot. I don't know why it was such a struggle for me. I would see someone I hadn't seen in a long time. They would ask how I was, and I would say "fine." In my head, I would tell myself they didn't really want to know the whole truth. They were just being polite. If I answered honestly, suddenly the moment would be awkward and it would feel like I was trying to get sympathy. I actually told people that it was ok to share about me with each other; gossip away and share my personal information, because I didn't want to share.

Jason's school began raising money for us. He organized multiple fund raisers on my behalf. They sold pink bracelets and sold pizza for lunch. It was really great of them, but a little surreal. I never imagined I'd be that person. I was the person they were having fundraisers for. I was the person efforts of help were devoted to. They had a pink day where students could wear pink instead of their school uniforms if they paid $1. The money went to us. It was an extraordinary blessing. Just as the bills started piling in, the blessings came and kept away the stress. I felt undeserving of this good will, but eternally thankful at the same time.

~

*Saturday, October 13, 2012*

*I know my Daddy didn't give me this cancer. I know He will heal me completely. I know He is with me and I can rest in Him and trust Him and lean on Him.*

*Today the weight of it all is heavy. The duties I have*

*before me are too many. I am tired and weary. Today is a*
*more difficult day than the others.*

*Perhaps I am carrying too much of this. Daddy, show me*
*how to let it go. Show me how to lean on you when my mind*
*tries to take it all in. Show me how to take one step at a time.*

*Thank you for being with me and loving me.*

That was my journal entry. Four days after I wrote that, I
was at peace. That was my journey. Some days I was up and
okay, some days I felt crushed, but at the end of each day I
knew that my Daddy had me and that He would carry me
through it all no matter what the future held and no matter
what kind of day I was having.

∾

### *Wonder*

*I don't wonder why*
    *I wonder who*
    *I am not exempt from this*
    *Who will my life touch?*
    *Who will I bless in this walk?*


*I don't wonder if*
    *I wonder how*
    *I know my Daddy heals my diseases*
    *What will that healing look like?*
    *What will it feel like?*

.  .  .

*I don't wonder when*
 *I wonder how long*
 *I know this will end one day*
 *How long will it really last?*
 *How much of my life will it try to steal?*


*I wonder...*
 *Will I break?*
 *Will I stand strong?*
 *Will I make it?*
 *Will I be victorious?*
 *Will I conquer my mind?*
 *Will I be a slave to it?*
 *Will I survive?*
 *Will I shine?*


*I want to stand strong.*
 *I long to be victorious.*
 *I strive to conquer my mind.*
 *I pray to shine.*

I began a new journal today. There is a beautiful picture of
a Yellowstone wolf on the cover.


*Sunday, October 14, 2012*

. . .

*The wolf on the front of this book inspires me. I choose to believe it's a female. Her intense gaze is saying "I am confident, I know where I'm going, you will not get in my way." There is nothing that can take her down. She is aware of her surroundings and conquers them. Nothing surprises her, nothing changes her determination or her purpose.*

*As I venture down this path, I desire to be like this wolf. I will remain in my pack, keep my confidence, keep my purpose and conquer this enemy that is trying to take me down.*

~

Even though my pneumonia diagnosis should have kept me down a few more days, I ventured off to school Monday morning after only 4 days of rest. Due to the difficulty in preparing for a sub and my desire to occupy my mind, it was simply easier to go back to work.

The last time I spoke with him, my dad informed me he wants to come down for my surgery. He doesn't visit or call, but suddenly when I am sick, sicker than he would have imagined, he wants to be here. Do I suddenly exist in a more real way because things are not peachy? If that fact is true, how sad that it took something like this to open his eyes. If that fact is true, will it last beyond my surgery into days of health once again? I saw his actions that October as an effort to connect and was thankful for it and prayerful that I would remember to be me and not try to be different in any way.

When I was 13, my parents divorced. My childhood is divided into two halves: before and after the divorce. Before the divorce, I understood my life, I could envision a future that looked like my present. I could predict each day. After the divorce, I searched. I wanted answers. Why did this happen? What was I supposed to do about my life now? Who was I supposed to be? Where did I live? What would my future entail?

My parents decided to divorce in August of 1990. They'd tried. Their marriage had been a struggle for at least half of their 15 years. They couldn't find a way through, so divorce was the answer. I still remember sitting down with them to hear the news. I don't remember if they said they were separating or if they were divorcing. It doesn't matter, divorce was the result. Even though I was only 13, I knew my devastation was more about having a broken family and becoming one of the divorce statistics than it was about the actual separation of my parents. My dad moved into our camper. The one my brother and I used to ride in on long drives to our camping destination. I think he kept it in the yard for a bit, but eventually he parked it at his work. It didn't take long for him to find a duplex close to his work which was 45 minutes from where we lived in the house with my mom. We were supposed to visit him every other weekend and on Tuesdays and Thursdays. We never saw him on a Tuesday or Thursday. In reality, it was inconvenient. He got off work at 5. We wouldn't have gotten to his duplex until after 6. We would have been forced to leave shortly after 8 in order to get home for a reasonable bedtime. Sometimes we saw him on his designated weekends. Sometimes my brother and I made plans with friends so we would be busy and couldn't go. If we did go, he often had made plans of his own and we didn't get his full attention. It may seem selfish to want his attention. We were supposed to see him 4 days out of the month. I was a teenager. Right or wrong, I expected his full attention.

Almost every vision and dream I had before the sit-down-conversation was lost or changed with the words, "We are getting a divorce." I came home to an empty house because my mom was working. I declined get-togethers with friends because it was my dad's weekend. My brother and I no longer fought over which of us would live in our child-hood home forever (once our parents died). I sought guidance and wisdom and a listening ear from anyone willing to give me some time and patience. I no longer dreamed of teaching in my familiar elementary school. I no longer could see my future mirroring my present. I know my parents didn't divorce us, but everything we had become familiar with, everything in our lives that made us feel safe was changed. It would have been possible for my parents to create a new safe place, a new place of familiarity and peace where we could continue to grow and thrive, but they didn't know how. And, at the time, I didn't understand the change that was taking place.

There have only been a few people who come out of a divorce unscathed and stronger. Most instances I know about involve pain and sadness, even if only for a little bit. My parents' divorce shocked me. It wasn't until the following months and years that the pain fully took effect. Because of my dad's own brokenness from the divorce, he couldn't see that when he left, thinking he was leaving my mom or his marriage, he left my brother and me too. He forgot we were separate from his marriage relationship. His own hurt kept him from us, kept him from reaching out to us. He did the best he understood, but I still felt abandoned. I had hoped the divorce would provide a special relationship between us; instead, he found ways to protect himself from the pain of rejection. He did what was best for him. I felt like an afterthought. His new wife didn't act like she liked me or that my brother and I existed at all. He often had to choose between her and us. I kept hoping to renew the relationship, especially after I had kids of my own. I wanted them to know and love their grandparents without any of my baggage. That proved more difficult as the years went on. Conversations about my motives happened behind my back, skewing all my actions. Even kind acts were viewed through a dark and cloudy lens.

This announcement of their coming for my surgery gave me a sliver of hope. However, it was a cautious hope since it was coupled with years of being ignored. I didn't immediately pick it up. I wanted to, but I knew it might not be real.

This season was primarily a mental battle. There were still questions waiting to be answered and uncertainties about the future. My faith was strong during this time, not because I had power to believe, but because I had power to remember. I remembered all that my Daddy had done in my life. He had blessed me with an amazing husband, two special daughters, a nice home, a wonderful job, a family and friends that cared for me. I remembered all the ways He had rescued me. There were many times in the early years of our marriage when there wasn't money for food or gas. Yet, we always paid our bills and were able to work with whatever was left. Most months, after the bills were paid, there was $20 for food, gas and any other surprising expenses. Yet, we never went hungry. Our cars didn't break down and our clothes lasted longer than our desire to wear them. I remembered all the times He had fulfilled His Word. His Word says He loves me. He shows me His love every day in the little thoughtful things I know are only Him loving me: phone calls, special moments, and helping me avoid car accidents. My entire life is a picture of how my Daddy has been with me through thick and thin. I am not strong enough to withstand any hard times. I am not good enough to deserve any easy or good times. I attribute my every breath to Him and to how faithful He has been throughout my life. My life is all the evidence I need to know I can count on Him like no other because He has never let me down. I remember. I believe and trust because He has proven trustworthy.

*"But they delight in the law of the Lord, meditating on it day and night. They are trees planted along the riverbank, bearing fruit each season. Their leaves never wither, and they prosper in all they do. For the Lord watches over the path of the godly." - Psalm 1:2-3, 6*

When I was in high school, I went to a church camp in western Washington, near Olympia. I remember bits and pieces about that camp. One mortifying moment involved my bathing suit falling down while trying to water ski. Mostly, I remember what the youth pastor said. He preached on Psalm 1. He accented the word *delight* and held it out like he was singing a song. He talked about being a tree by the river and being faithful, and faithful, and faithful, and faithful, and finally being fruitful because it was now the season for fruit. He talked about being successful in everything we do because the Lord watches over us. He painted a vivid picture by changing his voice like a comedian doing impressions, standing on his chair and accentuating all the important words. In all my years of going to church and listening to sermons, his sermon is the only one

I remember. I still get excited when I hear the words of those verses because they touched me so deeply at the time. Today, they still bring comfort.

My Daddy watches over me and cares for me like no other. I am planted securely. I am strong because of Him and will not lose my leaves. All those things may sound funny since I am not a leafy tree planted permanently by a stream, but think about it differently. He knows me. He loves me. He sees me. He knows what I am going through. He knows my fears. He knows my joys. He knows what will comfort me and He is the only one with me all the time. If I feel like I can't hear him, I open the Bible and read his words until they speak to me. He has set me where I am, wherever that may be. He has given me deep roots in my life and I am rooted in who He is in me so that I will not fall down and no wind or storm can knock me down. He has given me leaves of beauty and potential fruit that won't wither and die. Even if I feel naked or weak or feeble, my leaves are a sign of the strength and life I still have. I can stand firmly by this stream and take all that life brings. I can withstand whatever comes against me because, ultimately, I am not my own. I did not make myself strong and I do not have to remain strong on my own. I am because He is in me. That all may sound strange. All I know is that I am not strong enough to take on cancer, so every success I have is only because I trust the Father who made me and gives me strength to simply stand each day and on good days, do a little walking.

# Chapter 5

## *Passing Days*

I t was finally time for my genetic test. I have never had anything like this done before, so I didn't know what to expect. I went by myself because Jason couldn't take the day off of work. It felt like the plan was to see how many different rooms I could wait in. I began with the first person. She took my information, and then I waited. The next person came, then left. I waited. Then the next person came and we repeated the waiting dance. Finally, I was sent to wait in a little room. I waited for the lady who took my blood. At last, I went home to wait for the results.

The doctors asked me to get genetic testing because I am a 35-year old who should not have breast cancer. Both my grandmothers have had breast cancer, one of them had it twice, and my great-grandmother had breast cancer. Even though my mom never had it, there were enough people in my genetic line to warrant a test. Everybody has cancer cells in their bodies. A cancer cell is simply a cell that is a little messed up. Typically, when cells begin to degenerate, a person's body fights and kills those cells and all is well. There is a special gene that fights these cancer cells. For breast cancer, there are two main genes called the BRCA1 and BRCA2. You want these genes to be healthy. It is equivalent to a general who calls his troops together when an invader enters the land. Any mutation of this gene incapacitates the general. The soldiers don't fight, they don't send the invader away. Instead, the invader grows and takes over. When they conduct a genetic test they are looking to see if the gene is mutated. If it is, a person will just keep getting cancer.

In one of the rooms I waited in, a nice lady walked me through all the statistics. I have a 15% chance of having a mutation. I have a 15% chance of needing to remove my ovaries and breasts (if the gene is mutated, ovarian cancer is extremely likely in addition to breast cancer). But, I have an 85% chance of testing negative for the mutation. I have an 85% chance that this cancer is just some fluke thing and it can easily be wiped out. I have to wait two weeks for the results. In the meantime, I am a tree. In the meantime, I will hold the 85% chance, remember that chance, and remember that I am in bloom. My leaves shall not fall and my Daddy charts my path. I have nothing to worry about.

. . .

*Friday, October 19, 2012*
    *". . . But you, O Lord, are a shield about me; You are my*
*glory, the one who holds my head high . . . I lay down and*
*slept, yet I woke up in safety, for the Lord was watching over*
*me. I am not afraid of ten thousand enemies who surround*
*me on every side."*
    *- Psalm 3:3, 5*

I am protected.

By the 3rd week in October I was finally beginning to feel
better. I was still very weak from lack of activity and from
sporadically coughing. I celebrated sleeping 10 hours
straight on October 20th. It was the first time I had slept
through the night in over 4 weeks. I was also anticipating an
evening with friends. We went to a Boise State University
football game and dinner with our friends, Rick and Patti.
An evening with friends was the medicine I needed most.
They were very busy people, so I appreciated them putting
aside some time for us. When you are always fighting to feel
better, a day with friends can make you believe you might
actually be getting better. I don't remember spending a lot
of time talking about me, which was good. We just visited,
watched a good game and enjoyed being together. I can't
tell you who Boise State played. I know they won, and they
looked good in their all black uniforms. The most important
part of the day was being with friends who buoyed me more
than any medicine could.
    Since I was finally beginning to feel better (it takes a

long time to recover from pneumonia, longer than I wanted), we decided to go to church for the first time in weeks. At first, I wanted to sneak in and sneak out, but instead I stayed present and was rewarded with gentle love, encouragement and support. Patti encouraged me and shared that the prayer group was praying for miraculous healing. I assured her I'd take that prayer. Healing is always welcome. I imagined miraculous healing looked like waking up cancer free. As much as I appreciated the prayer, I didn't exactly see God doing that. I wrote, "I believe God will receive more glory from me going through this than from me being miraculously healed. That doesn't mean He won't heal me; it doesn't mean I will have to venture down the worst path. I envision a journey that will glorify Him and heal relationships. He's not making me sick. He is using this season when peoples' hearts have been softened to move. He is using this season when peoples' eyes are opened to reveal Himself. If a person learns about Him from all this, or leans closer to Him, He gets the glory."

As difficult as all this was, I knew I would be okay. I knew I needed to record my thoughts and prayers so that I would stay sane. If I had been left to my own devices to think freely about all the *what ifs,* or even to listen to some of the people around me, I would have collapsed like dirty laundry. I had to stay focused on the now, stay focused on God, and keep my mind clear of garbage that would clutter my steps and cloud my vision.

My daily writing ritual was similar to how you treat an old car that only responds to certain movements: before you start the car, pump the gas 3 times, put it in reverse then 1st gear, turn the wipers on and off once then turn the key twice. On the second turn it will start. If you neglect any step, the car just won't run. It was the same with my morning journal writing. I had to begin by sharing my feelings, physically and emotionally, then my doubts, then my fears, and finally a statement of faith that I trust my Daddy and it will be okay. Those daily movements helped me to walk through each day. They helped me take one more step.

~

*Monday, October 22, 2012*

*Before I was forced off the freeway, my journey began like many others' journeys. I traveled on small, safe roads until I learned enough to venture onto the busy freeway. Once on that fast-paced highway, I felt powerful, free, and successful. I traveled long distances. I watched others struggle on their own journeys, but the largest struggle I had to endure was a poorly managed road with potholes making my drive a bit uncomfortable. Sometimes those potholes beat up my car more than I would have liked, but I always made it to my destination in a short amount of time. Before long, I was cruising at top speeds again. I noticed the many exits along my journey, but I had a destination I was focused on. Those exits would only slow me down. Besides, the towns they led to weren't places anyone chose to go. Most people were forced onto those exits and off of the ultimate path to their chosen destination.*

*On Tuesday, September 18, 2012, I began to be pushed towards one of those exits. Its name was Cancer. I began to imagine what the town might look like if I went that way; I fought turning off my safe freeway. Eventually, I was forced off the freeway to the exit whose name had been hidden from me. As I slowed my car to stop at the light, I thought I got a glimpse of the town's name. I still didn't want to go there. I didn't see a place to eat or rest. I was forced to turn the opposite way I had planned and found myself on a 2-lane road that hadn't seen many cars. This road led away from the freeway. I kept straining my neck in all directions, wishing I was an owl, looking for a sign that would direct me back to the familiar road, knowing that with every minute that passed the sign leading me back to the freeway was less likely to appear. I thought about the people on the freeway. They had no idea what this little road was like. Some tried to imagine and understand, but this is a road that can only be experienced. I kept driving, slowly and cautiously looking for any sign that might take me back when I finally spotted it. On Monday, October 1, 2012, I read the sign welcoming me to the city of Breast Cancer. I wanted to turn around, but it was impossible. I was now so far from the freeway that the only way to get back was to travel on this one-way street through the entire town. I had to finish the journey.*

*I found a hotel to stay in called "Wait and See." I ate daily at the restaurant called "Hope." I took my coffee from a cafe called "Faith." I drank multiple cups a day. I found maps telling me how to maneuver through the town. They gave great directions: telling me when to turn, and which turns to take, but the routes always required the slowest, most uncertain movement.*

*My world slowed down in this town. The freeway was fast with everyone focusing on their destination. This town was filled with moments. Each moment was precious, each moment was lived. As much as I didn't want to be in this town, I enjoyed the pace. I enjoyed not being in a hurry. I enjoyed seeing the path in front of my feet. I noticed each rock, the different colors of soil, each flower smiling at me from the oddest places, and tall trees I had never seen on the fast-paced freeway. The days inched by like a slug seeking far-away food. Each day had value. Each person I spoke with had value: their time was worth gold to me, their words like sweet balm, their touch was a boost of energy helping me see my way through the town.*

*No one chooses to stay in the city of Breast Cancer. Everyone keeps moving, sometimes more slowly than others, but they move nonetheless. I know that on the outskirts of town, signs will lead me back to the freeway, but I might begin taking the hidden roads and enjoying the sights and the people more. I know I'll eventually make it to my destination, I might as well enjoy the trip.*

One of the phenomena of a situation like this rising in one's life is that time slows down. As one day passed to the next, I was amazed only a day had passed. The days were long, full of common activities, but also full of millions of thoughts and questions and attempts to control the thoughts and questions. On top of everything, I was in the waiting game. What would the genetic test show? What kind of surgery would I need? Would I need to order new boobs? I was in a state of limbo, wondering what the future held and not wanting to know at the same time. Knowing could be a relief, a simple surgery. . . radiation. . . done. Knowing could mean turning the familiar in my life on its head. If the test returned positive for a mutation, I would need to get a bilateral mastectomy. That meant they would remove both of my breasts completely. Fortunately, the insurance companies pay for reconstructive surgery, but that means two surgeries and I had heard some horror stories. I would love to no longer be a 32DDD. I would love to be a 32C, so I could wear normal clothes without having to get a size bigger just because my breasts are always trying to escape my clothes. I would finally be able to find supportive bras without spending an arm and a leg to try to hold up my boulders. I could even buy colorful bras at discount prices. But all those positives would be coupled with the undeniable fact that those breasts would not be the ones I'd come to know and understand over the last 35 years. It may still be my skin, but it wouldn't be the same. I'm not saying I would choose against the surgery because of a loss of my personal boobs. I'm saying I realized I would have to deal with the loss. I would have to adjust and cope and mentally walk myself through the journey. I would need time and space to grieve. That scared me. Smaller boobs excited me, adjusting to them scared me. These thoughts never escaped me. This mental argument and pro and con list never left my mind, except while I was teaching.

Teaching is an all-consuming task that takes every sense, thought, and physical ability. Attempting to think about anything else will knock you out and create an opportunity for the students to trample all over you. I thought my scary thoughts in the quiet of the bathroom, walking down the hall, sitting in my home in front of the fire with my coffee, lying in bed in the morning and in the evening, driving in my car, riding my bike, walking my dog, watching television, eating, and all the other times - except when I was teaching. These thoughts, this battle, this argument consumed my days and made them long. The tasks of the day were extended by every thought of *what if.* I knew I should trust, I knew it would be okay. That knowledge didn't stop the conversation in my mind forever extending my days. And, strangely, I was thankful for the long days. I was thankful time didn't fly, I was thankful to pass each day in a spiritual peace even if my mind fought it every step of the way.

On Friday, October 26, 2012 I wrote: Can I really do this? Can I really be strong enough to endure surgery, radiation, be a wife and mother, a friend and successful teacher?

I heard: *"You can't, but in Me you can."*

The initial stress of all this turned my cold into pneumonia. Once the pneumonia began to subside I acquired 3 cold sores (I always get cold sores during stressful times). On the outside I was calm, but this stress was obviously affecting me and my body refused to conceal it.

By the end of October my mental and emotional journey was a continuous roller coaster. I felt good and in control one moment, then ready to collapse under the pressure the next. I was constantly thinking about what was going on inside my body and what would be happening in a few weeks. On any given day, I didn't feel worried or scared, I just felt a heavy weight pressing down on me every second of every day. I was amazed how I could not feel worried, but at the same moment, could feel this extreme pressure. I even reflected that I wouldn't have been surprised if I had shrunk from the constant weight. I had no idea how to lessen the weight, or how to distract my mind or change my thoughts. I ventured that maybe I should stop trying to beat my thoughts away, and instead, embrace them and deal with them head on. I thought maybe I should attack them instead of avoiding them. I considered that plan. I discovered that I was afraid to engage my thoughts. I was afraid of where they would take me. I was afraid to say them out loud or write them down. Then they would exist for real and I could no longer pretend they didn't.

Ironically, that is the thing I love most about writing. I love that when you write it down it is down forever (or until you throw the paper away). I especially love that when you write your thoughts down they are no longer in your head, at least, that is how it works for me. I don't have to remember them. I don't have to recall what happened, when it happened, how I felt, or what I wanted. I write it and it's done. I write it and move on. Now, I'm terrified to write my thoughts down because they will be permanent and real, and I wasn't sure if I wanted to make them fully real. Then I might have to deal with them. Then I might have to admit something I'm not willing to admit.

I was rescued from my dilemma of dealing with reality by a book I was reading called *Jesus Calling* by Sarah Young. It said:

I am able to do far beyond all that you ask or imagine. Come to Me with positive expectations, knowing that there is no limit to what I can accomplish. Ask My Spirit to control your mind, so that you can think great thoughts of Me. Do not be discouraged by the fact that many of your prayers are yet unanswered. Time is a trainer, teaching you to wait upon Me, to trust Me in the dark. The more extreme your circumstances, the more likely you are to see My Power and Glory at work in the situation. Instead of letting difficulties draw you into worrying, try to view them as setting the scene for My glorious intervention. Keep your eyes and your mind wide open to all that I am doing in your life.

I was amazed at those words, and I was surprised at my amazement. I knew I should have known better by now. I've had a lot of experience watching God take care of my needs and issues throughout my life. He saved me from a potential life threatening car wreck when I was 17. I was driving to school in my '71 Chevy Nova on icy roads. I lived in a town north of Spokane, Washington and was used to the snow. I took and passed my driving test at 16 in six inches of fresh snow when everyone else canceled their driving tests.

Approximately a half a mile from the school lies a rather steep hill. I, after gaining one entire year of driving experience, accelerated up the hill with my 350 big block engine. The tail of my Nova moved like a fish. With my great 17-year old wisdom, I did it again. The car fishtailed again. Since I am a fast learner, I accelerated one more time. This time my blue Nova did a 180 and slid off the left side of the road, down a hill and into someone's driveway. In my state of shock, I opened the barbed wire gate that blocked my way, drove through, turned left and went back up the hill to school. I was shaken, but it wasn't until my drive home after school that I truly realized what happened. I had already noticed that my license plate, which originally was nestled in the back window, flew onto the floor of the front seat. Considering that my car didn't have seatbelts, I was thankful I didn't receive more of a jolt. I searched the side of the road for the location where my car must have slid off. The only car sized spot along the road that didn't have trees or steep cliffs was the spot where my car slid. In any other spot, I would have been seriously injured or dead. I believed with all my heart that God allowed my car to go to that spot to save me. He takes care of me and loves me. I knew that during this difficult time, He would take care of me just like He did then. This time, it simply took much more mind power. It took much more patience and waiting and trusting. I definitely know that He is trustworthy.

The first sentence that struck me from Sarah Young's book was, "...ask My Spirit to control your mind so you can think great thoughts of Me." I didn't have to control my thoughts, I could ask for help. When my mind wanted to travel down this dark, unknown path I could choose to think of all the great things about my Daddy instead. He is real and true, this imaginary path was not. "The more extreme our circumstances, the more likely you are to see My Power and Glory at work in the situation." This sentence encouraged me because my circumstances felt more extreme at this time. Many people have different "extreme" circumstances happen in their lives. Who's to say that in 5 years there won't be another circumstance that is even more extreme than the current one, but God promises His grace is sufficient for whatever circumstance we are in. I do not have the grace right now to go through *your* struggles, but He has given me the grace to go through mine no matter how difficult it seems at times.

In 2005, Jason had a sales job working as a personal trainer. His income was inconsistent and small and we needed more money. I had just weaned Abby and I offered to get a job. I declared the only job that would work was a waitress job. I ventured out to place my applications. Two hours later I was hired at Red Robin. I worked there for a total of 3 ½ years. In the beginning I enjoyed the time with other adults. It was a drastic change from my 4 years of being home with my young daughters. I grew dramatically during those 3 ½ years. I became more outgoing, I became more confident, I realized I was good at many things, I was respected by others, I had fun, and I began to relax. For 3 ½ years I served people. I served them their drinks, I served them their food, I served them whatever they needed or wanted. I served the happy, I served the grumpy, I served the laid back, I served the stoic. No matter what, I served with a smile. Many times people tipped graciously. Just as many times people tipped stingily.

In the state of Idaho in 2005 a server at a restaurant made $3.35 an hour. The state of Idaho takes a large portion of that so a server's wage consists almost entirely of tips. There were nights when I worked for more than 5 hours and made $20. There were nights when I made over $100 for working the same amount of time. It may average out okay at the end of the month, but if I had to pay a $60 power bill tomorrow and I made $20 today, it didn't matter how much I would make later in the week. The most difficult thing about being a server is giving every person the best service I can and then getting stiffed on the tip. I knew they didn't know what I got paid, but it was still difficult. I had the grace to do that job for 3 ½ years. At the end of that time I began hating that job. I hated how people treated me, I hated working for nothing. I was telling a friend and she said, "You don't have the grace for it anymore." What she said made perfect sense. I had the ability to put up with it all those years, but now it wasn't time for me to put up with it anymore. It was time for me to move on. A month later I had a second grade teaching job.

God gave me the grace to handle my circumstance in my time, not anyone else's circumstance or anyone else's time. People often wondered how I was dealing with this cancer journey. It was only by the grace of God.

The final most encouraging part of that passage was, "Keep your eyes and mind wide open to all that I am doing in your life." My focus had to be redirected from uncertainty and fear to revelation and hope. God was working. He had not abandoned me now, so He could show up later. He was with me each moment of each day strengthening and encouraging me. I needed to pay attention. I needed to stop trying to control my thoughts and feelings and, instead, release them to Him and then watch what wondrous things He would do. I prayed that I would walk this journey in the present and not try to look too far ahead. I knew I only needed to know one step at a time and even that wasn't revealed until I began moving my feet. I needed to be reminded of the past and how faithful God has always been. I needed to let go and trust. The battle was always raging. This poem I wrote gives a small glimpse into what my mental battle was every day:

### *My Mind…*

*my mind says what if?*
    *My Daddy says I Am.*
    *my mind says what's next?*
    *My Daddy says I Am with you.*
    *my mind says I can't.*
    *My Daddy says in Me you can.*
    *my mind says I have no strength.*
    *My Daddy says I Am your strength.*
    *my mind says Why?*

*My Daddy says I Am Glory.*
*my mind says I'm scared.*
*My Daddy says I Am with you.*
*my mind says it is dark.*
*My Daddy says I Am Light.*
*my mind says I am weary.*
*My Daddy says I Am rest.*
*my mind says this is heavy.*
*My Daddy says I will carry you.*
*my mind says I am weak.*
*My Daddy says I Am strong.*
*my mind says quit.*
*My Daddy says I love you.*
*my mind doesn't give up.*
*My Daddy says I don't grow tired.*
*my mind only speaks to me.*
*My Daddy says I hear every thought.*
*my mind tries to take me down.*
*My Daddy builds me up.*
*my mind travels to the unknown.*
*My Daddy knows all things*
*because of I Am, I can.*

All this may sound victorious. The words on the page make it appear that I had it all together. The very next day, after these great revelations, I woke up and immediately began the forbidden path with my mind again. I had read, "Fill up the spare moments of your life with praise and thanksgiving," (*Jesus Calling*), so I tried. I thanked God for what He had done. My back hurt, I had kinks in my neck, but when I began thanking God, peace filled me and I quickly fell back asleep. The battle never ends.

I came to appreciate the message *Jesus Calling* gave me each day. A fellow breast cancer survivor, Myrna, gave it to me. It seemed, each time I read it, I was encouraged with exactly the words I needed to hear to make it through that day.

It is now Monday, October 29th. It has only been a little over a month since I began this journey, but it feels like an eternity of months. I should be hearing the results from the genetic test any day, my surgery is only a few weeks away, and I can't turn my brain off from the *what ifs*. Each day I awake afresh with the weight of two fully loaded, oversized semis on my shoulders. Each day I sit with my journal and word by word, page by page, I set the burden down so I can function throughout the day. On this day the burden was fully present. I was tired. I was spent. I felt like quitting. I was tired of having one thing on my mind every waking moment. I was tired of moving forward and working so hard just to take another step. I was tired of being strong. . . so I read the message dated January 8th in *Jesus Calling*.

Softly I announce My Presence. Shimmering hues of radiance tap gently at your consciousness, seeking entrance. Though I have all Power in heaven and earth, I am infinitely tender with you. The weaker you are, the more gently I approach you. Let your weakness be a door to My Presence. Whenever you feel inadequate, remember that I am your ever-present Help.

Hope in me and you will be protected from depression and self-pity. Hope is like a golden cord connecting you to heaven. The more you cling to this cord, the more I bear the weight of your burdens; thus, you are lightened. Heaviness is not of My kingdom. Cling to hope and My rays of Light will reach you through the darkness.

I was, yet again, amazed. I felt weak. I felt the depression trying to press in. I felt the heaviness. He was there. He was with me. By placing all my hope in Him, I would be okay. I gave Him all my burdens, all my weariness, all my thoughts. He replaced them with joy, rest, and gratitude. I felt alone and broken on that Monday morning. I felt like I needed some guidance to help me through this, but at the time, the best I could do was to write it on the page, remove it from my head, give it to God and let go.

People say you must do something over and over again to make it permanent. It could be acquiring a new habit, believing a new idea, or learning a new job. The repetition helps you begin to master whatever you are trying to add to your life. On Tuesday, October 30th, after days of the emotional roller coaster, I awoke feeling better than I had felt in days. I felt at peace and ready to take on the obstacles the day held. The next day I leaned in to my Daddy the way I have for years. Whenever something has come along that was difficult or stressful or scary, I leaned on Him knowing that He had this. He wasn't surprised by anything happening in my life. He wasn't stumped about what to do. He loved me and He would help me through whatever terrible thing was trying to take me out.

For a few days, I felt strong. I finally wasn't trying to hold myself up. It takes many days of telling yourself that something is true before you actually believe it and can act on it. I was feeling like all those truths I had been telling myself for the past month were actually becoming a reality.

"I will not show you what is on the road ahead, but I will equip you for the journey" (*Jesus Calling*). This quote comes from Psalm 118. The rest of it praises God for everything He is and everything He has done. So many times on our journeys we want to know what will happen. How will everything get worked out? What job will I have? Who will I marry? What will my kids be like? Will I ever get out of debt? Can this relationship be mended? The questions don't stop. I am thankful God doesn't show me what will happen. I would probably protest or try to help Him if I knew what was coming. I am thankful that He has given me every tool to be victorious over whatever my life will bring me next. The future is still full of many questions, but I am equipped.

On Friday, November 2nd, some dear friends came to visit. We hadn't visited with them since this journey began. They were integral people in our lives when we were experiencing a season of rejection from our church. We shared some simple food and caught up on some events of the past few months. Jason shared his story with Steve while I found myself sharing everything with Kati. I shared the freeway analogy and my aspirations to be strong and powerful like a wolf. My trust in my friend was revealed in the fact that I was willing to share my soul. She was blown away by my writing and considered that perhaps writing would help her with all she's going through. I was blessed by their visit. I can see her eyes as she hears every word I say. I don't have to rush to the end of my story. I don't have to shorten it. She completely listened and heard my soul.

"I am always beside you helping you face today's waves" - *Jesus Calling*.

Yet another quote that spoke directly to my heart. Each day has many waves. Some of the waves are exciting and fun and some are terrifying. Honestly, all the waves look scary to me from the shore. They don't start to get exciting until I get into them and actually get to ride them. From the beach they always look larger than they really are. By the time I'm within reach of the waves, they begin to look ride-able and even a little inviting, no longer quite so daunting. I know my Daddy is taking those waves down before they take me down.

Today, the biggest wave I have to deal with is a lack of time. Daddy, will you give me clarity of mind to know what needs to be done and the efficiency to do it? Will you help me to remember and not forget what I need as I travel from place to place? Thank you for watching over me and making my day efficient. Thank you for taking down the big waves and letting me ride the little ones.

∼

On Tuesday, November 6th, over a month after my diagnosis, I was finally scheduled to meet with the geneticist to find out what my surgery was going to look like. I was not worried or stressed. I was at peace. I left school at 1:30 and drove straight to my brother-in-law and sister-in-law's house. My husband and I were meeting there to drive one car into town. We drove to downtown Boise for my appointment. We sat down in Christina's office, and after she assured us that she wouldn't make us wait, she reported that both tests were negative. You could hear the air expel as we sighed. You could see our shoulders relax down to their resting position. I had no idea the massive weight I was carrying around wondering about the results of that test. The relief was immense. Negative results meant I didn't have the mutated gene that would allow cancer cells to run rampant through my body. A negative result was positive news.

I found out later that my father-in-law and my mom bawled with relief when they heard the news. We were all carrying the burden. I would often forget that everyone around me was feeling their own pressures. They were wondering and worrying right along with me. I had tunnel vision. I could see my journey, my steps and I used all my strength, energy and focus to stay on track and not lose my head, or more accurately, lose my hope.

I had no doubt I could have handled the news if it had been different, but the relief of not having to handle it was equivalent to setting down a box of 20 five-pound weights that I had been carrying over my head. I called my grandma Hazel, in part to tell her, and in part to talk to her on Grandpa's birthday and let her know I was thinking about her. Grandpa Ray died in 1999, just after I started my first teaching job. I wanted to let my grandma know I remembered today was his day. We talked for a while, it was good to talk with someone who's been down this path. She has conquered breast cancer twice, I can do it!

. . .

"Rejoice today, refusing to worry about tomorrow" - *Jesus Calling*.

In this place where I am now, not worrying about tomorrow means not thinking about tomorrow. I need to practice actively rejoicing and praising out loud. I think that will dispel worry much faster than simply not thinking or trying not to think.

So here it goes, my attempt at rejoicing today in the midst of it all:

Today I am thankful. I am thankful for my cheerful puppy, Shelby, who greets me with her wiggles when I wake up in the morning and helps me start my day with a smile. I am thankful for my husband who is steadfast and has built a cozy fire for me to sit by. I am thankful for this delicious coffee that I can enjoy before I start my day.

I am thankful for my girls who are asleep in their beds. I enjoy their amazing spirits. I am thankful for my supportive family who has surrounded me with love. I am thankful for all my dear friends at school and at church.

I am thankful for our home and its protection. I am thankful for my job and that God has made me successful at it. I am thankful for my health insurance. Without it, we would be in dire financial trouble.

I am thankful God is with me every moment of every day. Thank You for never leaving my side and caring for everything about me. Thank You for your healing touch on my body and for a good doctor who puts patients first. I trust You will give me a great oncologist. Thank You for aligning everything in our lives so we always see Your hand.

∾

Friday, November 9th marked our 16th anniversary. Special days don't wait until cancer has passed. Sixteen years is a significant amount of time, but it doesn't feel like it. It feels like a breath of time. Jason and I were married on a Saturday in November, 1996. We had very little money so we kept the wedding simple and elicited the help of friends and family. The majority of our meager savings went to our Oregon Coast honeymoon. We were married in the evening with more candles than flowers. A family friend arranged beautiful white roses in simple bouquets. My college roommate and another family friend made our wedding cake. The lovely people from the church provided food for the reception. I wore my grandmother's 50 year old dress. Most things were borrowed, donated or homemade. It was simple and beautiful.

The next morning, we drove 9 hours to the house on the beach where we would spend the next two weeks. We played Monopoly, ate a lot of goldfish crackers, and spent hours on the beach. Jason liked looking for treasure, I liked walking on the sand. This was the year of the great ice storm in the Northwest. We got to enjoy the effects of that storm on the Oregon Ocean. The waves were dark and huge. The rickety stairs from the house to the beach almost caused me to be a very young widow when Jason fell down the cliff because of a broken step. We survived and brought back fond memories.

At an Enjoying Marriage class, we learned marriage is akin to two rivers that were once flowing separately suddenly merging. The merging of the rivers creates chaos. Sticks are flying, the water is muddy, rocks are rearranged and turmoil ensues. This is the metaphor for our first year of marriage. We brought all our baggage from our own parents and didn't understand that we had been toting it around or that we had the choice to leave it at the door. With each chaotic move of the rivers we learned about ourselves and one another and managed to find a way through. We know God put us together and no amount of flying sticks would undo that. We had to learn how to live together, how to give a little, how to take a little. We had to learn our roles with each other and in our home. We learned what the other recognized as love and caring and we learned how to show that. We learned to speak in a language the other understood.

We learned how to walk together through hard times, how to be there for one another. Most days we learned when to speak and when not to speak. This season is another tough one. It's the most difficult tough time we've ever had. I know that surviving it won't be a problem. We've already survived so much.

I praise God that most people can't tell by looking at us that we are in the midst of difficult days. The other storms in our lives have made us stronger and taught us that our Daddy always takes care of us. We have no doubts about making it through this season. We just lean-in together and keep walking.


We celebrated our anniversary in downtown Boise enjoying the culture, eating good food and buying some early Christmas presents. My husband tried to create some distractions to keep my mind off of everything. For the most part it worked. I still thought about surgery only a few days away, but not as often as I would have if I had been at home. I might have been useless at home looking for distractions more than enjoying the weekend.

.   .   .

The weight instantly got heavier when we walked through the door into the kitchen. I managed to keep most of the burden to myself, but I felt it down to the center of my bones. Being still and quiet was difficult. Being busy was difficult. This would be my first surgery. The longest amount of time I've spent in a hospital was when my girls were born. This was definitely different.

Surgery was scheduled for Monday, November 12th, my grandma Hazel's 86th birthday.

The surgery itself wouldn't necessarily be the end. There was still a chance that they might find more than they had originally seen. There was still a chance it had spread to my lymph nodes. They wouldn't know until the surgery. The surgery, which was scary by itself, could potentially be the beginning. It could also be the end or the beginning of the end. The unknown was still too tremendous to hold.

# Chapter 6

## *Surgery*

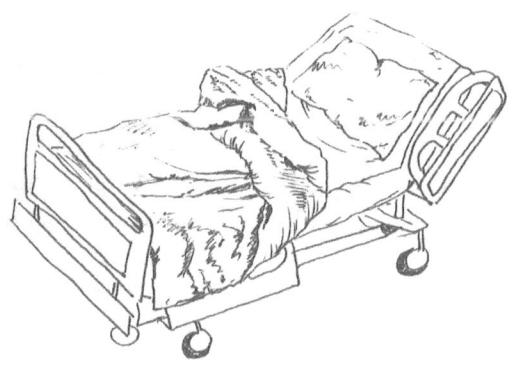

Jason and I left for the hospital early Monday morning. Most people weren't up and about yet. I was staring out the window, watching the street-lights, and I found myself wishing I had written down my thoughts before we left. I was having a difficult time processing how I felt about what lay ahead. I felt scared and slightly nervous. I knew I could do it. I often remembered what a friend said about making my body a living sacrifice, just letting the doctors do what they needed to do. I knew this, but I still felt the fear overtaking my body. I was frozen, yet focused and ready to get it over with. There was no end to feeling opposing emotions.

I began at the Breast Care Center (yes, that is the name on the building, a definite sign that there is too much breast cancer when they get their own building). This was the same place I had my second mammogram. They took more pictures than I could count and placed a wire in my breast. This wire was a roadmap for the doctor to know exactly where to go to find the cancer. The wire protruded out of my breast like a radio antennae, so they covered it with a bandage to protect it and keep it from being bumped or from moving. No one could see it under the bandage, but I was sure that antennae could pick up any signal.

Next, they wheeled me to the Nuclear Medicine Lab where I laid on a table that rolls back and forth. They injected me with blue dye and a radioactive solution. They rolled me under a camera so they could watch where the dye went. It quickly began traveling to one of my lymph nodes. They took many more pictures. The worst part was that I had to keep my arm over my head for over 30 minutes and it fell into a painful sleep. Now I was filled with blue dye, I had a numb arm, and I had an antennae sticking out of my boob.

Once that was over, I went to pre-op. They gave me an IV, asked questions, measured my blood pressure and took my temperature. Waiting for the next step, I laid there all alone for a few minutes. I stared at the pale yellow curtain and wondered again if they had made a mistake. This couldn't be real. This couldn't be happening to me. I have the best health of most people I know. The nurses went over my chart and proclaimed how healthy I was. The fact that I have cancer at 35 seemed made up. Maybe they looked at someone else's mammogram. Maybe they thought they found cancer, but it's not really there. How can someone so young and healthy get this sick? How was this real? But it was real, it was happening and nothing was going to change the imminent future.

This moment, alone and staring at the pale curtain that was the door and wall of my small room, was the only time I found myself crying. My thoughts panicked, maybe it's all a mistake. Tears threatened to come more fully when I realized the reality of it all, then I moved back to the moment where I knew I could do this. I was not alone. I would be victorious.

They gave me anti-nausea drugs. Then they gave me the best drug of all, the relaxing drug. As its name implies, it made me feel relaxed and peaceful. They wheeled me to the cold, uninviting operating room. It was large and sterile and filled with more people than I could identify. I wasn't able to see everything in that room clearly, and even though I wasn't fully coherent, I somehow knew that it was going to be okay. My scared factor would have soared without the help of the lovely relaxing drug fully doing its job. They put compression socks on my legs, then asked me to breathe deeply into the oxygen mask.

The next thing I remember, a nurse was waking me up telling me I did good. My immediate thought was, "I'm done, it's over?"

I fell right back to sleep. I woke up again, they said they'd call my husband. I went right back to sleep. I saw my husband come in, then I went back to sleep. Finally, I got to the point where I could stay awake for a few minutes. They decided it was time for me to go home.

Before we left, they informed me that the dye they injected into me would cause my urine to be blue. I went to the bathroom for the first time all day and peed royal blue pee, the color of a gemstone. I immediately got nauseous from standing up, or from the blue pee, and needed to sit down. This bout of nausea informed me that I had better not forget my barf bag for the ride home. It would be a long, 40 minute drive home. No one wants to pull over to puke and there is no guarantee Jason could do it before the nausea got the better of me.

I put the bag to use on the way home, then staggered into the house with my husband guiding me and all but holding me up. I promptly went straight to bed and right back to sleep.

My husband woke me up to give me more medicine at some time in the night, then I went right back to sleep. Sleep was coming easily. I could hear some of the rustlings of the family, but I didn't have the energy to interact with them. I finally fully woke up at about 6 AM. The phrase doesn't usually go that direction. Usually people say they finally went to sleep. I decided to move to the basement while everyone was still asleep and watch some TV and rest. My dad and his wife were watching the girls while we were at the hospital. It was a blessing they were there. Hannah got violently sick the night before we went to the hospital, and they were able to care for her so I could rest for my big day. Caring for her meant cleaning up the vomit covering the bathroom and not being able to go anywhere. They didn't seem happy to be stuck at home with the girls. I think they wanted to be at the hospital. We never told them which one, so even if Hannah had been healthy, they couldn't find us.

I heard my dad and his wife get up and prepare to leave the morning after my surgery. I was surprised they were leaving so soon. I really only saw them for a few hours. I was still in the basement. I gathered myself and made my way up the stairs. I was afraid they would leave without saying anything (no, this thought was not far-fetched). A few minutes after I found them, I said my good-byes, returned to the basement and rested with all my might for the remainder of the day.

It's incredible that a surgery where you essentially do nothing for a day can wear you down so much. It's a testament to the amount of work your body is doing while you are not watching.

"O Lord, I give my life to you. I trust in you, my God! ... for you are the God who saves me. All day long I put my hope in you." - Psalm 25:5

I can see how this experience might break a person. I know I am okay because I have full trust in my Daddy. He has me in all of this. He keeps my eyes on Him and not on what is happening. He keeps my focus in the moment rather than on anything past or future. He holds me. He comforts me. He loves me through it all.

I see the stickers that say "survive" or "cancer survivor." I've decided I don't like the word "survive" when it comes to my cancer. You might say you survived a shark attack, but "survive" sounds limiting to me. It creates a picture of just making it through, almost going down, but finally pulling through.

I will not survive this cancer attack, I will be victorious. I will win this battle because I do not fight this alone. In fact, most days I feel like I don't fight it at all. I am being carried through the battle. I see it, I feel it, but I rest in my Savior's arms who has already fought and won and who continues to take out each of my adversaries each day as they come at me.

I am victorious because of what He has already done for me. I am not a survivor who is barely living. I am victorious and fully alive and will come out on the other side of this stronger than before.

I am still home alone recovering from surgery. I am unable to wash dishes, sweep, vacuum or fold laundry. Yesterday, I cleaned out the dishwasher, but I was ordered not to do that today. I feel a little queasy today. I had to take some Metamucil which tasted like orange vomit. I think I held off my own vomit, but my body was thinking about it.

I know there is still more coming: surgery results, radiation. . . but I have been able to be free of those thoughts this week. Perhaps I am so preoccupied with getting better after surgery that my mind can't go there or perhaps it's just the grace of God. I sense everyone else around me is more concerned and aware than I am. I am simply going with the flow.

A friend came by on my third day after surgery. I watched her clean my house, and we had lunch together. It will always be painful to watch someone else clean my house. I wasn't raised to sit and watch. I was raised to help. I was raised to find something to do even if everything looked like it was done. I did it. I sat and watched and let someone else lovingly clean what I could not.

It was nice to have company. She encouraged me to start a blog with my writing. I'm sure that's a good idea, but it's scary and overwhelming. I want to write a book one day. Would that lead to it? Would a blog help me write a book one day? I suppose this would be a good time to write since I can't do much else. I've been wanting to write my story. Everyone has a story. I want to write mine. I have time on my hands, it would be wise to begin now. However, I'm very tired this morning, so rest may win out.

I like my job and I like teaching. I feel bad when I have to get a substitute. The students have a predictable day when I am there. Next week is only a 2 day week because Thanksgiving break begins on Wednesday. I was going to try to go back to school, but I decided yesterday not to. Everybody's happy with my decision: my husband, my mom, my principal, my fellow teachers. They didn't think I should go back to work so early. I think I would have been fine, but I won't turn down 2 extra days of recuperation.

My surgeon called. He said they got "clear margins" on the surgery which basically means they got all of the cancer. Also, all of the cancer they found was DCIS, the type of cancer that doesn't have the biological ability to spread. I love that. It's like worrying that a shark swimming in the water will bite you while you are standing on the beach. Once you realize the shark can't come on land, you feel much safer. Sharks are incapable of coming on the beach just like my cancer was unable to spread.

The really good news is I didn't need chemotherapy. Radiation treatment will begin in about a month. After 6 weeks of radiation treatment, I will be done. It is all a blessing. I still have a slightly deformed boob, but Jason announced yesterday that women with scars are sexy. If he's good with it, I'll be okay. Better to be a bit deformed and cancer free than to have perky breasts and be riddled with cancer.

On my fourth recovery day from cancer, I took the car to the mechanic. Actually, I didn't take it because I couldn't drive yet due to the strong medicine, so my father-in-law took me and the car. We walked to Flying M, a nice, unique coffee shop, while we waited for the repairs.

I did okay with the trip. I got a little extra sore just because of the uncharacteristic movement. I was tired too. It's incredible how a simple trip that is normally just a check on the "to-do" list can be so exhausting. It would be wise to increase my activity a little each day so my first day of school doesn't wipe me out. Of course, increasing my activity is the last thing I want to do. I'd rather simply rest and get better, rather than work to get better. It can be tough to know when to rest and when to work. Here comes another moment when I have to listen to my body, figure out what it needs and then follow through with what is most helpful for my health.

The Lord says, "I will guide you along the best pathway for your life." - Psalm 32:8

This is such a wonderful promise. If I remember it, I can relax and know that He is guiding me. I don't need to fret and worry, wherever He is guiding me is what is best for me. The problem I usually have is I think I know the best path for my life. Once I've traveled a little farther down the path, I realize I had no idea what the best path was and if I would have forced my agenda, I would have ended up in a place that was not best for me.

I can trust that this bout of cancer I am dealing with is what is best for me. He did not give me cancer, but He is walking with me down this path. If I listen to Him, He will teach me, love me and give me His best. I will be better and stronger. I will be prepared for what happens next down my path.

It has been a week since my surgery. We went to the store on Sunday. We were all getting a little stir crazy around the house. I quickly lost all stamina, was in extreme pain, got overheated and almost threw up.

This is starting to border on the line of sucking. I'm tired of being in pain. I'm tired of not sleeping well. I'm tired of lying around the house. I don't mind taking it easy, but I'm tired of being completely limited.

While I was lying awake in bed, I was thinking about surgery. Most surgeries come because a person has an injury. They are broken and the surgery fixes them. My surgery technically fixed me because it took out the cancer, but I didn't *feel* broken beforehand. I feel more broken now. I didn't have a broken bone that hurt and would eventually heal. I felt fine before (I know I wouldn't have stayed that way), so after the surgery I felt more beat up than I did before. It's a bit of an adjustment.

I have to adjust what I do, how much I do, and when I do things. I don't get to freely follow after everyone else. I have to pay attention to myself and sometimes say "no." I'm not used to this type of adjusting. I'm used to being more than capable of completing any and everything that comes my way. My limitations are taking some time to get used to.

I am not the only one adjusting to cancer entering my life. My husband has a whole new set of thoughts, worries, concerns, and decisions to deal with that he never had before. My husband confided in me over breakfast before my next doctor's appointment that he felt like he was trying to hold everything together. He was feeling overwhelmed and a little bit alone with his new burden. He was trying to make things easier on me which meant that he was silently taking on more duties and, especially, more worrying. He was trying to keep difficult things from me. We realized that we needed to figure out how to make it easier on him so he doesn't feel so stretched. The first step was in talking about it.

Everyone has their own way of dealing with difficult times. No one is right or wrong, but I also believe that no one can deal with those difficulties on their own. We must share our burden with someone, even if it's only by telling them. We can't and shouldn't ever carry our whole load alone.

# Chapter 7

## *Just a Lot of Things*

One of the biggest struggles I am dealing with is transitioning from being a healthy person to a "person with cancer." We met with the radiation oncologist. I was filling out another pile of paperwork when I realized I had taken the week off from thinking about all the cancer things. The paperwork brought me back, cutting this respite short. I had to check the "cancer" box on the forms I filled out for the radiation oncologist. Before my diagnosis, I didn't have to check any of those boxes. Now, I have to check the "cancer" box. I have to write the date of my lumpectomy and respond to all the people who are shocked that I have breast cancer at such a young age. Now I'm completely healthy . . . except for cancer.

I had a conversation with my dad about this. He had the same thing happen to him. About 12 years ago he was diagnosed with MS, and before that moment, he was completely healthy. Now he has the one box to check. It's crushing. You can't go back. You can't make it go away. For the rest of my life I will have to check the "cancer" box. I spent some time grieving this loss. It shouldn't have been a big deal, but it was.

The doctor explained the radiation process. He explained the risks and the options of radiation. He also explained he is uncomfortable putting a 35 year old through radiation treatment, but in the studies they've done, people without radiation treatment have had a much greater risk of the cancer returning than those who don't. The doctors and scientists have decided that the return of cancer, whether invasive or noninvasive, would be worse than any side effects of radiation. Regardless of what they think, I am more scared about the whole radiation process than I was before I walked in the door. I am more concerned about the sunburn on my skin, the tiredness it will cause, and the grocery list of side effects affecting other parts of my body.

They sent me home with pamphlets of information. I feel like I have a choice to either read up on it so I fully understand everything and perhaps become more scared, or I can sit back and trust the doctor's judgment. I know being educated can be a good thing, but I don't know if my mind can take this information in and send it to the right places of my brain. I think I need to call my grandmas and talk to them. If they can go through cancer treatment at 65 and 85 years old, I can do it at 35.

My radiologist also told me that my surgeon will probably be presenting my case to the tumor board. I never thought about how doctors might get together and discuss their cases. It makes sense. They probably share cases in which they want to hear other doctors' professional opinions. As teachers, we do this. We discuss the students we may need help reaching and seek how others have dealt with the same situation or what professional advice they may have. It helps to gather advice from others with experience. Sometimes the discussion itself reveals answers.

It's amazing to me that my case will be discussed among the surgeons. I felt kind of special in a weird way. If I have to have an illness, it may as well be a unique situation. I'd like to know the other doctors' recommendations for my treatment. How many cases like mine do they see?

There is so much going on. There is still so much I have to do before this is over. I'm going to be ok. I'm going to get through this amazingly. A year from now it will just be a memory.

∼

Why does the passing of time seem to change? Filled with its questions and unknowns, I felt every second of the month of October inch along. The month of November, filled with doctor's appointments and full days off of work, is racing. I'm afraid I will miss an entire day if I blink. Why does that happen? Why does time feel like it changes speed like a drunk driver on a windy highway? I haven't done anything differently. I'm not counting the days to some future event, I'm not wishing away the seconds, I'm not even busy. Why is it passing me by like a shooting star? It is fleeting. I feel like time is playing a game with me.

Once in a while time feels tangible. I can catch it, I can feel each moment. At other times, it hides, bolts or pretends to last longer than should be possible. I can't find more time. I can't save time. I have no control over time and its speed. My only choice is to enjoy the time I have and make wise choices with each moment. Time won't win this game if I simply sit back and enjoy the ride. Time won't trick me if I own my moments and choose to spend them in a way that makes me better and stronger.

In the midst of my healing and recovering and preparing for the next step, Uncle George died. It was a complete surprise. He was recovering from two knee surgeries when a hidden blood clot took him home. My grandma Hazel should not be burying a son. He was a rock that everyone leaned on. He was glue. He was one of the most consistent people I knew. He struggled with plenty, but never let any of it show. He was a big teddy bear. I can still see him walking into my grandma's kitchen for Thanksgiving. My grandma and mom were managing dinner preparations like professional jugglers. I can feel the heat from the stove. I can smell the turkey, potatoes and pies. I can see mischievousness in Uncle George's eyes. He was the first to start stealing pieces of food. He was the mastermind of each prank that happened in that home. He was a giant and he was a kid. When I was little, I was afraid of him; he usually had a big beard and he had a big voice. It took my shy, timid self time to see the truth. He was the best uncle. I could count on him to show up and always be the same. Around the age of 13, I started talking to him. He loved it. He loved that this once silent niece found her voice and I would gladly join in with his mischievousness.

I am thankful I spoke with him 2 days ago. I happened to call my mom while he was in the room. I'm thankful we went up to visit everyone in June. I'm thankful my girls knew him. I still can't believe he's gone. He is leaving behind a very large hole in this family. I don't know if it will be repaired.

I know my uncle is doing well. He's hanging out with his dad, Grandpa Ray, now and all the cousins' babies that didn't make their appearance with us. I know he's good. We are sad for the missing place he had previously filled in our lives. We are sad for a future without him.

I live about 400 miles away from the rest of the family. I want to go up there for the funeral, but I'm not quite strong enough for the trip and I've already missed too many days of work. I'm still recovering from surgery. I went Christmas shopping and lasted until hour four before I started fading and wishing to stop and lay down. Each day I try to do a bit more, but I'm not ready for that sort of trip. It's odd not being able to go to the funeral, but I know that is not where he is. I can say goodbye in my own way and in my own place. I have to make sure I am healthy first. I find myself in another moment when I put my health ahead of what some think I "should" do.

Later, my mom told me about my Uncle George's funeral. There were over 450 people, people he had impacted over his life. It didn't matter what he was going through in his own life, it never affected the kind of friend or person that he was. It was such an amazing legacy to leave.

I watched the end of "It's a Wonderful Life." Clarence, the angel, gives George a Bible. Inside the Bible, he writes:

"Dear George,

No man is a failure who has friends."

Let me always remember that it is the number of my friends and not the number of my things that make me successful.

It's been almost 2 weeks since my surgery. I don't feel that same heaviness on my body. I feel like I can almost cautiously be normal. Normal means I can complete the tasks of a day without having to take long breaks. I realize the pain may never fully go away. It's one of the daily mental battles I fight. This pain in my breast will probably be here, to some extent, for the rest of my life.

I'm going back to school tomorrow. I'm not concerned I won't make it through the day. I'm concerned my adrenaline will kick into gear and I will push too far. I fear I will make it through the day then be in extreme pain. Teaching requires an intense amount of attention. I have to know what each student is doing at all times, make sure they are on task which means getting them to do all the things they don't want to do, be aware of what I am teaching, be aware of how the students are receiving the information, and monitor their practice to make sure they understand. Typically, at the end of the day, the adrenaline is still carrying me and I appear to be full of energy. Once I get home, I crash with exhaustion. This is how a day flows when I am healthy. I'd prefer to be able to find a calm balance throughout the day and not fall back on adrenaline to survive. Teaching post surgery will give me an opportunity to try to learn to teach well without tapping into my adrenaline. I don't think I've ever done it before, but I need to begin tomorrow. I'm going to need to begin putting myself first and making wise choices to take care of myself.

It's time to think about Christmas cards. I started addressing envelopes. I'm sending everyone a picture of my daughters from the Oregon coast this past summer. They are sitting close together with their arms around each other with colorful buoys in the background. It makes my heart melt.

As I'm writing down people's names, I'm wondering if they know about what is going on with us. I wonder if they want to know. I wonder if their prayers and support would be helpful. I wonder how I would tell them. Many envelopes are sealed and ready to mail, but perhaps I'll add a message to those remaining unsealed cards. I realize again how much I appreciate others spreading the word about my cancer, but at the same time I wonder if they are spreading the word. Are they telling each other what is going on with me so I don't have to?

Part of me wants to walk through this journey silently, but maybe that is selfish. I would wish to know about friends and family traveling this trail. Why is it so difficult for me to tell them? Perhaps saying it still makes it too real. It's difficult to believe that after all this time, I am still having a tough time with the reality of this. Of cancer. Perhaps it's too fresh. Perhaps I need time to step away from it and look back, then maybe I'll be more willing to talk about it. It's sitting on me right now and I'm afraid to name it. It might take more interest in me if I say it out loud. It might become louder than it is. I'll figure out what to do about telling people. It's my choice either way. They'll be okay whether I tell them or not.

"Follow me one step at a time ... You see huge mountains looming and you start wondering how you're going to scale those heights ... I will equip you thoroughly for that strenuous climb. I will even give My angels charge over you, to preserve you in all your ways" - *Jesus Calling*.

Perhaps this is why October moved so slowly. I saw only large mountains ahead. Each one was taller than the next. Each one was covered in deep snow. The steep and slippery slope didn't look inviting. The mountains wanted to be left alone. Because I didn't know which of these mountains I would be climbing I kept my eyes down and focused on the path and my feet. I watched where my next step would be and nothing more. I couldn't consider climbing those mountains, and since I didn't know which one I would be climbing, I couldn't handle being overwhelmed with wonder and worry.

Now that I think I know which mountain is ahead, I have started looking at the mountains instead of my path. I've stopped focusing on my next step. Because my eyes are looking ahead to the daunting journey, I have more fear and weariness than anything else. Nothing has changed except where I focus my eyes.

∾

I made it through my first day back at work. I didn't have a bad day, but I didn't have a victorious day either. I felt isolated and alone. I struggled to talk about myself and couldn't honestly answer how I was doing. I ended up saying, "Okay." It was as if the only choices to the "How are you?" question were *good* or *bad* so I said, "Okay." I realize now I could have said weary, scared, cautious, heavy, hanging in there, determined, strong despite my weakness, hopeful for full recovery, or any number of more intelligent and truthful answers. I kept judging whether the person asking really wanted to know and responded accordingly, when in reality, I should simply have answered honestly no matter what.

When I did talk about it, someone interrupted with their own surgery story and I refused to compete in a conversation. I've met over a dozen people that have had breast cancer, they tell me they had it, but they don't regale their story. The fact that they have gone through this is all I need. All our stories are different. This person had an out-patient surgery, and interjected my story with "Me too!" then continued talking about herself. I felt isolated. Knowing that I looked normal on the outside, but wasn't normal on the inside made me feel like an alien in disguise. I imagine everybody looks at me and thinks I'm fine. I feel like I'm falling apart.

There came a day when I simply cried. I cried in front of my husband. I cried in my office. I cried in bed. I cried throughout the night. I cried while I wrote in my journal. The mountain ahead was too big. Radiation was coming and I was still healing from surgery. I was terrified of it and weary from the journey so far. Then the bills started coming in. I couldn't carry all of it. I couldn't carry the situation and the bills. I couldn't be strong enough for me and strong enough to stand up to the bill people. The cancer slogan is "survive." I didn't like that word. I wanted to be victorious, but on this particular day, I simply needed to survive.

I kept hearing the words, "I can't do this!" streaming through my head. Then I would immediately be reminded that in Him I can do all things. I knew I was not alone, this was simply one of those moments when I was struggling to stand, when I wondered if I was strong enough. I knew I'd be okay, maybe tomorrow, maybe the next day, maybe even later that day, but right at that moment I was weak. Praise God that when I am weak, He is strong.

There are plenty of extra burdens that come when you are diagnosed with cancer. There is the stress of surgery, the unknown results of treatment. The constant scheduling of different doctors for appointment after appointment, the medical bills, and trying to continue to be a wife, mother, daughter, friend, teacher, and coworker to the myriad of people in my life. As I got closer to the end of November, I felt the weight of each and every burden sitting on my shoulders. If I thought about it, I probably would have said I felt a little shorter. One or all of these things were on my mind constantly. I'm surprised I slept.

One day at the end of November, many of these burdens were lifted. I give God credit because they were out of my control. First, I called the insurance company and spoke to the most wonderful lady. She was very kind and explained everything to me in a way I could understand. She was patient with all my questions as she walked me through each insurance description and medical bill surrounding me on the floor of my pink room. She was a true blessing. God led me right to her to help decrease my stress.

The second lifted burden happened when I called my mom. I had to officially tell her I wouldn't be coming to my uncle's funeral. I had waited to see if I would start feeling better to make it official. Her burden lifting statement: "I didn't expect you to come." She already knew I should have stayed home and so did my aunt. Oh, the relief!

I want to remember how valuable these simple acts are to relieving a person's burden. You never know what they might be going through or struggling with. The simplest act of graciousness can make all the difference.

Seventeen days after my surgery, I felt like I was still trying to heal. Some days I struggled to keep my eyes open. I was healing and getting a little stronger each day, but I still felt weak. I managed to accomplish quite a bit in a day, then a point would come when I would have to stop because I was starting to ache.

Before the surgery people told me, "You'll be up and about right away." I was able to "be up," but it hurt or I was tired. I stayed completely down for 5 days after the surgery. I stayed partially down for 3 more days. The next 5 days, I paced myself, slowly easing myself back. Then it was time to go back to work. I was still trying to take it easy, but it was difficult. I had to wear a bra all the time. I had to stay warm because the cold caused pain. I couldn't stretch out my arm fully, lift anything heavy, or bump into anything. It's okay that the healing seemed to be going slowly, I simply wished the people hadn't told me that I would be up and about right away, so I didn't think I wasn't healing quickly enough or that I was weak because I still hurt. Everyone heals and recovers at different rates. As the days, weeks and years progressed, I would discover that I would do few things like everyone else. It is definitely a reminder to not compare our situations to others' situations. We can empathize and encourage, but everyone's journey will be completely different even if the events seem the same.

December 1st came, one of my favorite days. December brings my birthday, Christmas, a break from school and sometimes snow. It is the best time to stay inside and play games or sit by the fire: all my favorite things. On my 36th birthday, I was scheduled to get the CT scan that would map out the area they needed to radiate. Reality began again. I had a little time off from seeing doctors and thinking about cancer. It came rushing back on this day like shoppers the day after Thanksgiving. It was easier when there were no appointments. I could forget what was going on for short periods of time until a stabbing pain brought me back. I enjoyed those moments of forgetfulness.

I had to lie on an uncomfortable flat bed for the CT scan. Three lasers were aimed at me from around the room. One of them was aimed at my left side under my arm, the second was aimed at my right side under my other arm, and the third one was aimed directly at the middle of my sternum. Once I was lined up and the lasers were in place, I got my first tattoo. The lady tattooed me the old fashioned way, a needle with ink on it. I got 3 tattoos that day. Each one resembled a pencil mark located in the 3 places the lasers would aim while getting radiation treatment. During treatment, they will use those marks to make sure I am in exactly the same place each time. It is important for it to be accurate or they could radiate the wrong area.

I felt anxious about radiation. What would it do to me?

How would it affect me at my job since I have to get radiation treatment every day? What side effects would I get? They said you feel like you have a sunburn and get tired. Perhaps I won't get all the side effects they told me about. Perhaps this will be easy for me.

The unknown was upon me again. The unknown is a hooded figure slowly shuffling towards you in the middle of the night. I needed to remember to trust and surrender my worries. No matter what happened, I needed to remember I will be okay.

On December 6th, a lady from the Mountain States Tumor Institute, a place that is lovingly called MSTI (misty), called to let me know that my radiation would begin on Thursday, December 11th. My cancer surgery happened on my grandma Hazel's birthday, and my first day of radiation would happen on my husband's birthday.

I was not mentally ready for radiation treatment. I didn't know what it was going to do to me, and I was fearful. In my head, I was sure I could handle it fine because I handled everything else fine, but I was still terrified. Perhaps I was scared of the unknown. Perhaps I was not giving it to my Daddy and the fact that I wasn't letting go was causing me anxiety and fear.

At this point, my weariness was affecting my memory. I got overwhelmed easily. I cried at the drop of a hat. I knew I needed something from my Daddy, but I didn't know what it was. I couldn't put into words my weaknesses and needs, I just knew they existed. I felt like my teaching was lacking, my housework didn't get done, and I felt like I just barely squeaked through each day without having any measurable accomplishments.

People around me had their own stresses so I didn't dare

add mine to theirs. I simply continued to trust. Then I read another excerpt from the *Jesus Calling* book, "Trust Me and don't be afraid for I am your strength and song."

It is daunting when the mountain looms. It is terrifying when you feel you are entering a cave without a light, but I have learned (and when I forget, I am reminded), that with a little faith and trust, I come out okay. I simply have to keep moving.

December 11th, my first day of radiation treatment, arrived. I planned to leave school about 30 minutes early each day, so I could get to treatment on time. I already had an educational aide in my room during that time. She would simply finish the day with my students and send them home, so I could rush out the door.

On this particular day, I felt tired and was feeling a little sick. I had to ignore my feelings because I had work to do. I had my radiation treatment to begin. I found it interesting that I called it "my" radiation treatment as if I wanted to claim it, to make sure no one else claimed it. I suppose it was true, it didn't belong to anyone else.

Once I began treatment, I couldn't stop. It was a 6 ½ week process with no break. I went to treatment 5 days a week. It was a 35 minute drive each way. I didn't get to take a day off, I couldn't call in sick. I hated that I was afraid of the side effects: skin irritation, hair loss, tiredness... I wished I could believe I wouldn't feel any of those. I wished I didn't have to worry about what soap I would use for the next 6 weeks or which bra I would wear or that I had to stop shaving my armpits.

They told me my skin would be irritated so I needed to use a mild soap and stop shaving. I would have to wear a sports bra because a regular one would hurt. I was devastated. Thankfully, it was winter and no one would see my hairy armpits, but the bra thing was more difficult. I am what most would call blessed in the chest department; although, I don't always feel that way. Going without a supportive bra while still working was unbearable to think about. I kept wishing everything could be "normal." I wished I could have a day where I didn't think about cancer. I wished my life didn't have to be turned upside down for 6 ½ weeks.

I had no magic lamp. None of these wishes were going to come true. Yet, I knew I would be okay. I just didn't know how hard I wanted to work at all of this. I had two days of feeling strong and normal the week before. I would have a new definition of strength after this was over. I would be okay, only because I wouldn't go through this alone.

December 12, 2012: "As your thinking goes, so goes your entire being" - *Jesus Calling*.

It's time for me to take this to heart. My thinking has been pure fear this past week: fear of what might or could happen as a result of radiation. But what will happen will happen, I will manage, then it will be over and I will get better. I do not need to dread the next 6 weeks. I need to walk one day at a time knowing my Daddy gives me grace enough for each day, each moment. I need to stop trying to tackle all of it at once, relax and take one day at a time. He has given me strength for today. My pity party is over.

∾

They told me when I started treatment I might notice side effects after a few weeks, I probably wouldn't notice right away. Within the first 2 days of treatment I was exhausted and my skin was agitated with a burning sensation. I wasn't surprised when whatever side effects were mentioned, I got in full force right from the beginning.

I had the flu. I only managed 5 days of radiation treatment before I got sick. The night before the flu showed up, I went to bed with monumental plans to tackle household tasks since my surgeon gave me the thumbs up to do whatever I wanted. My plans were thwarted when I woke up with a stomach ache soon followed by vomiting. I spent the day resting, nibbling crackers, drinking soda, and waiting for the next signal that I needed to run to the bathroom. The next day, I spent recovering my strength and feeling the effects of a day without food. I had to think about going back to work while being completely behind in everything. I wasn't sure I could do this schedule: put in minimal time at work, go to radiation treatment, go to bed early, get sick on the weekend, then repeat.

I feel blessed to have a wonderful family who is trying to help me. My husband's school put on a benefit concert for us on Friday night. It was strange being the one they were raising money for. They raised almost $900. I felt blessed. Together with their pizza sales, they gave us $1000 towards medical bills. That is half of our current bill. I am already stressed over what's happening to my body. I am thankful the school has helped minimize the money stress for now.

· · ·

On Friday, January 11th, the Notus High School decided to donate all proceeds of their 4 basketball games: JV girls, JV boys, varsity girls, and varsity boys, to me. They also had 3 baskets of goodies up for silent auction, again with the proceeds going to me. It's indescribably surreal to be the center of something like that. We walked into the gym (after 4 years of teaching at this school, this was my first basketball game) and looked at the full "home" stands. Fortunately, a student of Jason's, was saving a whole bench and graciously let us sit there. I noticed a number of people wearing pink. Even though none of those people came up to me and said a word, their conscious decision to wear pink when the school colors were blue and white felt equivalent to giving me a hug or an encouraging smile. We watched the end of the boys' JV game. They won by 2 right at the buzzer. Jason went across the gym to visit with his parents and I was left alone, not sure what to do with myself. Should I try to visit with these people? Should I go sit with my family? I just sat there watching.

After watching the varsity girls warm up, Mr. Christensen began announcing what was happening tonight. He shared that the proceeds from the games were going to me in order to help pay doctor bills. He shared that they appreciate me and hope for the best for everything. Jackson's gas station (a gas station we can see from our house) donated a basket that the varsity girls presented to me. Each varsity girl wore pink socks. The cheerleaders sported pink socks and wore pink ribbons in their hair. The entire girls' basketball team began walking across the gym towards me. I reluctantly (reluctantly because I would prefer to go unnoticed) rose from my seat and met them on the floor. All I could see as they walked across the floor were their enormous smiles.

They walked with such pride. I graciously received the pink basket and shared my thanks. These girls began hugging me. I didn't even know one of their names, but you wouldn't have known that by their hugs. Eventually, I was in the midst of a group hug. I didn't do what I normally do, I didn't shy away, I didn't mentally flee. I stayed. I enjoyed the moment and I hugged them back. I didn't know these girls. Not one of them had been in my class as a student, but they knew me and they loved me and cared for me.

I enjoyed the game. I stayed for the varsity boys game. A neighbor and senior on the team came up to where I was sitting and gave me a hug before the game began. The girls' coach and elementary PE teacher walked by where I was sitting. His eyes said I hope you're ok, I'm on your side. He reached his hand out to me. For a brief moment, I saw what they saw. They see this relatively young person dealing with the C-word. For anyone who hasn't had cancer, this word, this disease is one of the worst. They see me, they see that I'm managing this and they have the utmost compassion for me. They don't know what to say, so they wear pink. They don't know how to help, so they bid on the baskets or come to a basketball game. They don't know what to do, so they hug me. I interpret what they do as their way to find hope. Their actions, no matter how small, mean the world to me. I receive their attempts to support me. I feel every ounce of hope they are wishing on me. I want them to know that their small efforts speak volumes to me.

Hundreds of people were supporting me Friday night. They told me they were behind me, they were pulling for me, my victory meant everything to them. They were cheering for me just like they cheered for their kids to win those games. Each time I completed a radiation treatment, they applauded as the basketball went swish. Each time I got up in the morning and came to work, they cheered for my fast break. Each time I smiled in the midst of everything, they gave me a high five or a pat on the back. "Good game" they said.

# Chapter 8

## *Radiation*

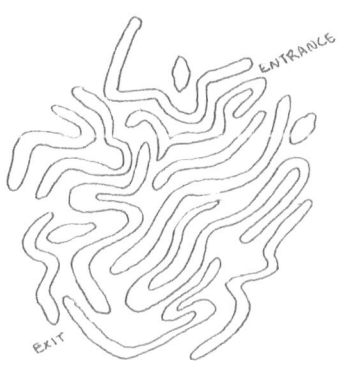

I t is day 15 of radiation treatment. I always arrive early. I check in, they know my name. I don't say it. When the secretary sees me, she checks her computer then tells me I am checked in. The other secretary tells me she'll let them know I am here. I walk to the back of the waiting area towards the offices. I turn left down the hallway and am immediately lost even though I've been here 15 times. I follow the signs leading me back to the small radiation oncology waiting room at the end of the hallway that turns more times than I can remember. After I make the final left turn, I recognize the big doors and chairs in the waiting room, and know I have arrived. I quickly scan the waiting room, hoping nobody notices I am looking at them. I turn right to go to the women's dressing rooms. I look at both rooms. One of the rooms is towards the back so no one will walk by me, but the one in the front tends to have the hospital gown that fits. I choose which dressing room to walk into and yank the brown and tan curtain over to the opposite wall, trying to close the gaps that won't really close. Even though my breasts have been seen by many over the last 3 months, I don't need to add a fellow radiation patient to the list. I take a gown down from the shelf. It's a faded light pink top with pink flowers on it. It has short sleeves, a snap at the top by my collar bone and a snap in the middle of my breast bone. The bottom two-thirds of the shirt is open. It's my job to try to keep that part closed. I take off my coat, I take off the scarf that is hiding the fact I no longer wear a bra. I take off my shirt. Finally, I take off the cami tank top with the shelf bra built in. I fold my clothes and place them in the 4 inch by 3 foot locker. I close the locker, lock it and remove the key attached to the red, spiral, jelly bracelet. I always use the same locker. I don't know why. It wouldn't bother me if someone else used it and I had to choose a different one, but I use the same one anyway. It's on the far right. That way I would only have one locker neighbor if there was anybody else using the lockers. It's comical that there are 10 lockers. I'm sure there are never more than 2 people coming and going at a time based on the 15 minutes per person radiation schedule. Maybe since the lockers are so small, some people have to use more than one to store their things.

After my clothes are safely locked away, I go out into the small waiting room. It's a long, narrow room. It fits about 8 chairs lined up along one wall facing the opposite wall which, surprisingly, holds a counter where I could have coffee, juice or water if I wanted. I'm never there long enough to enjoy the beverages, but it's nice they are available. The television is mounted above the beverages, and I tend to watch what is on even after the patient before me releases the power of the remote. I sit down, carefully checking my two snaps and the large opening, making sure nothing is hanging out. I always know when something has escaped because people look at me funny or they get uncomfortable. I sit and wait.

I went to a church ski camp in Olympia, Washington when I was 13. This was the same camp where the pastor taught about Psalm 1, the tree planted by water that will bear fruit in season. They gave water skiing lessons in addition to all the other typical camp events. My first time skiing, I went with a small group. I don't remember all the instructions, but I know I got up. It was so fun that the next time the leaders went out, I wanted to go. This second time, I was the only skier, the only camper, the only girl in the boat. I water skied, felt very good, and climbed into the boat when I finished. I sat on the back seat, pleased and ready to head back. The two male leaders kept saying "um" and acting uncomfortable and almost pointing. I looked down. One entire breast had come out of my swimsuit. I fixed it. I don't remember anything after that mortifying moment. Now, I recognize those uncomfortable "um"s and don't take so long to remedy the problem. It hasn't happened since then, but I'm ready.

Before long, I hear footsteps from farther down the hallway. It's likely my turn since I'm the only one here. The lady smiles and tells me they are ready as if this is going to be fun. We walk past the sign that says something like, "This is a treatment area, please don't come back here." This room or enclave on the right side of the giant door has a long tall counter and 2 computer screens where the two ladies will monitor my treatment and watch me. They ask for my name and birthday. They already know the answer. It's how they identify that I am the right person. I think this is comical. Who came up with this system? Are there a lot of people trying to get radiation treatment under someone else's name? Is that why they started this protocol in the first place? Are the technicians having difficulty with their memories in that they wouldn't recognize a patient from one day to the next? If these are really problems, is my recitation of my name and birthday really the best way of identification? Couldn't I easily tell another person the answer to that? I recite my name and birthday. It takes me a moment to remember, then it flows off my tongue quite easily as if I've always known the answer to that question.

I follow the technician through the 12-inch thick door, the first sign that this treatment is dangerous. This door keeps the radiation in the room. The room is large, too large for the big machine, another sign of the danger. The radiation needs plenty of space to disperse so it won't affect the people coming in and out. Now begins the worst part. I am getting used to it after 15 days, but not really. I get to take off my shirt, which already revealed too much. Yep, take it off. The machine, although very powerful, can't get through my shirt. I take it off and use it to cover the right breast, the one that doesn't need the radiation. It might be more modest to only have one breast hanging out for all to see than two. I know this isn't true, but I do it anyway. The technician will even arrange the shirt over my right breast nicely so I am more fully covered. My right breast is fully covered, my left breast is sitting all by itself completely revealed for all to see. I sit on the table. It's probably supposed to be a bed, but it's hard and flat like a table. I lay down and place my head in the plastic head thing that has been adjusted just for my height. I raise up my knees so they can put a blue cushion-pillow-thing under them. It's supposed to make me more comfortable. They put a strap, a blue rubber loop, around my feet so I won't cross them. If I cross my feet, I will change position and that would ruin the treatment. I raise my arms, revealing my hairy armpits which I'm not allowed to shave (I can shave the right side, but that would be weird) and grasp the handlebars behind my head, also set just for me. The technicians line up my tattoos with the lasers around the room. They set the table to the correct height, it feels like 5 feet up in the air, calling out numbers and watching the lighted ruler that displays on my chest. I visit with the technicians a little, it makes the process and my lonely boob feel a little less horrible.

They say, "Here we go," and exit the room, being sure to fully close the mammoth door and leave me alone with the machine. The machine moves into place. There is a lit scene of mountains and streams covered with trees and a little snow, but it's not exactly in my line of vision and I can't find anything interesting or curious in the picture so I look at the white tiles on the ceiling or the green cross formed by laser lights embedded in the ceiling. The machine hovers over my right side angled at the right side of my left breast. It makes static noises as the metal tube-looking things change position. Then it makes a high pitched buzz as it zaps me with an invisible dose of radiation. It gets staticky again then makes a lower pitched buzz as it zaps me with a different invisible dose of radiation. I have counted the seconds. The first dose takes 8 seconds. The second dose takes 10 seconds. The machine sings static again and shifts to the left side of my body. It moves slightly below the table where I can't see the metal tubes anymore. The technician comes in and moves the table so I am in the correct position. She leaves me alone and I wait for the static again. The machine does its zapping again, this time zapping the left side of my left breast. I count 10 seconds for the high and 8 seconds for the low. The machine moves right over the center of my body. I know that I am finished, but I stay in my awkward position waiting until the technician graciously says, "You can put your arms down." I try to nonchalantly cover up with the pink shirt. I wait impatiently for the technicians to lower the table when I would prefer to jump off it. I lie there as she removes the pillow from under my knees and the rubber loop from my feet. Once the table is lowered, I sit up, put my feet on the floor and dress in my pretty pink shirt. Once again, there is a little small talk followed by, "I'll see you tomorrow." I walk out of the bomb proof room into the small waiting room. No one is there because I am the last patient for the day. I unlock my clothes, choose another dressing room and put myself back together. The trip out is much like the trip in. I look for clues that I am heading in the right direction through the maze of doors and scenic mountain pictures. Once I know I am heading the right way, I walk a little faster, slip out the doors and begin going home. I will do this again tomorrow and the next day. I have 18 days left. The last day will have only one difference from all the others. No one will say, "I will see you tomorrow."

"Thank Me for the conditions that are requiring you to be still. . . Instead of resenting the limitations of a weakened body, search for My way in the midst of these circumstances. . . Quietness and trust enhance your awareness of My Presence with you. Do not despise these simple ways of seeing Me. . . My strength and power show themselves most effectively in weakness." - *Jesus Calling*

These words reminded me to find things to be thankful for while recovering from surgery and receiving radiation treatment. I had to learn to slow down and enjoy the quiet, enjoy the moments of sitting, and soak in the moments of rest. I had to learn to do what I could and accept not doing what I couldn't. One day towards the end of December, I sat with my youngest and helped her with her homework. I didn't rush away. I was wholly present. Most days I would have already gone to bed, but I found the energy to help her and was blessed with special time with my little one.

I was thankful for the help I was getting from others and was learning how to sit back and accept the gifts of time and energy that those around me offered. I was aware then, and am still aware now, that I only operate and achieve anything by the grace of God. I have no strength of my own. God gives me everything I need to accomplish what is before me each day. It is only through Him that I am victorious.

. . .

Each of us has good days and bad days. When I was about a month into my cancer treatment, and it had been about 3 months since my diagnosis, I reflected on my level of energy. I went to a Christmas party and people were surprised and pleased to see me. They were surprised I felt well enough to join the party. They were pleased because they were encouraged to see me out. Later, a friend called and told me I was strong and an encouragement to people around me.

At the time that I was in the midst of all of this, I did not feel any of these things. I felt a little slower, a little less energetic, a little more tired and a little more pain. I simply walked forward through my life one step at a time. The treatment for cancer and the idea of dealing with cancer took more from me than the actual cancer.

I imagined that on the day I became 100% myself again I would say, "Wow, I wasn't feeling well all those days." I would be able to tell a definite difference between the beginning of this and the end. Because I hadn't felt well for over 3 months, I couldn't compare my healthy self to my present self. I had no idea how this cancer had really affected me. I had no way of holding my health of summer next to this new state in winter to measure the change. When a cold steals 3 days of health, you are very aware on day 4 of the difference. These moments weren't close enough together for me to fully compare. I simply moved forward at the pace I could move and did what I could do. I didn't get down on myself for not being able to do something I used to be able to do. I had a new normal I had to learn to accept on a daily basis.

We all have days when we don't feel completely whole. Sometimes we are ill, sometimes our mind is full or weary, sometimes our hearts ache. We have to keep going. We know there will come a day when we feel better. We simply need to keep moving and do our best during those difficult days. We also need to remember that many people around us may be having difficult days. Most of the time, we won't be able to tell by looking at them. They are trying to keep moving in the midst of their difficult days also. We have a choice to hinder them on their journey or help them.

People kept telling me how strong I was, but I felt anything but strong. I wanted to be able to see myself through someone else's eyes. In most people's eyes I saw compassion, but sometimes there was pity or fear. I hoped being strong was a good thing and that people didn't think I was seeking their praise. I'd rather be strong than be too weak, fall apart all the time, and need people to carry me. Most people didn't know how to help me, so I got all my strength from my Daddy. They didn't have to worry about it. They could simply watch me walk.

After about 2 weeks of radiation treatment, I was scheduled to meet with the medical oncologist. Before having cancer I didn't know there were different kinds of oncologists. A radiation oncologist deals with radiation treatment and a medical oncologist deals with medical treatment which includes chemotherapy and any other medication. We talked for a few minutes when we met. He noticed my Ossie's Surf Shop sweatshirt from Newport, Oregon, so we talked about surfing and vacations. Due to my unique situation, I had a choice about whether or not I took medication for hormone control after my radiation treatment was complete. The choice he gave me was based on my fear. The doctor asked me what I was more anxious about: side effects of medication or the return of cancer.

This may have been the first time I really had a choice about my treatment. I told him that the side effects of the medication concerned me more than the return of cancer. This medication wouldn't help it go away. It would possibly reduce its chance of returning. I rarely take medication, so I usually endure more side effects because my body is unfamiliar with medicine. Once I shared my answer with him, he encouraged me to continue to live healthy and don't go nuts trying to overdo it. He told me to go surfing.

It has taken me a few years to learn what this "live healthy" advice looks like for me. It looks different for everyone. I had to find the things in my life that make me healthy, not the things that make others healthy. I had to find a way to keep my mind clear and focused on what would benefit me. I had to find a way to eat what made me feel well. I had to find exercises that would give my body energy and I had to find fun activities that would bring me joy and peace.

As you journey through your life, make choices that make you whole and happy and productive. Make choices that fit who you are and what will make you the best version of yourself.

$\sim$

I was 35 when I was diagnosed with breast cancer. I was teaching 3rd grade at the time. I did not have the ability or the desire to take a leave from work while I went through treatment. Most people who are diagnosed with cancer are older and are often already retired from their jobs. They have the ability to focus on treatment and rest. Each day, I went to work, taught 34 third graders, drove 35 minutes to radiation treatment and 35 minutes home. I ate dinner and crawled into bed at about 6:30 in the evening. It took everything I had to maintain this routine.

Every little extra germ made me sick. I had to stay away from large groups. If anyone was sick, I contracted whatever they were carrying. In the midst of all of this difficulty, the thoughts I had during this time were of staying relaxed and trying to enjoy each day. I chose not to stress about anything or worry about accomplishing tasks. I felt blessed and content.

It is our mindset that helps us get through the toughest days. We have to control our thoughts. We have to choose what we focus on and choose to focus on what will give us strength and help us to accomplish whatever lies ahead.

As 2012 came to a close, I reflected on all of the happenings that occurred in the previous 12 months. I realized it had been a year where we experienced a lot of loss and sickness. In 2012 my girls' two beta fish died, our beloved dog of 12 years, Kobie, died of bone cancer, I got pneumonia and cancer, my uncle died, and my grandma got really sick. Normally our years aren't filled with this much sickness and sadness. During this time in our lives, when living was at its most difficult and trying, our family was at its strongest. Our family came together to show strength and togetherness. Our family became one. We learned to lean on one another, trust one another and believe in one another. The difficult events of the year didn't determine who we were. How we got through those events determined our true identity.

During this time we became, and still are, an extremely united family. We are not perfect, we are united and respectful to one another. We haven't always been this way, but we are this way now.

Don't shy away from the difficult times that come into

your lives. Rally together around those you love and care about and learn how to lean on each other. Learn how to be weak and let others be strong and to be strong so others can be weak. Don't shy away from talking about the hard stuff. You may be amazed what you learn about yourself and the ones you love.

# Chapter 9

## *Unapologetic*

I never would have wished for breast cancer to enter my life, but I am grateful it was the catalyst to unite my family in the most precious way. As I write this, it has been almost 5 years since my initial diagnosis and we are still close. We enjoy each other and let each other be who we were made to be.

2012 is ending. A new year means new beginnings to most people. They can begin fresh, forget about their failures and try to do or be something new. To me, it's a new day just like all the others. Each day I have a choice to begin fresh, to learn from yesterday's mistakes and to come a little closer to being the person I want to be. A new year is a great time to start that, but so is each day. If I fail on day two of the New Year I have to wait until the next year. Instead, on my system, I simply begin again tomorrow.

So in this new year, I want to walk through and be completely present in each day. I want to accept each moment as a gift and treasure it. I want to learn from my mistakes quickly and move forward. I do not want to miss a day because I'm looking forward to or dreading a different day. I want to live to my fullest, not caring if I please everyone. I only care if I am loving, compassionate, kind and generous. I don't want to judge myself harshly, but instead be gracious with myself.

God has put me where He has put me. He will give me the grace to do what is before me and the strength to stand each day. These so-called negative things that come my way will not knock me down, but make me stronger. I will be victorious and, upon reflection, the path I cross will be overflowing with blessings.

In my mind, the path is muddy and dark, but when I look back, flowers are overflowing the path, squeezing together and rejoicing like teenage girls at a pop concert. I have made it a pattern in my life to remember to look back at the path I have just walked and to gaze at the blossoming flowers. After our first dog, Kobie, died, we got a new dog. Kobie's death was sad and painful. Kobie was Jason's dog, he was devoted to him and would follow him everywhere. Eliza, our other dog, wasn't the same after he died. Jason was up in Yellowstone taking a class about wolves for his master's degree. He learned that wolves are pack animals. When they lose their pack, they can become ill. Eliza was part labrador and part border collie. She had spent her life keeping Kobie in line and watching out for the family. She needed a job. In July of 2012, the girls and I drove to Twin Falls with Eliza to meet Shelby and see if she was a good fit for our family. She was a year and half old. Her owner had died and the little boy she lived with was allergic. Upon meeting us, she continually barked at sweet Eliza and we wondered if this adoption would be a good idea. Shelby was sprinting with her dump truck of energy, back and forth down this long patch of grass. Every time she passed Eliza, she would stop and bark at her. We were thinking this won't work, we were full of uncertainty. We didn't want to make the wrong decision. On the next pass, Eliza turned and nipped Shelby in the heels saying "knock it off." Shelby stopped. That was the deciding factor. Eliza was boss. She would keep Shelby in line. We wrote the check and took the two dogs home. Because Jason was in Montana, Shelby became my dog. We walked or ran together every day. I threw her the ball whenever she had too much energy. Not only is she a blessing, but she came just before this cancer journey. She is a gift on my tough days. I didn't want to lose Kobie and there was nothing good about it. Once we looked back, we could see the blessing of Shelby growing from that muddy, dark time.

I know that all seemingly negative or difficult things will reveal something beautiful in my life. I simply need to look back every once in a while, after I've walked through the mire, and see what God has done to the path He carried me through. He always does it, I can count on Him to do it again and again.

The most difficult part of having cancer is the battle that goes on in my brain. I can cope with the daily schedule of going to treatment. I can manage the pain. I can even figure out how to dress. The problem is my mind. It goes to places of despair or pity. It doesn't let me sleep. When I wake up, the battle immediately begins again. I can't escape it. I know, I give my thoughts to God. I know, I focus on His truths. Those things work. What I'm saying is that I don't get a break from the battle. If I let down my guard for even a breath my mind takes me to places I prefer to avoid. That's why mornings are difficult. I must begin the battle the moment I wake up and sometimes the *thought enemy* gets a jab in as I'm just becoming fully aware of the arrival of a new day.

It's an exhausting battle. It's a continuous battle. It's one that people don't know I'm having. They can't see my battle. They only see my actions. They cannot see the war going on in my head. They can't see the casualties that have occurred. It's the only thing no one else can understand. It's my battle and I have to fight it alone every day. I know I will win. Sometimes I get weary, but in the end I will win.

I survived my first day back at school despite an extremely short fuse. I'm beginning to have a little more pain on my breast from radiation. It hurts when it moves. If you know very much about breasts, they move all the time. It's getting red and a little blistery. My doctor is looking at changing my schedule to give my skin a break. I only have 18 days to go.

My gynecologist called me last night. I really appreciated it. She had my chart out for a couple of weeks and had been thinking of me. I told her that I appreciated her obeying her gut by sending me to get a mammogram. Without that recommendation they wouldn't have caught this cancer. She's taking a new job, which I'm sad about, but I will trust my Daddy to give me a new doctor that is just as good or better.

"My life has been an example to many because You have been my peace and protection." - Psalm 71:7

I believe the level of peace one has is equivalent to the amount of trust one puts in God. If I surrender fully to Him all my issues and concerns, then I trust Him and I no longer worry because I know He has it.

I'm having much more pain now. My skin is red, my breast is extra large and my nipple hurts. I don't know if all this is typical or not. Regardless, I trust my Daddy. I trust that He's taking care of me and He will not release me from His hand.

I am weary. I struggled to not fall asleep driving home from treatment yesterday. I tried to go to bed early, but I couldn't fall asleep. Going to sleep is difficult. I am tired enough, but my mind struggles in those quiet moments before sleep. It's not busy, it just struggles.

*Friday, January 4, 2013*
    *Daddy, I know you are in all of this with me. I know you*

*are making up for parts of me that aren't working. Help me to remember that you are there throughout each day, help me to lean and depend on You. Draw my thoughts to what I can be thankful for. Help me to be that example of peace. I don't want to do this. I don't want to have radiation and everything that goes with that. Help me to be thankful for my job, the health you have given me and to remember that You love and care for me and none of these other things matter.*

I'm tired. After 10 hours of sleep, I still feel weak and groggy as if I could sleep 10 more hours. If my body truly needs this much sleep, I can understand why I am struggling through the week, especially when you add the exhaustion of teaching. I can typically handle a lot. Right now, I can only handle the minimum. I'm tired of being tired. I only have a few more weeks left of radiation. I don't want the weeks to go by fast, but I'm anxious to be done.

When the media portrays a person with cancer, they always address their chemotherapy treatment. I know that chemotherapy wreaks havoc on one's body. Because of this media attention, I thought radiation would be easy, no one talks about radiation treatment. I assumed I would sail through it with no problems. I didn't. Radiation beat me up. From the first day, I was tired, I hurt, I felt like I had an intense sunburn. As the weeks went on, it got worse. Some days, I was on the verge of sleeping in the car on my way home after treatment. I ate dinner, went to bed and repeated the same steps the next day. When there were only a few weeks left, the pain got so bad that it hurt whenever I moved. My skin was turning to a pink, painful, leather. I was going to bed earlier and earlier. I was losing patience with my students.

I never imagined myself with failed health, especially at 36. I read in Psalm 73:26, "My health may fail, and my spirit may grow weak, but God remains the strength of my heart." I knew that I would get better eventually. At the time, I did not feel like myself. I was tired every moment. I was in pain. I, who was normally very efficient, couldn't focus enough to function. It hurt to clean out the dishwasher. I was tired, so tired. I fell asleep while driving. My eyes closed and I couldn't remember portions of my trip. It may have only been for a second at a time, but it still happened. I considered taking a pillow to school and napping under my desk while students were at lunch. I rested and napped all weekend trying to store up rest like a chipmunk stores up nuts. I had dandelion seed-sized energy, most of which I saved for school, so my family received the leftovers. These were all unexpected and unwelcome outcomes of radiation treatment.

However, throughout this pain and exhaustion storm, God remained my strength. I stepped out of bed in the morning because of Him. I accomplished basic tasks because He gave me strength. I had hope in full healing because I knew he was healing me. I rested and had peace in this season because He was present. I was not good at having cancer, but He gave me grace to walk through it.

∾

After a snowstorm, I thought the roads would be slick and dangerous when I went into town for my radiation treatment, so I gave myself an extra half hour. In the end, I arrived 30 minutes early. In addition, they were 15 minutes late. I read a great article in a magazine and visited with 3 people. Anita's husband is scheduled for radiation right before me. We've been visiting for a few weeks now. She is a nice lady. They make a good couple, supporting each other. Jim's prostate cancer came back. They are hoping they can get it with radiation.

I met another lady who I haven't seen before. I don't know her name. She has 2 days left of radiation and has already finished 2 bouts of chemotherapy. She just got out of a 12 day stay in the hospital for pneumonia. She blessed me. She was very positive and upbeat about everything. She smiled a large sparsely toothed smile. Her bright, blue eyes lit up her pale face and she graciously reminded me to chill with her presence. I may have been extra miserable last week because school started or because my body was adjusting or because my treatments were depleting me. No matter what it was, I felt gloomy and negative. This lady, who has been through much more than me, reminded me to be thankful and hopeful and smile my way through this journey.

The third person I visited with was a blonde lady, not much older than me. She had her CT scan, where they prepare the map for radiation treatment, and I saw the same fear reflected on her face I had on my face when I first entered the building. Lord, I would love to meet her again. I want to encourage her and be a person she can talk to. I've gone through this journey by talking to God. I didn't feel as comfortable meeting with a group of older women and talking about my situation and I would guess she wouldn't either. I'm thankful for these people: a friend, an encourager and hopefully one I get to encourage.

~

People throughout the Earth have difficulties in life pursuing them like hungry wolves. Hopefully, we learn a few things from those difficult times. Hopefully, we become a little stronger. Cancer was the first difficulty in my life that compelled me to stop and seriously ponder my priorities about myself. People are comfortable speaking about life and family priorities, but my struggle was prioritizing myself. I can be rather unyielding about the standards I set for myself. I judged myself against my imagined image of others. I believed I must act a certain way or live a certain way. When I had 9 days left of radiation treatment, I found myself reflecting on how cancer had changed the way I judged myself.

One of the greatest lessons I learned over the 4 months since my cancer diagnosis was to be kinder and less judgmental of myself. I was and am in the process of learning to lower my expectations and increase the grace I give myself. Cancer reduced my ability to work as hard as before. I didn't berate myself for that weakness. I did what I was capable of, then I released the rest. No amount of worrying could complete my tasks. I let go and praised myself for what I accomplished, not what I failed to do. I didn't look the same as before. I couldn't wear stylish clothes or make my figure the best it could be. I learned to show myself grace and not be overly concerned with my looks.

I tired quickly at night. I allowed myself to go to sleep, regardless of the time. Dishes were waiting to be done, I turned my back on them until I had the strength to clean them. While at home, I was either wearing sweats or pajamas because they were comfortable. I didn't change when someone came by in order to impress them. As I stopped being concerned about what I thought of myself, I cared less what others thought of me.

I did my hair in a way that was functional, a way that made me feel good even if it wasn't the best style. I painted my fingernails any color I wanted. I wore the shoes I wanted to wear even if they were giant unstylish snow boots. Sometimes I wore makeup in public, sometimes I didn't. I was finally learning to do things because I desired to do them, not to impress the strangers surrounding me. My Christmas tree was still standing on January 17th, and I didn't rush to take it down so others wouldn't judge me. When I had the energy to take it down, I took it down.

I wasn't able to exercise, but I stopped judging my shape. My hair was gray, I didn't plan to dye it. There was no one out there I needed to impress. I needed to be unashamedly myself, to be comfortable living in my skin and to give myself room to breathe. Today, I am still nurturing these skills. I am still practicing kindness to myself. This may be the most valuable gift I could have received during this journey.

It's unfortunate it requires a good shaking of our lives for us to truly get our priorities straightened out. I wonder if anyone has figured out how to put life and all its demands into perspective without a minor earthquake.

Most of this part of the story about my cancer journey was written in a notebook with a wolf on the cover. The wolf is a Yellowstone gray wolf. Its eyes are confident and direct. It is not worried or scared. As I filled the last page of the journal, I decided that I could be as strong and confident as the wolf in the picture. Every journey has its share of battles.

Fighting the battle is the fatiguing part, but it is possible to be victorious: one day, one step, one moment at a time.

"I am the wolf. I am strong. I am part of my pack. I am confident. Whatever comes my way I will deal with and keep moving. I am not concerned with everyone else's problems. I will help, but they won't take me down. The only thing that will take me out is death; since I am still alive, I will live. I will eat, sleep and enjoy every gift that comes my way. Troubles are merely in my path. I will go over or around. I am the wolf. I am victorious."

Along this journey, I found myself being drawn to owls. I studied them with my students and without thinking about it, I found myself choosing items with owls on them. An owl's ears are asymmetrical and their faces are shaped like a satellite dish so they can hear each sound and identify where the sounds are coming from. Owls are good listeners. Their heads can turn 270°, so they can easily see what is happening around them. Owls are observant. Their wings are specially made to allow them to move silently through the night. An owl is unobtrusive and patient. It regurgitates the remains of its food, allowing the leisure scientist to easily see what it eats. The owl is transparent, it has nothing to hide. I can imagine it sitting on a branch watching and listening. The owl is a picture of peace.

Perhaps I'm drawn to the owl because that's how I wish to be seen: wise, attentive, observant, unobtrusive and patient. I want to be at peace. Perhaps I am drawn to the owl because I am already these things. Perhaps I am becoming these things as the owl becomes part of me.

∼

On Thursday, January 17, 2013, I met with a social worker who is a part of the cancer support system at MSTI. After talking to him, I realized I was coping with all that was happening to me quite well. Each time I felt overwhelmed, I wrote and God carried me through the fire.

Two days after my meeting with the social worker, I woke up with extreme pain and blisters on my breast. I had about a week and a half left of radiation. Whenever anything touched it, it burned. When it hurt, I simply wanted to lie still until the pain went away, but I had plans to finally put away Christmas ornaments. I couldn't sit and be still and get the ornaments put away at the same time.

This new problem arose on a day when I was very near the end of my radiation treatment. The treatment was wreaking havoc with my skin. Yet, on this same day, I wrote that I felt blessed and at peace. The house was a mess, I was tired and sore, but those things didn't determine my state of mind. I was cared for, loved and surrounded by people who saw me and not my "stuff."

∼

Cancer took a toll on my mind and my body. Radiation continued to take more from me. Somehow, I continually found my feet and kept walking. I found the blessings in the storm and focused on those things. I thought about what was most important and let everything else slide away.

When I had 4 days of radiation left, I began to think I was actually going to make it through the situation. I was anxious to begin healing. I was excited to finally be on the healing path.

During the last week, the radiation technicians started doing the booster for my treatment which meant they would only treat the area where the cancer was and not my entire left side. This news meant that part of my body could begin to heal. A rash was beginning to grow all over the treated area. The cream I put on it was helping, but I was definitely ready to halt the damaging process. It was wonderful to know that from this point on, I would be getting better. I was hoping that I would heal unusually quickly.

At this point, I felt emotionally stronger than I was last fall when the journey began. I felt like it took a lot more to stress me out. I was currently taking things with ease that would have previously ruffled my feathers. I hoped the change was permanent. I liked having smoother feathers.

The rash from radiation was all over my chest, under my armpit and on my ribs. It itched terribly and ached down deep. I was thankful this was happening at the end of my treatment. I knew all these difficulties would be over soon because my radiation treatment would soon end. I had 3 days left to go. I looked forward to the end of treatment, the end of daily trips across town, the end of repeatedly damaging my skin. I knew it wasn't really the end like I wanted it to be. Recovery was going to be difficult. My body would take months to fully heal, but the end of daily treatments meant the beginning of healing and the beginning of being whole once again. Healing means each day I should have less pain than the day before, have less weariness and have a little more strength.

This journey was like a mountain range. I began to climb a mountain. I reached the top, felt victorious then walked down the other side. As soon as I reached the bottom and thought I could rest in the valley, another mountain loomed before me. I steadily climbed, carefully putting one foot in front of another. I stopped to rest a lot on this journey, mentally and physically. The rest gave me enough strength to take a few more steps.

During this time, I was reading *Pilgrim's Progress*. In the book, there is a character named Christian who is on a spiritual journey. When he stops to rest, he loses something very important. When I read that, it sounded like he was being punished for resting. I don't think God does that. His Word says that He will give us rest which means He will give us a needed reprieve, but I also think it means that when we need to rest, He welcomes us to rest. He encourages us to sit in the quiet with Him and gather our strength to continue our journey. God is not a workaholic. He is gentle and gracious with us. He would like us to faithfully walk the path before us, but He doesn't ask us to walk until our feet bleed.

~

The rash began to spread like mold on old bread. It was sneaking to the other side of my chest, up to my collar bone, down my ribs and towards my back. I didn't know what caused it, but I hoped it would go away soon.

Two days after I noticed the rash spreading I got extremely itchy. My chest, my legs, my ears, my face. . . everything was itchy. It felt like ants were crawling up and down my skin. This was my last day of radiation. The end was within my reach. The cancer diagnosis came in October, the surgery came in November, radiation consumed all of December and January. As January came to a close, so did everything they needed to do to me. From now on, my only job was to heal. At least, that was *my* plan.

The next morning I felt like a blowfish. My face was swollen and puffy. I was reacting to something. The doctor thought it was the antibiotics she gave me for the rash. It could have been the Benadryl I took the other night. It doesn't matter which it was. My eyes were squinty little slits sitting above my puffy cheeks.

It felt like my body decided it was done. It was weary of fighting all the foreign attacks and substances and it had finally given up. The best plan I could think of was to keep all foreign material away for a time.

Thankfully, my radiation was finished. The technicians called me one of the "nice ones" and they were sad I was finished and no longer returning to greet them with my name and birthday. I'm glad I was a positive moment in their day. I'm thankful I didn't make their day more difficult. I also found out my radiation oncologist was telling other patients about this teacher who got so tired from treatment she went home from work and went directly to bed (yes, that was me). I made my mark. I had no idea that my situation wasn't typical. I had no idea I would be an encouragement for others; they could say at least they didn't experience what I did or perhaps it was a cautious tale that things could get more difficult.

# Chapter 10

## *Moving Forward*

**M**y pain woke me up at 1:30 in the morning. I shouldn't claim the pain, it's not mine. It was a pain in my face that could only be described as burning, worse than any sunburn I've ever had. The only relief I could find was under a cool, wet washcloth. I stayed home from work so I could go see the doctor. I still could have done my job, but it would have been at the expense of my health.

I was scared the doctor wouldn't know how to fix me. I was afraid they would say it was still a reaction to the antibiotics and I needed to wait longer. I needed to be better, no pain, no puffiness.

This week was supposed to be the beginning of my healing, instead, it became the beginning of what felt like the worst experience of this journey so far. My face was swollen like I was allergic to bee stings and I got stung by a bee the size of a hummingbird. My eyes were squinty. I had to use forehead muscles to open them. The skin on my cheeks was dry and stretched. You could sand a piece of wood by rubbing it back and forth on my cheek. My mouth was squeezed in by my plump cheeks as if I was pursing my lips or preparing for a kiss. All of this caused throbbing pain from my forehead to my chin.

I had no body image issues with a scarred or lumpy breast. This puffy face made me want to wear a mask. I felt ugly enough to be cast in a Batman movie. I was tired of having physical problems. I was weary of constant pain. I wanted to be fixed. I simply wanted someone to make me better. I didn't count on a balloon face as a side effect to anything they did to my boob. They are not attached. I understood the pain in my arm, my chest, even my back, but not my face. I guess I hadn't dealt with my vanity yet. I had to be hideous for a week. I'm sure smiling made me look better, but I didn't want to smile, I didn't want anyone looking at me. I thought about wearing a ski mask or letting my hair hang in my face. My wish: "Oh, to escape would be bliss."

I left the doctor's office with a prescription for steroids. I was still in intense pain. I had ice packs on my face all day long. I literally laid my face on an ice pack. I took one with me on my trip to the doctor. I began driving down the road holding this giant white ice pack on my face. I quickly found that wasn't going to work, not because people were probably looking at me because I looked crazy, but because it wasn't very safe. I had a difficult time seeing and I was driving on cold roads with one hand. Remembering it was January and 34 degrees outside, I rolled down the window. I hate to be cold. It can be 80 degrees outside and if the air feels chilly, I will roll up the windows, but here I was driving with my windows down and I wasn't cold at all due to the fire burning on my face.

After I saw the doctor, I went to the pharmacy in Costco to pick up my prescription. I walked in with my balloon face and picked up some steroids. The pharmacist was very empathetic and hoped I would get better soon. Her compassion reminded me I still had a hideous Halloween-ready puffy face. I drove home with the window open looking forward to my ice pillow when I got home.

The steroids worked. The puffiness started to subside. I was getting better. After a couple of doses of steroids I found a wrinkle on my face. Oh! the joy at finding a wrinkle under my eye. I had no wrinkles on my face all week. I had been a balloon like what Shrek and Fiona did to the snake and the frog. I am thankful for wrinkles. I am thankful I can feel the pain in my breast again. (The pain in my face distracted me from my radiation burning breast.) I am thankful I can open my eyes. I am thankful I will be able to go back to work. I need to remember this. I need to remember what the opposite of health feels like so that I will be thankful for my health and not squander my energy. On days when I simply don't want to go to school, I need to remember how horrible it feels to be forced to give my students a substitute.

This event reminded me not to take my health or energy for granted. Please don't let me forget when I am tempted to squander it all in laziness. I was utterly miserable before the medication kicked in. I couldn't even read or write. I spent the morning with an ice pack over my whole face. I was blessed once I was able to write again. I was blessed to be enjoying the warm fire. I was thankful I had a nice shower and the ability to get dressed. I want to remember to be thankful!

I am thankful for the healing and safe keeping. I am thankful the swelling is going down in my face. I trust that I will continue to heal. I'm thankful that the damaging part is finally finished.

I'm getting better. My balloon face is gone. The wrinkles are in full effect just like a deflated balloon with its stretched out wrinkles. My body is trying to heal the damage done to my breast and the surrounding areas from surgery and radiation. The healing is painful, but I'm thankful it's healing.

I realized, if I let it, this experience of cancer, surgery, radiation treatment and everything else this has entailed has taught me to be excessively less concerned with perfection than I previously was.

First, I was weak and tired from pneumonia. I couldn't keep up with the house. I was sore and limited from surgery. People came over and saw dirt and clutter when in the past I would have cleaned it up before they arrived.

Second, radiation and its mandatory "no bra, no shaving the armpit, swollen breast era" made me less concerned about my appearance. I dressed in layers, didn't look as thin and definitely didn't have a flattering figure.

Finally, the allergic era took away all vanity about my face. When your face resembles a puffer fish, your eyes are playing peek-a-boo, and in the healing process you peel like a sunburnt elephant, one begins to be less concerned about one's looks.

Perhaps after this experience, I will be more relaxed, less vain and more gracious with myself. Perhaps I will have learned something if I don't forget my new lessons. I feel that I'm at a place where I could easily choose the thankful path. In all things there is something to complain and whine about, but there is equally something to be thankful for. In any situation, I can always be thankful that my face has not become a party decoration. I can always be thankful I am not in burning, fiery pain. I can always be thankful for people who love and care for me. I can be thankful for my home, my transportation, my dogs. I can be thankful I can walk, see, hear, speak, and feel. No matter the situation there is much to be thankful for.

I know this has been preached before. I don't think most of us believe it. I think we say, "I know, I should be thankful for . . . ," but really, in the moment, we feel better when we complain. We don't want people to say, "At least you're not . . ." Being thankful is different than diminishing the difficulty. If we are not careful about our thankfulness, or lack thereof, we become cranky old farts at the age of 40 and all our friends want to stay away. Or, we can find the silver lining and sing about it like a Disney princess while everyone wonders when we turned into a cartoon character.

Perhaps being a positive, thankful, whimsical cartoon character is equivalent to having a joyful, light-hearted attitude. I want to remember this. My face itches, but I'm so thankful it's not 5 times bigger. My boob hurts, but I'm thankful I have no more radiation treatments. My house is filthy, but I'm thankful my family doesn't really care.

I was told once the word, "but," erases everything you said before it. Usually people say, "I love you, but . . ." I'm going to do it the other way around. I don't have to be blind to reality, I can recognize it, yet choose to focus on the amazing. For example, sometimes life can be shitty, but I'm glad I'm alive. What a great place to put a "but."

At the end of the most difficult part of the journey and the beginning of the healing process, I wrote:

*I'm getting there. This journey has helped me see the truth of me and my world and my role in it. Without this journey, I would still be lost or blind or both.*

I was learning to write the truth, telling myself the truth and being okay with it. Reality doesn't change just because you don't want to believe it's reality. I was in that place of choice. I was finished with all the really crazy parts of breast cancer. I was at a crossroads and it was time to make a choice. I could choose to be a part of the breast cancer community, go to groups and fundraisers and such, or I could pretend it didn't happen, it was not a part of me, and only remember the journey when I have a doctor's appointment.

I believe if I chose to forget this difficult journey, I would be lying to myself and cheating myself of growth and revelation. Yes, the worst was over. Yes, they couldn't heal me any more than they already did, but the experience still formed me and put its stamp on me. If I ignored that transformation, I would be ignoring a piece of myself.

Truth is knowing oneself and accepting oneself, scars and all. My story may inspire someone, but not if I ignore it. My story may empower me, but not if I pretend it never happened. My story may encourage someone, but not if I don't tell it.

My story doesn't end here. I had days where I felt amazing and days where I was tired and weary. My body still surprised me by developing unexpected issues whenever it wanted. Daily, I fought the mental battle to stand, to run, to move forward even if I didn't feel like it. Daily, I celebrated what I could do and accepted what I couldn't. Most of the time I didn't believe my limitations would be forever which made it easier to move forward one day at a time.

It has been almost 5 years since my diagnosis. This is the point where the doctors stop seeing me regularly. It is good news. I am cancer free. I am not free of the experience or the effects on my mind and body. I hope people who go through difficult times like this take it easy on themselves, give themselves room to rest and to heal, and remember that it is okay to have a bad day and it is okay to let others help.

# Chapter 11

## *M.S. (Major Shit)*

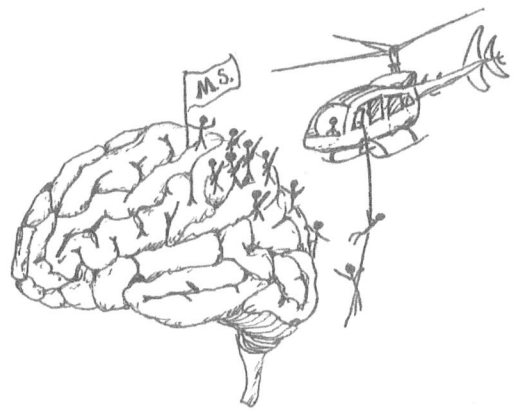

This story isn't about Multiple Sclerosis. In this story, MS sits in the backseat. It participates in every turn, hill climb and rutted road. It attempts to whisper directions. Some are heard, some are ignored.

In January of 2015, days after the 2 year anniversary of my last radiation treatment in 2013, I woke up to what I would later learn was the beginning of a brand new road I would never be able to leave. It turns out there are more people on this road than I thought, but it is still very lonely.

I was feeling particularly healthy. I felt like my body was finally finished fighting the effects of cancer and treatment. I had considerably more energy than I remembered having for years. I partied with my 2 girls to the new "Just Dance" they had received for Christmas. On this Friday night, I was sweating in the basement with my girls, laughing and so grateful I was finally getting better.

The next day, on a wintery Saturday morning, I woke up with the left side of my face frozen. It wasn't numb. It wasn't tingly. It was immobile. My left arm also felt a little weak. I could talk as well as someone who can only move half their face. I could think and write. I knew it couldn't be a stroke. Other than the coffee I kept dribbling down my chin, I could function just fine.

Jason's perspective was a little different. He could see my crooked face. He could see that I wasn't getting better as the day wore on. He was filled with worry. He could see my sagging face and could hear my slurred speech. All my reassurances that I was fine, since my brain was functioning fully, were not silencing his fears. I completed Sudoku puzzles to demonstrate the functionality of my brain. I couldn't be having a stroke and solving complicated puzzles, right? I conceded to going to the doctor when my symptoms didn't improve. Quick Care saw my face and sent me to Emergency. When you walk into a medical office with a sagging face, they get into action quickly. For the first time in my experience, the Emergency Room quickly conducted many tests, and they collected my family history. If it hadn't been for my family history, they would have diagnosed me with Bell's Palsy and sent me home. Once they discovered my dad has MS, they sent me to get a brain MRI. Everyone in the hospital was pretty confident it was probably MS, but they would need to wait for the neurologist to view the results and report back. The seconds moved in slow motion while we waited for the results. After a few hours of trying to wait patiently, but really waiting impatiently, MS was the final diagnosis.

There were lesions on my brain. They sent me home and informed me the neurologist would contact me on Monday to tell me the next steps. In February 2015, I was officially diagnosed with Multiple Sclerosis. They gave me an infusion of steroids to reduce the inflammation. It took a long time for my face to regain its ability to move. It took longer for my left hand to regain its function. I dropped my coffee cup while walking, I dropped a piece of paper in my classroom, and I dropped my dinner plate right into the trash. I couldn't multitask while holding something in my left hand. It needed all my brain's attention to move or hold something. Even today, it is a bit slower than my right hand.

My doctor prescribed Tecfidera to manage MS. I reacted instantly with frustrating flushing that stole my focus and stomach pain that left me doubled over and in tears. After a drastic change in my diet, I was able to minimize the side effects of that medication.

For me, MS was different than cancer. With cancer, you have the hope of vanquishing it. It may take time and pain, but there is hope of winning the battle. With MS, you just hope the enemy doesn't get any closer. They stand prepared near the horizon and you see them every day. You can't hear what the generals are saying. You can't see what new formations they may be practicing. You keep throwing out just enough munitions to keep them from moving forward. Then one night, while you weren't looking, they took the small town to the west. "It's time to rethink the battle plan. They figured out our weakness."

I manage MS by taking my medication, drastically reducing and sometimes eliminating dairy and gluten from my diet, exercising, sleeping as well as I can, and managing my energy. The onset of MS meant that in the course of a day, I have about half the energy others have. If I overdo it too early in the morning, I will not have enough to finish the day. I have learned to pace myself. I have learned that I must have one day on the weekend when I don't go anywhere. I must put my health first.

For the rest of my life, every blessed and difficult moment will be accompanied by MS.

# Chapter 12

## *Going With the Flow*

On Tuesday, June 12, 2018, I got a phone call from the Breast Cancer Diagnostic Center. I had a mammogram the day before. They called today. I immediately knew it wasn't good. The tears came without warning.

I knew.

They wanted to see me again.

They saw something on my right breast (not the left like last time), and they needed to have a closer look at it.

Since 2012, I have had many successful mammograms. A successful mammogram looks like showing up to the appointment, letting my melons become pancakes, and going home with no other contact. It has been almost 6 years of successful mammograms. Now, all I could think was, "This is too familiar." I was aware this could be nothing, but I'd been in this place before. This story has all been told. I wasn't sure I could do it again.

Time, the great healer, calmed me. Less than 12 hours after the call I felt okay. I wasn't worried. I wasn't over-thinking anything anymore. I was simply waiting to know which direction on this road I would have to travel. Would I travel the familiar and difficult road or the unknown, never traveled road of ease?

Out loud I told myself, Jason, and my loved ones, "Right now, nothing is actually wrong with me." There was still a chance the mammogram showed a fatty tissue or it was a faulty picture. But my mind was planning the next steps for cancer. I knew the step after the follow up mammogram was a biopsy order. I already had a surgeon. Then . . . radiation . . . or chemotherapy . . . or something different. I didn't really know if I could handle another dose of radiation. I did know that adding Multiple Sclerosis into the equation made each layer more difficult and complex. I did know I wouldn't stop exercising.

Just after my MS diagnosis in 2015, Jason needed an outlet. He discovered CrossFit. This discovery has its own story. Ultimately, it saved us. Because of the health issues that don't seem to leave me alone and my husband's need to "do something," CrossFit solved both our issues. I know exercise was keeping a recurrence at bay and helping me maintain strength amidst a disease that wants to steal my muscles. My entire family has been exercising together since 2015. This exercise gave me community, connection and a strength I have never known before.

I kept telling myself I wasn't scared of the outcome. I knew both paths before me. I had been down one before and the other one looked just like the one I had been traveling on for the past 5 years. I wasn't worried. I reminded myself God had me even if I had to go down the cancer road again.

The next day I wanted to scream. I had been taking every action I felt I could to be healthy and it didn't seem to help.

I had back surgery because of a herniated disc in 2017 and still had scars and pain. I still had scars on my breast. I still had MS. People everywhere were killing their bodies while I fought to keep away the diseases with the healthiest choices. After the MS diagnosis, I omitted certain foods from my diet. I felt like every time I started to get ahead, started to get stronger, something would push me back again.

Either I have bad luck or an enemy is set on coming after me. I thought, perhaps I am making a difference in people's lives and someone is trying to stop me, or perhaps going through difficulties is how I impact lives best. I don't think there is an answer other than this is my journey, and the only choice I have is to walk in it.

I had to share the news with someone. I told my mom and my best friend, Kelly. I decided not to tell anyone else yet, it was only a follow up mammogram. I tell my mom most things. My mom knew this happens all the time and wasn't worried yet. She also understood it was traumatic for me.

When my family began doing CrossFit in 2015, I found Kelly. I was drawn to her. I couldn't and still can't describe why I was drawn to her. I just wanted to be near her and talk to her. Once we became neighbors, our friendship went into overdrive. We could see each other in a moment's notice for a nice walk, a moment by the pool, a game of tennis, or a backyard drink. We had innumerable differences in our past, but precious similarities in our present. We are both a nine on the Enneagram which means we are peacemakers, we let others win, we put ourselves last. We challenged each other to grow. We challenged each other to do uncomfortable things.

We have a two person book club called the Novel Gang. We read books, and talk about them while reading them. When we are finished, we go out to discuss the book again. We share our struggles, our hopes and our fears. We are completely real with one another and are never scared away by one another's bigness or smallness. Kelly is one of my soul friends. When we connected, I felt understood and seen in a way I had never been before. Even when we don't talk all the time, I can sense my soul friend's dark and light days from afar. Kelly was my rock during my cancer season. I knew she was there. I knew I could depend on her. I knew she would always listen and hear me and never try to fix me. She was the only one I confided in outside of my family. I've learned I need someone who isn't family to share these things with. I need someone who is impartial and doesn't see me as a daughter, wife or mom. I need someone who can be outside that circle.

I know I *can* do this again.

I know I don't want to.

I also know God shines bright when I go through these difficulties because I have nothing and must depend fully on Him.

A month has passed since that phone call. Most of the time I'm fine. Every once in a while panic sets in. I know I *can* handle all this again, but I don't want to. I don't want to fight another cancer battle.

On Friday, June 15, 2018, my ultrasound showed a mass in my right breast that was 13 millimeters at its widest point. No one knew what it was, so I was scheduled for a biopsy the following week. Even after all this, we still didn't know anything. We waited to find out the details of the biopsy and now we needed to wait a bit more.

Since we were moving on to the next step in the journey, my husband and I decided to tell his parents. My mother-in-law is a prayer warrior. She will pray for you and her prayers are often answered. Both of my in-laws are loving and caring above everything else. We knew they would want to know what was going on. On our way home from the doctor's office, we stopped by their house.

We told them within minutes of sitting down on their large gray couch. I could see their broken-heartedness for us and their worry. We talked a bit more. I reminded them nothing was actually wrong right now. We technically had nothing to grieve yet. They wanted to hold onto that, but it was still difficult. On our way out the door, we were giving hugs and saying "good-byes." While my husband was hugging his dad, he broke down in tears. It was sweet and vulnerable, a place I know he hates being. The smallest acts of love and compassion have the most power to break our walls of protection and let the grief, pain, and fear flow freely away from our hearts into the loving arms of others.

We told our girls when we got home. Hannah was 16 and Abigail had just turned 14. I found myself saying, "*Right now*, it's nothing." *Right now* is where I tried to help people sit. *Right now* is where we can cling to hope. *Right now* is where we can pretend it will all be okay.

I realized the pain of dealing with cancer was too great to handle *right now*. The hope that it was nothing felt out of reach. Even though I helped others live in the realities of *right now*, I had to pretend it was neither good nor bad. It was neither malignant nor benign. It just was, and I had to move forward with as little pain and fear as I could. It may have seemed odd to those around me. It was how I coped. It is how I cope.

∾

The day after the ultrasound I was still okay. I had fleeting moments of emotions.

My mom said she had a good feeling about this. I told her I didn't think I was that lucky.

At every turn I have come across the worst case scenario - not really the worst, but definitely not a break. I am beginning to feel I am destined to go through shit. Just last year, some back pain and pain in my leg nagged me until I could no longer walk, sit or stand without intense pain. The only solution to the pain that kept me in a recliner for a month was back surgery. There was no easy way out of that.

I was searching for hope in any corner so I did some research. According to the way the radiologist marked my ultrasound on the report, I discovered there was a 30% chance my lump was cancer. It could also be a fibrous cyst caused by hormones in women ages 40-45.

I am 41.

The odds were in my favor.

There was a 70% chance this lump was benign. These statistics provided a sliver of hope. Except, this thing in me was present a year ago and they said it was benign then and now it has grown.

Except, I simply haven't been all that lucky.

As I think through my initial plans for the summer, I am determined to enjoy myself even if shit happens. I am a teacher. I take my summers very seriously. The past few years I have taken extra care of myself in the summer. I exercise more, play in the water more, enjoy nature more, and conserve my fleeting energy more. The school year takes all of me and summers are for recharging my battery. I don't want this development to change my plans. I don't want to have to stop being in the sun, going to the pool or stand-up paddle boarding.

I feel my breasts, or see them when I get dressed, and I almost feel like they are out to get me. They are this entity determined to make things difficult. They seem to have a mind of their own, and when these difficulties happen I feel disconnected and sad when I recognize they are there, silently causing emotional distress.

Just 3 days after the ultrasound, I woke up feeling the weight of these past months bearing down on my whole being. I woke up and felt more pain in my right breast and I felt lumps everywhere, scaring me. I'm about a week from starting my period so it could be that, but that fact doesn't comfort me. The primary prayer on my lips is, "I don't want to do this. I don't want to have surgery and cancer treatment. I don't want to give up my summer." I know I *can*. I know God is by my side and He will give me the strength to keep walking. I simply don't want to, and I'm terrified I'm going to have to go through it all again.

I feel like I am sitting at the edge of a cliff where one strong blow of wind will knock me into the pit of depression. I can see the darkness and sometimes it feels welcoming. I can see myself giving up and simply lying down and letting the sadness wash over me. But I know I won't. I will keep writing and freeing myself from burdens. I will keep exercising to stay strong. I will keep eating and talking and sleeping and walking. I will keep praying and hoping and I will stay away from the darkness. I will not let it overtake me even though it would be easier.

So, here I am today, feeling like I've been in a fight, looking for tasks that will distract me while I wait for the next fight.

It is Tuesday, June 19, 2018. Tomorrow is the biopsy. I didn't wake with the heavy burden today like I have most days. I have thoughts, but they aren't weighing me down.

I did a lot of sewing yesterday. That helped.

I got to exercise today. That helped.

I've been doing a lot of yoga to ease my muscle soreness. That helps.

I have a lot to do today.

Remaining busy and distracted is on the top of my list.

Wednesday, June 20, 2018, arrived along with my biopsy appointment. It has been almost 6 years since the last time I had to do this, and the memory is fresh and vivid. I felt fine about it, but I worked hard to distract myself all day. I did yoga, went to the neighborhood pool and generally tried to stay busy.

This time they used an ultrasound to guide the biopsy. They wouldn't have to clamp, take pictures, readjust, clamp, take pictures, readjust, repeat. I laid on my back on a bed with cushions and a pillow. This alone was a huge improvement from the table with the holes in 2012. My boob didn't have to hang through a hole like a cow's udder. I could actually be in a comfortable position. Either this biopsy was different or someone figured out a better way to do this over the past 6 years. Because of the ultrasound, I saw everything that was happening. I could actually see the needle go into my breast on the screen. I could see it enter the mass and come back out. The nurse talked to me most of the time, which was a welcome distraction. The black and white ultrasound images didn't affect me the same as seeing actual skin and blood.

They completed the whole procedure in 38 minutes. I sat up when it was over and felt a little light headed. I wasn't surprised. It is fairly common for me to get light-headed. When I was a junior in high school, I donated blood for the first time. My light-headedness kept me on the make-shift bed for almost an hour. I don't volunteer for things that may affect me like this. I move slowly and am always aware my head and body may not be ready to move at the same time.

I felt calmer after this biopsy compared to the biopsy 6 years ago. It wasn't as traumatic of an experience. It wasn't as scary. I made it home. I kept the ice on according to the directions all night, 20 minutes each hour. I took Tylenol just in case the pain would sneak in and surprise me and I tried with all my might to be normal. This attempt at normalcy was an attempt to not require others to stop and care for me. It meant I tried to do things for myself. I rested, but tried to continue as if I hadn't just returned from a procedure.

I slept carefully. I slept somewhat on my back for part of the night. I couldn't lie on my left side because my right breast would move down due to gravity. I could feel it pull on the incision and it hurt. I discovered it was safe to carefully lie on my right side.

I felt a bit foggy and tired. I thought I needed to rest so I wouldn't feel as wiped out as last time. I remember being completely down after the last biopsy and didn't want that experience again. I would have liked it if everyone left for a bit and stopped watching me so closely, but other than that, all was well. I like to be left alone when I'm not feeling well. I can completely sit into myself and rest. I don't have to attempt to be okay if I'm not. I don't have to pretend or fake how I'm feeling when I'm alone.

I spent the entire next day down and resting. I didn't feel horrible, but I felt run-down like I'd just completed a Monster Mash workout. These are triple workouts, they consist of 3 different AMRAPS. An AMRAP means As Many Reps As Possible, so the plan is to do as much as you can in the amount of time that is allotted. We often participated in them on Sundays at Snake River CrossFit. These workouts make you feel like you suddenly aged 20 years and can no longer move or speak. A Monster Mash is essentially 3 workouts sandwiched together into one day. In a few years I will learn these workouts were designed for athletes preparing for competition, not middle-aged people just trying to slow down the inevitable aging process. This information, which we didn't have at the time, would explain why it took days to recover from these vicious Monster Mashes.

My body ached from sitting, but I knew I needed to give it a chance to heal. The only way I know to do that is through complete rest which means recliner and TV. I wonder how people are able to rest and heal without television sometimes. It helps to have a distraction. If I feel tired, I purposely choose a show or movie I am familiar with, so I can fall asleep. It takes too much effort to read or do other activities. Television helps me to settle in, and relax my mind and my body without feeling bored, irritated or annoyed at being forced to stay down. Just 8 months ago, I was forced to stay down and in a recliner for a month. No hyperbole, I was in excruciating pain from a herniated disc pressing on my sciatic nerve. Standing, walking and sitting were impossible without tears and cringes. The strongest medicine barely touched the pain. I conducted the construction of Thanksgiving dinner from my chair in the living room. They were kind, but I'm guessing receiving instructions from the other room about where the pans were was eliciting some sighs from my family, but they kept it to themselves. The end of November included surgery and relief. The months between that surgery and this biopsy were spent recovering, walking and starting to exercise again. I had to remind myself every day that I was starting over.

During the biopsy procedure, the nurse kept talking about surgery. I hoped it was just talk and not a "knowing" that surgery was coming. I was very much in the present. I couldn't even look at that path right then. My footprints had barely disappeared from the last time I was there. I didn't have the strength to consider what stepping on that cancer path again would do to me.

I felt anxious and sad Friday morning, June 22, 2018. I needed help calming down. Just 6 years ago, I received the "you have cancer" call. I'm continuously expecting another call, either informing me I have cancer again or, miraculously, the mass was benign and normal.

I called my mom. I shared my frustrations with her, many of which had nothing to do with this biopsy. In the middle of our conversation, a lady from Dr. Smith's office called. She said my biopsy was okay.

I breathed.

I thanked her.

I got back on the phone with my mom and shared the news.

She yelled and celebrated, proclaiming she knew it!

She just knew this wasn't like last time.

I cried.

A dam broke inside me and every fear came flooding out. I was thankful I was with my mom even if only on the phone. She knows how to let me cry. Even if I had wanted to stop crying, I couldn't. It was finally okay to let go. I didn't have to steel myself for the worst and make myself strong for a difficult journey. I could breathe again.

. . .

Years from now, when I read these words again, I hope the relief is clear. It was like being told your husband has died, then he walks through the door. I had been steeling myself for the worst. I had been rearranging my summer in my mind, grieving over lost activities I had planned. I had imagined conversations with all my friends, doctors' appointments, restrictions, undoing the health I had been achieving... Suddenly, those possibilities were gone, and I was given permission to continue as I had planned. I would not be walking down the familiar path of 2012. I would walk down a path I had never seen before. I've known a few women who have had benign breast biopsies. My very first biopsy, at the age of 35, revealed cancer. I've never known what it is like to have extra testing and then be free to continue life as usual. My experience was that a biopsy was the beginning of 5 months of difficulties. For the first time, I just got to go back to life.

I cried.

On Saturday, June 23, we loaded ourselves into the car and drove to the Oregon Coast for our annual surf trip. Our journey was the beginning of a celebration. It started last night with Matt and Kelly, our dear friends. Just having them around brought me peace. My peace continued on this day with the ocean. I was free to celebrate my health. I was free to continue being healthy. I was free to be me. This bandage on my breast from my biopsy doesn't mar me anymore. I will take it off in a few days and move on. This day will not be the beginning of a difficult journey.

.   .   .

I followed my mom's friend, Betty's, advice. I went down to the ocean, put my feet in the water, faced the ocean, lifted up my arms and let it all go. It felt liberating. It would have felt better if I wasn't concerned about what people thought.

I thought about the ocean and its power. We can't do anything to change or control it. It can be gentle or vicious and all we can do is literally go with the flow. We can figure out how to ride it and become one with it or fight it and lose to the waves and tides. I think my peacemaker tendency gives me an advantage. I don't like conflict or turmoil so when it is thrust upon me, I settle in and do all I can to meld with the situation, to flow and not fight.

I took the rest of my bandage off. Each day I am a step closer to losing the marks that remind me of a difficult 2 weeks of this summer.

# Chapter 13

## *Silent and Screaming*

oday is Tuesday, June 23, 2020. It has been almost exactly 2 years since the mammogram that ended in a call-back that ended up setting me free for the summer. It has been almost 8 years since the mammogram that changed my life. It is the day scheduled for my yearly mammogram. I always dread these days. I hate standing half exposed. I hate getting squished in all directions. I am too familiar with them. I hate the hidden, faint whisper that they could find something in me that doesn't belong.

The receptionist was the same one I had last year for my yearly check-up. Last year, since I was a little early to my appointment, she asked me to wait while she sent an email. I didn't inform her she could send her email after she checked me in or she could ask me to wait a moment and not tell me she was sending an email making me and my time feel unimportant. I decided I wouldn't make the mistake of arriving early again. This year, after I arrived on time, she told me she was having a bad day. I appreciate that she is honest, but in a place of business, especially a hospital, your first job is to make the patients feel comfortable, not to share your bad mood. I am definitely not comfortable hearing about your bad day as I am preparing for my dreaded mammogram.

She checked me in, then sent me to an extra sweet technician named Misti who took care of me the rest of the time. She updated my history, awed by all that she had to add to my paperwork about previous breast cancer and family history. She was kind and more than made up for the receptionist who checked me in.

We chatted about weight gain - she called me skinny.

She noticed and complimented my dragonfly and pansy tattoo.

She exclaimed cuteness over my white belt with the cut-out stencils of butterflies.

She resolved I was "granola." I heard it in an endearing tone rather than a judging tone. Apparently, my free hair, lack of make-up and simple style make me "down to earth." I welcomed the compliment.

She asked me to take my right arm out of my shirt so she could take pictures of and squish my right breast. Next, it was time for the left side. I hugged the machine, turned my head, held my breath and waited for the pictures. She showed me my breast on the screen. She was amazed at how my breast had shrunk over the past year. I was thrilled. Shrinkage that shows up on a mammogram means I have lost a lot of fat. I must be doing something right.

I walked away, satisfied I completed my mammogram, and content that Misti made it a delightful experience. I told her so. She appreciated me also. Apparently, some women come in very grumpy and angry and there is nothing she can do to appease them.

I walked out of the hospital wearing my COVID-required mask. As soon as I was clear of the doors, I removed my mask, breathed the fresh air, got into my car, and drove to Stewart's for our Novel Gang book club with my best friend, Kelly. I told her about the receptionist, Misti and my shrinking boobs. We also took some time to talk about the book over some good food and drinks.

I had a missed call on Monday, June 29th from St. Luke's with no message. I have their number programmed into my phone. I don't know what that means. How many people have a hospital switchboard programmed into their phones? I freaked out for a minute. Why else would they be calling? I attempted to call back, but the number I had was for a switchboard. On the 30th I was expecting them to call again around 10 am. I made sure I had my phone with me and turned on in case they chose to call.


They did ... while I was vacuuming.

This time I worked harder to reach the caller.


I found the number for the mammogram people, and they were busy, so I left a message. I was beginning my warm-up before my workout. Once I finished with the warm-up, and was ready to begin my 15 minute AMRAP of jumping pull-ups, reverse lunges and burpees, I thought I would call again. I didn't want them to call while I was 10 minutes in and be forced to stop in the middle. I also wanted to end this.


This time my call was answered.


In her calm, kind, nothing-is-out-of-the-usual voice, the receptionist informed me they wanted me to come back for a diagnostic mammogram and an ultrasound.

I knew it was them trying to contact me.

This was why I knew to call mammogram services.

I wasn't surprised.


I stayed "all business" on the phone and scheduled an appointment for next Tuesday, July 7th at 7:45 AM. I confirmed the location and time, writing them beneath the instructions for my workout on our metal white board in the garage. I hung up and immediately broke into a million pieces. I sat alone on the bench in my garage, crying into my hands. I'm not sure why I cried. They may have been tears of fear of what may be ahead, weariness that I can't seem to escape the roller coaster of hope and dread, hopelessness because I work so hard to be healthy, only to be welcomed by yet another obstacle.

Right now it doesn't matter if everything will be alright. In this moment, on a black bench, I was transported to 2012 when this same scenario changed my life completely. That time and all the feelings that come with it are always just below the surface like an underground river.


I have succeeded in caring for myself.

I have succeeded in living each day and each moment as fully as I can.

I have succeeded in fighting for each piece of health I have.

I have *not* succeeded in forgetting how painful and difficult this journey was 8 years ago.


I still have scars. Some you can see and some are only visible to me. My superpower is disguising the damage and making everything appear to be together and whole.

I remind myself I know I can handle whatever comes, but again, I don't *want* to. I was less bothered this time than last time, but I still felt broken. I still felt terrified. I determined to stay strong and be me and keep walking.

∼

I broke down again while telling Jason. My body remembered and recognized the words. The tears flowed without my permission. I hadn't had the diagnostic ultrasound yet. I told him I wasn't worried. Either direction, I knew what to do. I knew how to manage and be strong. I thought the difficulty I was experiencing came more from remembering trauma than from the current events. I was experiencing Post Traumatic Stress. I was in limbo while I waited to find out what the next 6 months would hold. It could be nothing again. It could be cancer again. I was simply tired of finding a surprise around every corner.

Each time I was on my way to health, personal excellence, and freedom from pain, something else tried to come in and steal those things from me. It makes me tired. I will never quit, but it makes a part of me down deep want to give up. It never stops being difficult.

I asked Kelly to join me for a walk. I told her about my "call back." I needed to tell someone who wouldn't try to fix me.

She listened.
    She was sorry.
    She didn't know what else to say, she was just there.

The day before my diagnostic mammogram and ultrasound was especially difficult. The coming appointment was eating away at me. I kept busy and finally escaped for some Novel Gang time with Kelly about our book, *Eleanor*

*Oliphant is Completely Fine.* I needed that escape. I needed to visit and talk with someone who wasn't worried about me as openly as my family. We hadn't told the girls yet. I would later learn that was a mistake for myself and for them.

This unknown sneaks up on me. It's a silent monster (Heavy Harold) that follows me around. Every once in a while it walks beside me and I feel it try to take my hand. Then it walks in front of me and I can see it clearly looking back, reminding me it is there. The worst is when it sits on my shoulders and whispers possible futures in my ear. Its presence makes me tired. It feels heavy. I want it to leave me alone.

The monster analogy has been very helpful to me. At any given moment I can tell you where the monster is and you can know my state. On July 4th, 2020, he spent most of the day behind me, but I had a moment where he was on my shoulder. I felt his heavy feet weighing me down. Right now he is sitting next to me. I feel unsettled. I went to bed early last night even after taking a nap while we were watching "Independence Day" with Will Smith. I woke up early this morning aware that Heavy Harold had not left.

Tuesday, July 7, 2020, arrived and so did the diagnostic ultrasound. Nothing new was discovered during the ultrasound except there was a mass in my right breast. On the ultrasound it looked huge, but I'm sure it was magnified. They said I need a biopsy. I wasn't surprised. If something unknown is there, they can't discover if it's malignant or benign unless they biopsy it. It's interesting that the first time this happened they *asked* if I wanted to do a biopsy. Now, they just tell me a biopsy is the next step.

I *was* surprised at how much better I felt. When I returned home with the news (Jason couldn't come to the hospital because of COVID), Jason told the girls what was going on. I felt relieved they finally knew and I didn't have to hide anymore. I didn't realize the toll it would take on me to keep a secret from them. Hannah was 18, almost 19. Abigail was 16. They could see something was off with me. Hannah spent almost a week worrying about me. I spent that time trying to avoid eye contact so she wouldn't be able to see the pain and worry in my eyes. It didn't work. Once they finally knew, I could breathe and include them in this journey. They were very young in 2012, and they didn't need to be included in the same way they needed it in 2020. I don't plan on keeping that kind of secret again. It was too painful for all of us. This moment of disconnect illustrated the kind of relationship we have. We are a family that shares stories, feelings and time. We enjoy being together and being a part of each other's' lives. Keeping this secret went against all we have become as a family over the years.

I was also surprised at how long it took them to schedule my biopsy. Apparently, Nampa St. Luke's doesn't have their act together quite like Boise St. Luke's. I attribute it to the fact that they have been operating Breast Care Services for fewer years. On July 9th, I eventually called the scheduler myself and got the ball rolling. I told them I was leaving town on Sunday the 12th and really wanted to try and get this biopsy in before I left.

The scheduler, I don't remember her name, understood my situation and promised to do what she could. It may sound like I had a few days before I had to leave, but July 9th fell on a Thursday. The only opening I had left to check this off my list before my vacation was on Friday, the 10th.

She called back while I was walking to the pool with Abby. She performed the miracle no one else could. She scheduled my biopsy for 8 AM on Friday, the 10th. She gave me the instructions to the Breast Care Services building in Meridian. She gave me instructions on eating and medication. I was infinitely grateful to her for working for me.

Once Abby and I got settled at the pool, I texted Jason, my mom and Kelly and updated them on the next step in the journey. It was time to call the others. I hadn't told anyone else about the diagnostic mammogram. Now that a biopsy was scheduled, it was time.

I learned something very important during these conversations about responding to someone who has shared their "news" with you: Do not require the person dealing with a difficult situation to comfort you about that situation.

In 2020, I began gaining an extensive emotional vocabulary thanks to books and podcasts by Brené Brown and Marc Brackett. When the world shut down, I went for long walks and listened to the podcast, Unlocking Us. I bought almost every book mentioned. I dove into words by these authors that filled my soul and made me feel fully seen. I also learned how to be a friend, how to be myself around others and how to stop worrying if I was too much for people. I never had a problem "being a friend" before. I struggled with being my whole emotional-deep-thinking-self freely without worrying what others thought of me.

This new awareness meant that I knew exactly what I was feeling. It meant that people's words fully affected me and I could articulate how. It also meant that I understood. I understood them, their uncertainty, their fear, their heart. I knew everyone was doing the best they knew how. I describe what was helpful and what wasn't to benefit those who read my story. Some may learn better ways to respond to those in pain. Some may learn I see you. I understand how so few words make anything better and usually just make you feel more alone.

It is important to comfort the hurting. It is important to stand with the one in pain. The moment you are in pain and you are hurting, don't demand that the one going through the horrible situation comforts you. Find your comfort in others then come back to love on the one in pain.

One of the best responses that makes me feel seen is, "I'm sorry, that sucks, I'm here for you." Some responses make me feel responsible to comfort you. It's okay to cry, we can cry together. I welcome your compassionate tears. I don't have room for your pity tears. I, the person preparing for the procedure, should never be put in a position to assuage your fears about what is happening to me. I want your support, but I don't want your worries and fears. This happened in one of my conversations. It felt heavy. I didn't see the other person negatively. I wasn't angry. I simply felt them hand me their burden. I had to consciously refuse to pick it up. I had plenty. I chose not to take theirs also.

≈

I'm going into this biopsy with my eyes wide open. I experienced the same thing 2 years ago. The difference between this time and all the other times is I must go alone because of COVID. Going alone also means I don't have to worry about how anyone else is doing. I'll get my results next Wednesday, then I'll proceed from there.

I'm not scared or worried *right now*.

I'm simply going to keep walking and take whatever comes on this journey.

~

On Friday, July 10, 2020, I woke at 2 AM, unable to go back to sleep. There are worse things. Today, I will repeat the biopsy experience. I'm comforted that it will resemble the experience of 2 years ago and not the experience of 8 years ago.

I got out of bed, started the coffee, then filled the hours with reading and writing until my appointment. You may have your own list of ideas why I was up 5 hours before I needed to be. As far as I could tell, I didn't feel anxious. I *was* nervous about arriving on time. After checking the traffic and seeing 2 accidents on the freeway, I decided to leave early. At 7 AM, I drove myself to Meridian St. Luke's. I went alone because the world was currently in the middle of a pandemic. Thousands of people were dying because their bodies couldn't take the stress of this virus. Because of this, we wore masks and attended doctor's appointments alone.

I arrived promptly at 7:24 just as my electronic map predicted. Neither the accidents nor the morning traffic and construction hindered my travel. I decided to sit in the car and finish reading *Dance with Anger* by Harriet Learner for 15 minutes before entering the Breast Care Services building adorned with the pink ribbon. The receptionist at St. Luke's in Nampa taught me never to arrive too early; I may be forced to wait for someone to send an email or hear how today is difficult for them. Sometimes I am okay with these things, but I knew I didn't have the capacity for it on this day.

The receptionist, Janet, who checked me in was confused about my claim that my "out-of-pocket" had been paid and I didn't need to pay the copay. After I used the restroom, I overheard her attempting to find the answer about my out-of-pocket from her colleague. I struggled to help her understand the differences between deductibles, copays and out-of-pocket. After being diagnosed with MS in 2015, I started taking Tecfidera. The medication reduces my white blood cells so they don't attack the myelin sheath protecting my nerves. That medication is paid for by an assistance program for the first few months of the year. It gets credited to my insurance as though I paid for it. Since it costs about $8000 a month, my out-of-pocket is taken care of rather quickly. Once my out-of-pocket has been met, the insurance takes over the payments and any other medical expenses that accrue are 100% covered. I didn't explain the MS part to her, but I explained the other. She understood, or at least pretended to understand. In my mind, I suggested she learn a bit more about insurance if she is going to be in charge of the desk where people check in with their insurance cards and their copays.

I was finally called to the back. A nice nurse took me into a little room with a computer and went over my information and explained what was going to happen. She gave me a pink gown and took me to the room. She was very sweet and compassionate. She made me feel comfortable. When working with people who are about to have a procedure which could be scary or which could bring a scary result, you need the kindest, sweetest, most compassionate helpers.

It was time for the biopsy. I went into another room with a computer on a cart and a bed. It was a rather small room, but bigger than the room in 2018. Once 4 people were in there it felt a little crowded. I stood in the room waiting to be told what to do. The assistant who helped the doctor with the biopsy had poor communication skills and was shocked to see my breast dangling when she asked me to take my right arm out of my sleeve. She meant for me to drape the gown over my breast once my arm was freed like a towel after a shower. She shouldn't have been surprised I hadn't read her mind. Another awkward moment with hospital gowns and breasts hanging around.

The doctor, Dr. A. was nice and remembered me from two years ago. We talked about the hospital workers' new plexi-glass eye shields, COVID, kids struggling socially because they can't see their friends at school, and all the things that have come about in this unprecedented time. I'm thankful much of life can still continue with the simple assistance of a mask. It was a reminder cancer doesn't care what else may be going on in your life. It will come and interrupt whenever it wants. It doesn't seem wise to deal with potential cancer in the midst of a global pandemic, but there are no rules.

Dr. A. numbed the area then began the procedure - my breasts are so dense she had trouble getting the needle all the way to the site located deep in the center where the mass was located. On the ultrasound the needle resembled someone trying to poke through a stubborn water balloon that just moved away instead of allowing itself to be pierced. I was able to watch everything on the screen as I did two years ago. With each biopsy I am grateful to avoid the experience of 2012.

I felt more discomfort this time than 2 years ago. The pressure of the ultrasound on my breast left a pinched feeling deep inside. The presence of that pain unnerved me. I also felt it for about 30 seconds early that morning while I was reading. I told the nice nurse about it when I arrived. She decided it was psychosomatic. I was more anxious to be finished with this biopsy than I was last time. I had more pain than last time. I wasn't as eager to watch the procedure on the ultrasound as I was last time. I wanted to be finished. It didn't matter that these 3 biopsies spanned 8 years. I was tired of doing this. I was done.

Dr. A. took samples and deposited the clip to mark the spot. I'd been conquered again! I'd forgotten about the loud clicking sound when they grab a sample. It is jarring because of the noise and because you feel a bit of a jerk. It sounds like the amplified click of a giant pen. The nice nurse put pressure on my breast to stop the bleeding for 5 minutes. She bandaged me. I woozily sat up and removed my mask to drink my cranberry juice. Removing my mask in a doctor's office felt the equivalent to removing my gown. I felt exposed as I sat on the edge of the bed feeling slightly lightheaded. I was trying to figure out why. They didn't draw blood, they didn't give me medication. They numbed the area and poked me with needles - was it the trauma that upset my equilibrium?

I participated in another mammogram to make sure they did it correctly. Before I could finish getting dressed to leave, the nurse returned and told me they didn't get the clip in exactly the right area and they needed to insert another one. I went back to the little room and the bed and prepared for another round of poking.

This time I draped the gown correctly, no more shocking hanging breasts.

I had another mammogram.

They poked me again.

They inserted a second clip.

This time I waited while they checked the mammogram before getting dressed.

Finally, I was allowed to dress and leave. Next time I want to remember to wear a sports bra. I loosened my bra strap to make room for my bandage and the new pink ice pack I placed inside the cup. Then I walked with my sweatshirt held high to my chest to disguise the large deformed looking right breast under my loose T-shirt which screamed, "Life Happens, Coffee Helps." After texting all the important people to tell them I was finished and on my way, I drove myself home, alone.

Hannah was prepared to take care of me as soon as I walked in the door. I didn't feel like I needed to rest, but my instructions said I should, so I spent the day on the couch. I iced my breast for 20 minutes of each hour. When my timer rang, the girls began to recognize I either needed the pink ice bag from the freezer or I needed to return it so they jumped up to help. I took Tylenol every 4 hours just in case it started hurting once the numbing medicine wore off. My family and I watched movies and Survivor. I survived another biopsy.

All that was left was to wait for the results. The day after my biopsy I packed for our trip to the Oregon Coast. I still tried to take it easy so I wouldn't hurt myself and impede my healing. As I was preparing to write instructions for watering the plants for my in-laws, I rummaged through the unorganized desk looking for a sticky note. In the dark bedroom, I found a blue notecard disguised as a sticky note. I opened it:

Tomorrow's plans I do not know,
    I only know this minute;
    But He will say, "This is the way,
    Don't be afraid, walk in it."

For a moment I felt encouraged. I paused, I breathed. I felt peace. I needed only to walk in right now.

We arrived on the coast at about 2 PM on Sunday, July 12th. We drove 9 ½ hours from Caldwell, Idaho to Newport, Oregon, stopping only for gas and absolutely necessary bathroom breaks. Shelby sensed where we were going and was uncharacteristically patient unless the car slowed or stopped. Then she was eager to be free of her kennel, either to relieve herself or to check if we had finally arrived.

The packing and preparing to leave portion of this trip was the calmest it has ever been. We have been loading our car to travel to the Oregon Coast every year since 2007. That year, Abby celebrated her 3rd birthday by riding her new skateboard down coastal neighborhood roads. In 2007, we barely had enough money to carry us through each month, but we decided we needed a special vacation for our family. We decided it was more important than anything else.

We had an old Nissan Sentra that was too old and tired to travel to Oregon, in addition to being a bit small. We had a 1999 GMC Jimmy that we actually loved, but it had regular oil leaks and was going to cost too much in repairs if we kept it much longer. We traded the navy blue Jimmy with the heated leather seats in for a white 2006 Chevy Malibu Maxx. The Malibu was a sedan with a huge open trunk, large enough to store 2 weeks of luggage. We bought it thinking about how it would help us get to the coast.

On that first trip, we put every gallon of gas and morsel of food we ate on the credit card. It took us a few months to pay it off once we returned, but that first trip began a tradition. Every year, we loaded up our vehicle and headed to the Oregon Coast. Each year, we charged less and less until the miraculous year when we had the money to pay for the trip before we went. This yearly trip was a mile post marking how our financial world was improving, how our girls were growing, and any other changes in our lives. For me, it often marked the end or the beginning of a health venture.

In 2012, we bought a white 2005 Toyota 4Runner so we could include our dog, Eliza, on our trip to the coast and load our new surfboards on the top rack. The following 2 years, we packed 2 dogs, Eliza and Shelby, 3 surfboards, 4 people and all their clothes into the 4Runner - the 4Runner we bought with the intention to haul our things to the coast once a year. In 2015, we were back to one dog, Shelby. Our precious Eliza died the previous fall. We even made the trip the year I spent much of the summer in Montana gradu-ating with my masters. I started my Masters of Science in Science Education (MSSE) in 2014. During the summer of 2017, I attended in person classes for 3 weeks which concluded with my graduation ceremony on July 7th. While I was in Montana, Jason and the girls moved us from our house in Notus to our new house in Caldwell. They joined me in Montana for my graduation and we all drove back to our new home. Even though that was a very busy summer, we still went to Oregon in October of that year.

While we were packing, it was common to hear Jason ask, more than 24 hours before it was time to leave, if our bags were ready yet. It was common for him to pace. It was common for him to be anxious for us to leave. But, this time he wasn't. After reflecting, I realized it must have been because we'd had sufficient time to settle after the end of the school year. This trip wasn't a hasty escape, but a reprieve from the mundane quiet brought on by an unexpected quar-antine with an expectation of beach and surf.

Jason was patient while packing and not once did he anxiously ask if our bags were ready yet. When the morning we left didn't go as planned, because the sprinklers wouldn't shut off, he calmly made arrangements and didn't get frus-trated about the half hour delay to our schedule.

Driving away from home accompanied by patience and peace was the first treat of this trip. I later found out this patience and calm was intentional on his part. He was grateful we could take this vacation when so many people had to cancel theirs or could no longer afford them. We were blessed, during COVID, to take a vacation to the coast. The primary evidence of a pandemic was illustrated in the scarcity of out-of-state license plates on the road.

Over the years, we've rented different houses along the

coast. Our first house was a tiny rental with a deck over-looking the beach. It had a wood stove, no dishwasher and no washer and dryer. I still have a vivid memory of sitting at the wood table drinking Rogue Dead Guy Ale and playing a card game. We rented another house on South Beach called Windside. We rented Kolby's Run and Dungeness at Beverly Beach. We stayed in Hawker's Nest at Agate Beach. We stayed at Applegate, a nice two story house, located towards the headland at Otter Rock. It had a perfect fenced-in yard for the dogs. Then we found Sally's Place. For the past 8 years we have been renting the same house. It doesn't belong to us, but it feels like home. It is familiar, cozy, and allows us to look at the ocean any time we want. We walk about a quarter of a mile to the beach and are free to surf or just enjoy the ocean. The girls stay in a yurt out back. We know where everything is and where everything goes. We enjoy the luxuries of a dishwasher and a washer and dryer. It has become our second home.

On the first Monday morning on the coast, I was feeling annoyed with my family. I was eager for them to figure out what they were doing and get down to the beach for their surfing session so I could be alone. I had to stay out of the water for 5 to 7 days because of my biopsy. I also felt tender and didn't think a run would be wise, so I waited.

I was definitely affected more by this biopsy than the one 2 years ago. My breast ached and I still couldn't extend my arm comfortably. I realized it may be awhile before I was in full working order and I didn't feel like having anyone watching me as I tried to figure out what I wanted to do.

Tuesday, July 14th drug on. I felt the weight of tomor-row's phone call pressing down on me like an officer pressing the thumb for a clear fingerprint. I felt immobile. I felt scared. I felt tired. Tomorrow they will tell me if the lump in my right breast is cancerous or not. I find out if I get to continue my summer as if nothing significant has happened like I did in 2018, or if everything for the next 5 years changes again like it did in 2012.

I felt like hiding.

I felt like crying until there were no more tears.

Instead, I go to sleep, wake up, have coffee, read a little, write a little, go for a walk, eat and wait for the phone call.

I know everything might be fine - again.

In fact, there is a 70% chance that the lump is benign.

I know that right now there is nothing to be concerned about.

Right now there is nothing.

It's just that right now I feel a bit of everything.

All my senses are heightened, yet numb at the same time.

I am silent and screaming.

I crawled into bed holding my breath and trying to hold myself together. Jason was inviting me to him and I had to admit out loud I didn't feel well. I had to tell him about the weight sitting on me. He listened. He held my hand. After minutes of silence passed with mute tears streaking down my face, he quietly told me I can tell him things.

I thought, "Why don't I?"

.   .   .

I strained to explain,
>I think I don't like saying it out loud.
>A part of me is afraid my thoughts are wrong.
>I know we know nothing.
>At the moment all is well.

There seems no logical reason to feel the weight of a result that currently has no positive or negative value.

A part of me is afraid I shouldn't feel this way, yet at the same time my feelings are real and there is no "should."

It seems that in the end I need to be better at sharing. I know it isn't right, kind, or healthy to bear burdens alone, yet it seems to be the way I tend to operate.

I have learned if someone genuinely asks how I am, I will respond truthfully. I know I am ultimately afraid of being misunderstood or not heard at all. That fear keeps me alone in my deep emotions and alone in my journey. It keeps everyone outside of my wall wondering what is going on with me and how to reach me. It's not fair to those who care and it makes me weary.

The phone call with the results will determine whether tomorrow is just another day or it is the beginning of a new difficult journey. I've accepted both possibilities, I just want to know which way to step. I've been standing at this fork in the road for over 2 weeks, keenly aware of what lies down each path. I'm waiting to be told which way to turn. Standing here wondering, hoping, and dreading is making me weary and sad. I'm ready to begin walking again. I'm ready to move forward. I'm ready to accept the directions and finish the journey.

# Chapter 14

## *The Fog*

While I waited for the results call on this warm Wednesday morning, I sat on the picnic table on the grass watching the waves below me. In just a few hours, I would learn if I would walk the path I stumbled down in 2012, or if I would be allowed to skip down the path from 2018.

My girls were surfing together. It doesn't matter how old they are, the sight of them doing something together always touches my heart and brings me joy.

We arrived at our special house on the Oregon Coast just 5 days ago. This was our 14th summer coming here to surf and enjoy the ocean. This little picnic table I'm on sits atop the cliff overlooking the beach and the headland. I can see far out into the ocean and I can see 100 feet down to the beach. I thought of Alicia Keys' words in her book and how she said songs spoke to her soul. The only song I could remember at that moment was, "It is Well with My Soul."

When peace like a river
    Attendeth my way
    When sorrows like sea billows roll
    Whatever my lot
    Thou has taught
    Me to say
    It is well,
    It is well, with my soul

I knew there were more verses, but I could only remember this one and I sang it over and over. It was true. I was scared. I was overwhelmed. But, despite my feelings, I knew where I stood with my Daddy. I knew I could trust Him. I knew He didn't cause this, but He would give me everything I needed to endure it.

The phone rang at 2:30. When she asked if I wanted to put the phone on speaker, I knew what she was going to tell me. A deep unknown, irrational, almost imperceptible part of me hoped I could make it untrue if I kept the call to myself. I listened and took notes calmly, like a business transaction, while my family ached and waited in the background. I know they wanted to know, but I did what *I* needed. I needed to have the nurse to myself and the pen in my hand as I recorded. It was "Ductal Carcinoma Invasive Stage 1" this time. This meant the cells looked funny. Stage 3 meant they didn't look like cells at all. It's hormone receptive again: I may need to consider hormone blockers this time.

She told me about the surgeon my doctor recommended since my surgeon from 2012 retired. "She's wonderful!" she said. The surgeon's name was Dr. M. She was kind, gentle and sensitive as she told me what would happen next and wondered if I had questions. I didn't . . . yet. Her name was Shaanti and she's my Nurse Navigator. She's on my team.

I hung up the phone and told the strained, concerned faces of my family I had cancer. Again. Jason hugged me and cried. The girls stood off, uncertain, tearing up, but waiting their turn. I hugged everyone. Before I could settle in with the news fully, the phone rang for me to schedule my appointment with the surgeon. I was scheduled to see her on July 30th.

Before I stopped for the day and really let this news sink in, I knew I had to make some phone calls. Four people were waiting to hear the results. I went to the yurt (a dome-shaped permanent tent), out behind the house, so I could be alone with each of these precious people. That would also leave some time for my family to process this news without worrying about me.

When I got to the yurt, I had a brief release of my own tears. They erupted from me, a volcano with too much pressure. Once I gathered myself, I called my mom. She responded with, "Fuck!" She admitted she didn't feel as good about this one as she did the last one. I didn't either. We talked for a bit. Lew got on the phone and I immediately started crying. His kind voice, and the way I know he is there like a concrete wall, steadfast and stable, broke every dam and tore down each brick wall I was beginning to build. I lost all control. He said, "You can call me Papa, you can call me Dad, you can call me whatever, I am here."

My mom married Lew in 1998. They had known each other for years. Before my parents divorced, my mom went to Bible Study with Lew's wife and my dad played basketball with Lew. Lew spent years caring for his wife while she suffered from lymphoma. My mom and Lew rescued each other when they married about a year after his wife's death. My mom finally found someone who loved her just as she was. Lew found the same. It was an extra blessing that my mom knew his wife and Lew never had to pretend to forget her. Lew is steadfast. He is dependable. He has been forced up many difficult mountains in his life and he understands. If my dad forgot to show up or forgot who I was or forgot to pay attention to me, I could count on Lew to be there and fill the shoes left behind.

I called Kelly next. I could feel the air leave her like a shrinking bounce house. She admitted she didn't have words or know the words to say. Her presence sitting with me was all I needed.

I called Norma, my mother-in-law. She said she's here for whatever we need. She also told me to get some rest. I'm not sure why she always thinks I need rest or that rest will help. I think "get some rest" is code for I want you to be okay, I want you to take care of yourself, and I hope a little rest will be the best medicine.

I called my brother next, knowing he may not answer since he was at work. He picked up on the second ring. I told him. He said something like, "I'm sorry, Sis." There is something magical that happens inside me when he calls me "Sis."

My brother, Bryan, is almost 3 years younger. He is the opposite of me. He is energetic, loud and full of energy. In elementary school, he was friends with more of my class-mates than I was. My brother was typical in that he found a plethora of ways to pester and annoy me. I just wanted to be left alone. He was not typical in that he was full of life and adored his big sister. Now that we are grown with families, he still treats me with that same adoration. On this day, it blessed me. The love of my little brother filled my cup.

He shared some of his day with me. I was unapologetically honest with him. I reflected with him that we both see each other at a very different age than we are because we didn't talk much for 25 years. He's still 10 years old in my mind. We know each other's essence and are not blinded or confused by the different masks we've learned to wear. I think it's good we see each other in this raw way.

I was going to stop calling people after Bryan, but I was on a roll, so I called my grandma Martha minutes before she left for dinner. Her experience with cancer must have been different than mine. Her response to me made surgery and radiation sound like getting your teeth cleaned. It also felt like she forgot I'd already done this. She told me hard times draw you closer to God. I disagree with her opinion on hard times. Primarily, this statement illustrates she does not know me. Secondly, that statement implies we go through difficult times in order to learn to be closer to God. I've learned to see God as the ultimate and most wonderful father. I use the term "Daddy" because father sounds too formal. "Daddy" reminds me that we are God's children and the Bible tells us that He loves us. I've seen my husband love our children. He would never purposefully make their lives difficult so they would run to him and lean on him more. If he did, we would say he was cruel. Just because our Daddy is a big God doesn't mean he manipulates us to draw near to him by putting us through trials.

Quite honestly, I wouldn't consider anyone who did that loving.

Finally, I finished the phone conversations by calling my dad. I heard the sincerity of his, "Sorry." I heard his compassion. I was grateful for his prayers. I accept what I get.

After the difficult phone calls, I returned to my family. The gray cloud sat heavy, but I tried to keep moving. We ate dinner and we played games. I told the girls they didn't need to worry about talking to me. They can ask or tell me anything.

Hannah remembers the first time this happened in 2012 well and probably has her own Post-Traumatic Stress from it. Abby doesn't remember. This is a new journey for her.

Cancer. I have it. Again.

People scoff at me when I tell them I know I can handle this, I just don't "want" to. They think, "Of course you don't want to." I don't think they understand. I know how to do hard things. I'm quite good at them. I know how to lean in, how to trust, how to be strong, how to fight, how to listen to my body. I'm capable of this and perhaps even good at it.

I also know how difficult being tough is. I know how lonely it is. I know how people will misunderstand strength for health. They will misunderstand will-power for ease. I will be fighting with all my might while they watch and feel sorry. There is nothing they can do. There is so little that will make this burden lighter.

I am going into this with greater understanding than the first time. I know this road and familiarity helps a bit. This just isn't something you want to be familiar with.

I forgot how cancer sits on you and never goes away. In the quietest moments it whispers, "I am here." In the pauses in conversations, in the stillness of a restroom, during the first light of morning, in your child's smile, between the joke and the punch line. In each quiet moment, it interjects its ugly head and won't let you forget.

I feel equally like quitting and fighting hard, escaping and attacking. The feelings are at a continual tug of war in my soul. I don't want anyone to see me and I want everyone to see me. I want to proceed with life as usual and scream from the rooftops and wake everyone to the knowledge of what I am going through. It's a world of opposites, of all-ins and all-outs, I need you and I want you to leave me alone.

It has only been a day since I got the news. The mental journey is the most difficult battle right now. During the day, thoughts sneak in.

I want to rewind to the day before I had cancer.

I want to escape this.

I don't want to go down this path.

~

I watched the ocean as the sun descended. The ocean is wild and has no regard for anything around it. The waves crash on the rocks, breaking them apart or smoothing their rough edges. The wind blows the spray from each wave in whichever direction it pleases. The large brown pelicans scout and dive for fish swimming unsuspectingly below the surface. The whales spout their breath then dive for more food or dive to play and swim in the depths. The sun sets. But the ocean doesn't stop. It howls, it roars, it beats the sand. It is furious and unapologetic.

~

Two days after the call, I sat on the deck with my coffee, watching the fog roll past me and take over the Yaquina Headland to the south of me. This headland still holds one of the few remaining working lighthouses. The fog wrapped its long white hand around the headland. In the beginning, only the lighthouse protruded through the space in the hand like a piercing. Each moment the fog-hand moved, sometimes sweeping the whole area and hiding the green trees in a blanket of white, sometimes opening small windows through its fingers to glimpse the brown cliffs. The sun and the hand battled as the morning inched along. Each minute the hand faded a little as the sun reached higher in the sky. Eventually, only fragments of the imposing hand remained behind, sitting between the hills and resting on the shore.

I watched this power struggle from a fogless cliff a few miles north. I watched, thankful the fog had passed me by, wishing that in this analogy I was really in that safe fogless chair, when in reality I am the headland. Cancer is the fog. I know the sun (Son) will win. I'm dreading the dark and the wait. I won't be able to see the fog gradually lift and move and ultimately lose the battle. I will only see that I can't see until it finally clears.

I cannot express how dearly I just want to walk north, away from the headland to the space that stays protected from the dark and the fog.

I know while in the fog I must have more faith. I must trust more. I must believe this is temporary and will pass with the rising of the sun.

Right now, I am dreading dealing with and talking to people. Cancer is on the inside. People can't see it. They can't see it steal your peace. They can't see it terrify every cell in your soul. They hear the word and connect it to someone they knew who died or lost their hair or who was on TV. They don't know. Worse, they often don't want to know. They will judge and measure my every move, deciding if I am strong or weak, giving fault for both. They will desire to support me until it goes on too long and they have become bored - why isn't this over yet? You should be better by now. They will be afraid because they don't understand. It will be my job to know who wants to know how I am and what I need and who wants to hear me answer, "I'm fine."

There are so many aspects I am dreading. I remember being weak and tired, will I be weak and tired again? I remember holding myself together with duct tape, is there a better glue?

~

I am relishing being here at the coast and having a week of a peaceful place before I begin this harried journey. My mind has no peace, but at least I don't have to take action right now.

Deep down, I am terrified about what I have to do. Deeper down, I know I will just do it.

I'm tired of holding my breath.

I'm tired of remembering with each breath.

Can I really do this?

~

I finally went for a run on the beach. It felt amazing! Every once in a while the truth would rise up in me and I felt myself push my legs harder in an unconscious attempt to flee something or run to something. I ran on the hard sand with the sound of waves crashing next to me. I had a playlist called "Fun" playing in my ears created from songs that either made me want to sing or dance each time they played.

I wished to run completely alone, but I waved or said, "Good morning!" to the people I passed. I saw what they saw, a girl running on the beach. I also saw what they didn't, a girl running to free herself from the shackles of cancer. I ran far enough down the beach that I would be able to walk a good distance back. I turned off my music and breathed in the sea air and soaked in the sounds of the ocean. I felt strong again - moving always makes me feel better.

Later, after I showered and Jason and I went out for

cheese curds, my mom texted me with a picture of the dock and lake where she is. She said, "Water is healing ... heal your mind and your body will follow. You couldn't be in a better place right now."

Jason wondered if I should try to get a virtual appointment with my surgeon to get things rolling faster. In addition to not feeling like virtual would be enough for me, I needed to finish being *here* before I had to fully travel down the cancer road. I needed to enjoy the ocean, feed my soul, grieve and gather strength and energy to deal with cancer, to deal with COVID, to begin a new school year, to deal with this hand life has dealt me. This moment is my calm before the storm. Unlike most life storms, I know this one is coming and I will fully rest and prepare. I read a beautiful excerpt from *The Book of Longings* by Sue Monk Kidd today:

"To avoid a fear emboldens it . . . When I tell you all will be well, I don't mean that life won't bring you tragedy. Life will be life. I only mean you will be well in spite of it. All shall be well, no matter what."

I know I will be well throughout and at the end of this journey. My difficulty right now is my desire to avoid the journey.

These times are always very tough for Jason. This time it is more difficult because of COVID. Peoples' beliefs about it and its restrictions have reduced the people in Jason's life that he feels he can trust. Lew reached out to him. Lew understands tragedy. When he was 18, Lew lost his leg in a grain elevator accident. He has lived with 1 leg for almost 50 years. He had to grieve that loss as a young man. He had to create new visions of his future and make adjustments so he could keep living because it wasn't an option to stop. About 25 years ago his wife died from lymphoma. She suffered for many years. Lew cared for her and watched her die a little each day. He took care of her, his young son, his home and his career. He understands. It meant everything to Jason when Lew called him.

In light of this, Jason observed that people who go through hard things are drawn closer together. I realized that may be the purpose for the hard and terrible things in our lives - it isn't to draw us closer to God, even though that inevitably happens. The purpose is to draw us closer to each other. We can have true compassion and love for one another when we share pain. As a parent, I love it when my girls are close, when they talk to each other and encourage each other. I bet our Daddy feels the same. He can't physically hug us the way another person can. When we let ourselves be loved and cared for by others, we are letting ourselves be loved by God. If God is love then wherever there is love, He is there. He is in the hug. He is in the kind word. He is in the heart-broken tears.

～

I have a new dilemma playing out in my head and heart. I need to decide what kind of story I will tell - not write, tell. What story will I tell with my life?

I will write the truth. I will write every thought and feeling because it is in those deep places where people can connect and see themselves. What will I tell? I can be honest, I can be hopeful and positive or I can be persecuted. The honest story answers truly to the question of how I am doing. It doesn't hide behind a smile when there is pain. It doesn't pretend to have energy when there is none. The persecuted story lets everything be as it is. This is difficult. I am tired. I can't, or don't want to, try and feel well. The hopeful story allows truth to dwell inside me, but portrays hope and light for everyone else. The hopeful story feels everything, but shares what is good and beautiful. I'm reminded of the verse in Philippians. I will record it here, but first I want to reveal my decision. The best testimony of God's love and strength in me is to tell the hopeful story. It is to truly smile, to truly believe and know God is with me even in the darkness. The people around me are worried and if I am broken and weak they will worry more. They need to be encouraged that I will be okay with whatever happens. Therefore, I must remind myself: lean into God and trust Him above all else. I must seek my own "Knowing" (thanks Glennon Doyle) and do what God whispers to my soul. Everyone has a story. I must live my own story.

These verses are my prayer. I need to remember them daily.

"Celebrate God all day, every day. I mean revel in Him! Make it as clear as you can to all you meet that you're on their side, working with them and not against them. Help them see that the Master is about to arrive. He could show up any minute!

"Don't fret or worry. Instead of worrying, pray. Let petitions and praises shape your worries into prayers, letting God know your concerns. Before you know it, a sense of God's wholeness, everything coming together for good, will come and settle you down."

. . .

It's wonderful what happens when Christ displaces worry at the center of your life.

"Summing it all up, friends, I'd say you'll do best by filling your minds and meditating on things true, noble, reputable, authentic, compelling, gracious - the best, not the worst; the beautiful, not the ugly; things to praise, not things to curse. Put into practice what you learned from me, what you heard and saw and realized. Do that, and God, who makes everything work together, will work you into his most excellent harmonies.

"I'm glad in God, far happier than you would ever guess ... Actually, I don't have a sense of needing anything personally. I've learned by now to be quite content whatever my circumstances - I'm just as happy with little as with much, with much as with little. I've found the recipe for being happy whether full or hungry, hands full or hands empty. Whatever I have, wherever I am, I can make it through anything in the One who makes me who I am."

Philippians 4:4-14

I will think of these things: true, noble, reputable, authentic, compelling, gracious, the best, the beautiful, things to praise. I will be content and put all my trust in my Daddy.

When people ask, "How are you?" I will smile big and say, "Hopeful."

That answer is honest every moment of every day. That answer is positive, it will not bring anyone down. That answer is an invitation; the hearer can ask for more or simply accept it. That answer is also a prayer I send up with each moment knowing there is always hope.

I will shine God's light and love. I will give him my pain and fears and give everyone else hope.

On this Sunday morning, there is a strip of fog moving parallel to the beach. Once it reaches Yaquina Head, south of us, it engulfs the land. We can see it moving and we have a protected fogless bubble around us to watch the action.

As the sun is moving higher in the sky, it takes turns shining on different areas. It takes a moment to illuminate the Dragon Nose headland. Then it shines its spotlight on Otter Rock in the middle of the bay. Sometimes, it illuminates a particular spot on the beach.

Because the thick fog blocks the light, it appears as though there is only light in a few places or that the light is absent. The sun has not left. It shines continually. The obstruction of light comes from the moisture on the land and in the sea. The temperatures of the air, land, and sea are different. When they mix, they create moisture which shows itself as fog. We can't see through it. While in the fog, we have to believe the sun is there because we can't see it.

Actually, we can know the sun shines when we see the fog. Without it, we would have no fog because nothing would be heating the air. We may not directly see the sun, but we know it is present by the way it affects the air around us.

I may be in the fog. I may not be able to see far ahead of me right now, but I know the Son has not left me. The fog is evidence of the Son's presence illuminating the smallest areas, guiding my way one light at a time.

I keep thinking about the possibility of getting a mastectomy. I think of people I know who have had them and wonder if I should hear their stories and use them to guide my decision. Then I wonder if I simply need to dig deep and seek the path that is best for only me.

I kept dreading going through the same journey I went through before. I need to remember I am a different person than I was in 2012, and this will be a different journey. I can't let the past determine my future.

# Chapter 15

## *Hopeful*

I decided to surf today. We arrived at the beach 7 days ago. I have given my breast ample time to heal from the biopsy. Tomorrow is supposed to be bigger waves, so today would be better than tomorrow to surf. I don't love the big waves. I am a once a year surfer. I'd rather have the guaranteed success than the terrifying risk. I took Shelby down to let her run first. I walked about a half of a mile. She ran at least 3 times that. She ran out to the waves to see if she recognized the surfers. She ran ahead to check out the birds. She ran to the trench filled with pools of water. It looked like she was checking on everything down on the beach, making sure all was in its place. I also think she was checking to see if I hid the ball anywhere. She is considerably older this year and, like most older people, she doesn't know how to pace herself. Her mind and heart are still a puppy and she can't wait to play, but her body has other ideas. She will chase the ball until she is unable to walk and in extreme pain if I let her.

I walked back up to the house once Shelby was worn out. I passed the girls coming down the hill and handed over the blue stocking cap I was wearing so Abby could easily carry my too-wide board down the 100 steps on her head. I met Jason at the house, preparing to go down to the beach with his board. In my mind, I was planning to join all of them, but I didn't say anything. They would be disappointed if I changed my mind and I needed to be certain before I said anything.

I rinsed the sand off of Shelby in the outdoor shower. She knows the routine. She doesn't like it, but she knows to stand still while I rinse her legs and belly and sometimes her head. Fortunately, it is warm water. I donned my black and blue swimsuit and my matching Roxy wetsuit. I put sunscreen on the only part of my skin that would be showing, my face.

When I arrived at the beach, Abby saw me first. We waved at each other. It only took a minute and she was coming out of the water, soon followed by Hannah and Jason. These 3 don't easily leave the ocean. The fact that they came out to greet me felt like a welcoming home even though I never left.

They were smiling. I was smiling. We were glad I was there. I was glad I surprised them. Abby gave me my board so I could go out. Jason decided to take a break so Abby took his board. We three girls headed out to surf.

After a couple of wipe-outs, I stayed in the white water and practiced popping up. Popping up means quickly getting to your feet when a wave starts pushing you. I couldn't remember what it felt like. I couldn't remember where I should sit on the board. I couldn't remember what the waves felt like when they pushed me. I needed to go through the motions over and over again for a few minutes so my body would remember again. I popped up a few times, then I was finally ready to paddle out a bit further. I am pretty decent at getting up and riding waves that crash just behind me. I'm not as good at riding waves that crash under me. Those waves are the best, I'm just not as familiar with what I'm supposed to do. If we lived by the ocean, I'd eventually figure it out. I took a big wipe out on one of those waves, one of the waves a more accomplished surfer would have ridden expertly. I knew what I did wrong and what to do next time, but I didn't know how to tell my body. After the wipe out, I found a wave I knew I could catch and caught it right away. It is akin to getting back on the horse. I needed a successful ride in order to be willing to keep trying and possibly failing.

I realized, after riding the first few waves, that my fear coming from my memory of surfing was much greater than the actual surfing experience. I remember walking into waves that knocked me back farther than I moved forward. I remember being cold, being scared a wave would push me down, and being terrified of being thrown head first into the white water while my board flew the opposite direction (the surfers name this head first trip under the waves pearling).

The actual experience wasn't as terrible as my memories. I walked into the waves just fine. I got pushed back a little, but then I moved forward again. I got cold, but not too cold. When I moved in the water I warmed up. I pearled badly. I was rolling under the wave while my board grazed my head. I came up. I was alright. I headed back out to find another wave. All the scary things happened, and I survived, and it didn't keep me from trying again.

Before I decided to surf, I was dealing with my fear. I was telling myself I would be okay if I chose not to surf. Then I remembered a moment when I caught a great wave and rode it to the shore like a pro. Those few seconds of ecstasy, of feeling on top of the world, of using the power of the ocean to fly were worth all the pummeling and cold. It was the memory of joy and success that drove me to step into my wetsuit. I rode some waves. I wiped out a few times. I felt cold. When I was satisfied with my surf experience, not craving more or dreading more, I grabbed my board and began the half-mile pilgrimage to the house. I dominated the 100 steps and the hill to the driveway. I felt strong, capable and victorious.

It is possible my fear of this next cancer journey is based on my memory of the last time I experienced it. I remember the weariness, the pain, the weight, the complications. I need to remember the strength, the determination, the support and the victory. I am not the same person I was 8 years ago. I am stronger. I am more sure of myself. I am already a survivor. I am not the same, just as the waves are not the same. I will enter this adventure with hope, looking for the successful ride, looking for the victories, knowing that after each wipe out, I just have to get up again and find the next wave.

The morning after my first ride of this trip, and my revelation about fears and memories, the fog was on top of us. I could only see to the edge of the cliff. I could hear the ocean, but could see no sign of it. In that moment, I knew two things. I knew the ocean's openness and power was there even though I couldn't see it, and I knew the sun would come and burn the fog off. This moment where I could only see 30 feet in front of me was temporary. This coming season was temporary.

My mom told me I was a "rock" for everyone. She said I am strong and wise and all she feels like she can do is be there. I told her that is all I need. I have to do this journey - me and God - and I just need people who show up and let me be. I don't need advice or guidance, just ears and hearts. It touched me that she shared how she sees me. I'm thankful she lets me share my journey even if sometimes I am wrong.

Hannah and I were alone one evening when Jason took Abby on a date. Hannah's stomach hurt which meant she had heavy things on her mind. She was concerned she has been a bad sister because she has had a difficult time transitioning from big protective sister to sister/friend. She told me how she and Abby talked and she's going to try. I assured her that's all she can do. We discussed a few more things and finally got to the last thing that was bothering her: me.

I already knew she had taken up a larger portion to help me. Her shoulders were sinking under the burden. Unfortunately, my mom didn't help by telling her she would have to be strong for me. I explained that was wrong. I told her God and I will figure this out. I shared my "hopeful" plan and the story of the fog. I reminded her I am not the same person I was 8 years ago. I told her I will be fine. In 2012, someone told Hannah she would have to step up and be helpful. She was 11. She believed them and stepped up. She put too much pressure on herself. I didn't know it at the time, I learned it later. This time, I implored her to take her job of being a first year college student and beginning the next chapter of her life seriously - that is the only expectation I had. If she desired to help, great! If not, that was great too. I do not need her strength. I need her to do "her." I think this helped. I saw the burden lift. I will need to remind her often of these truths.

The ocean continues to tell stories. This morning the tide is out the farthest it has been since we arrived. The rocks, whose evidence of existence is usually only found in the way they make the water above them behave, are actually visible. The other rocks protrude out of the water like neglected, hairy warts. Otter Rock stands tall in the middle of the cove with a bed of rocks at its side.

I love it when the tide is out. Much more of the beach and rocks are visible. We see evidence of their existence in the way the water moves when it is high, but it is thrilling to actually see them. Each day the water molds and shapes the land to make something new. Sometimes it's deeper, sometimes it's smoother. Yesterday there was a collection of pools that meandered down the beach. You could see how the water had shaved edges, created rivers and made its way through the easiest path it could.

There is so much that goes on beneath the surface of the ocean, we only see its effects. When the tide recedes, we get a glimpse of the ocean's secrets until it washes in again, hiding them once more. Only those who rise early get to see the secrets. Only those who sit quietly watching and waiting glimpse the hidden. The curtain is pulled back for a moment. What will we discover? Are we patient enough to look into the deep?

≋

*Wednesday, July 22, 2020*

*Today, I realized I am going to rock this! It doesn't matter what lies ahead, I have it. I have gone through much worse. It won't be fun or pleasant or easy, but I will be victorious!*

I recorded those words because they were true and I wanted to claim them when I had them. I didn't want to lose them. The most difficult part of the past 2 weeks was waiting for the verdict. Once I heard that cancer had returned, I could move forward. I could step out of the fog onto the path. So far, on this path, I have thought, spoken and written. I have taken the information I know, along with my memories of 2012, along with who I am, and I traveled a path of wild beauty to find my strength, my power, my animal in whatever form it takes. I will take all of that with me on the part of the path that will demand all of me. I've had the trees, the ocean, the beach and the wild animals to comfort me and help me find myself. Soon, they will go and I will be left with myself. This next section of the path is crowded. It is filled with many people, too many tasks and not enough wildness. I will have to look to myself to survive the demands and obstacles. I will have to find the wild in myself to comfort and carry me through.

This past spring, at the beginning of the pandemic, I read *Untamed* by Glennon Doyle. My reflection reminds me of each Unlocking Us podcast I listened to with Brene ' Brown in the middle of March when COVID changed our world. My Daddy knew what was ahead on my path and He had been preparing me, giving me tools and a vision and showing me how powerful I am.

That is an example of a kind and loving Father. He may not remove the cancer because we live in a fallen world where things like this happen. Cancer is coming. But He can prepare me, talk with me, teach me and hold up a mirror to show me my strength. He can remind me of what I have overcome and that nothing on my journey will be too much for us to conquer. He can give me the news while I'm away from home and sitting on the Oregon shore listening to the chipmunks, birds, wind and roar of the unstoppable waves. He can surround me with people who love me. He can give me peace in the storm. He can prepare my mind and heart for this journey while my soul is at peace. He can show his love for me in each simple act and moment. Everything is not going to be fine, but I am full of hope and everything will be and so will I.

It is time to go home. The morning greeted me with a colorful sky, a mist covered ocean and glassy, gray blue waves running to the shore. I'm thankful for this time here. I'm thankful for the waves and birds and ocean air healing me and giving me a plan going forward. I'm thankful I've gained the determination and strength to fight again. I will not lie down and let everything happen to me. I will purposefully keep stepping on my path. I will purposefully speak truth and act in my best interests. I will purposefully love and have compassion even when love and compassion are not returned.

I will be the snow leopard who survives extinction, who cares for her family, who is beautiful, dangerous, fierce and wise.

Gratitude filled me when I arrived home, but it was different. I could feel the weight of the decisions and events of the coming months sitting heavily on everyone's shoulders. Abby is dreading going back to school with few trustworthy friends. Hannah is anxious, yet excited about beginning college. Jason and I are uncertain about a year with COVID, blended learning and a "normal" we have never experienced. Everyone is aware that the next few months will sit under the umbrella of cancer. While we sit under these heavy burdens and attempt to trudge forward, Shelby is sad. She just misses her walks on the beach.

My mind no longer goes to all the poetic places it did on the beach. I either don't look at things with the same open spirit or there is less to see. It is probably a bit of both.

It's time to start telling more people. I asked Meg if she was free for a walk, knowing I would tell her the news. I gravitate to friends I can be completely honest with about my emotions and who I am. I seek friends who I can tell the whole story to, not just the highlights or the best parts. My neighbor and friend, Meg was someone I could depend on. She expected me to be completely honest and I needed that expectation. Meg and her honesty drove me to seek out the truth in all my moments. I was drawn to her and her family from across our church many years ago before I was diagnosed with MS. I would look at her in awe and wonder. We didn't always get to see each other because our schedules didn't align, but I knew she expected my truth. I need friends like that around me.

She happened to be at the neighborhood park with her kids. After just a few minutes of pleasantries, I told her the news. She was shocked. She was sorry. She was looking for words of comfort. She was distracted by her kids trying to play with a dead bird. I tried to visit for a little bit. What I really wanted to do was say, "I have cancer!" then run away. But I stayed.

I shared I was in a good place.

I shared I was hopeful.

One anxiety I have is about school, but I have to trust it will work out. She asked if we could live off one income. There is no way, but I think I was more surprised at the idea I might quit my job to deal with this. In addition to the income, I need the distraction and purpose of my job. It doesn't matter how difficult my job is, I still need, and even want, to do it. I don't know why that question made me uncomfortable. Perhaps it felt personal. Perhaps it simply surprised me. This question made sense, but it was the farthest thing from my mind. I had already prepared myself to walk through all this. I hadn't considered avoiding any of it.

I escaped as soon as I could. I didn't escape because of

Meg. Telling people you have cancer feels like standing naked in front of them. I needed to be less vulnerable.

I'm still not exactly sure how those conversations are supposed to go. What do I say to the "I'm sorries?" They are not wrong in saying them. I'm just not sure how to respond. Saying, "That's okay," feels wrong. Maybe I should say, "Thank you," because I do appreciate the expression of sympathy, care, concern, love, and all the other caring emotions. I'm in a healthy mental place right now. Do I talk about that fact or do I just show it in my actions? It feels weird to tell someone I'm going to rock this. I know I want to be a light. I know in a fight between myself and all that cancer brings I want to stand with my arm in the air and the belt around my waist. What does that look like? Is it words? Is it actions? Is it both? How do I become amazing, but stay real? How do I endure pain and doubt and remain hopeful? How do I shine while covered in mud?

It was time for Kelly and my annual trip down the meanders in McCall on stand-up paddle boards. We made COVID adjustments to our normal routine, but other than that, it was just as amazing as usual. We paddled until our stomachs growled in protest, then sat on our special piece of sand to have lunch. She had these nifty foldable chairs so we didn't have to sit on our life jackets. Our butts were in the chairs, our feet in the cool water just like "Toes" from The Zac Brown Band. We shared veggies, nuts, cheese, fruit, meat and veggie chips.

I tried to take in everything on our trip: the trees, the flowing grass, the flowers dangling into the water, the birds fleeing from us, the fish swimming in the shade, the rocks and dead fallen trees magnified under the surface. I tried to breathe in the air, store up each sight, and let the peace of the water and smooth paddling heal my soul. We talked a bit, but we were quiet more. I was relaxed and comfortable in my skin, recognizing my own power and self to be enough. Not feeling lacking in any way. I made decisions that were good for me.

After paddling, we had a drink and cheese curds at Snake River Brewery. When her dad and his wife, Chris, joined us, I discovered a truth that existed 8 years ago and hasn't changed. I don't care who knows I have cancer, I just don't want to tell them. Kelly's dad asked how I was. At first, I didn't know he knew and wasn't sure how to answer.

"How are you?"

"I'm well. Oh, by the way, I have cancer."

That's a guaranteed way to make someone uncomfortable and end the conversation.

Later in the conversation, I deduced he knew. My gratefulness knew no bounds. I could speak freely, but I didn't have to be the one to toss the grenade. Later, I thanked Kelly for telling him.

I am going to have to work on answering "hopeful" when people ask how I am. It isn't a habit yet. It's going to take practice. That word will create a door to the truth and the other person can choose to open it or not.

On Wednesday, July 29, 2020 I had 3 meetings at school. Two of them were regarding how we are preparing to teach during COVID. The third was a scheduled time for me to tell Heather, my principal, I have cancer. That "telling people piece" isn't getting easier. Her response was heartbreakingly compassionate. Her eyes showed grief for me. Her heart was reflected in the tenderness in her voice. It took everything in my being to stay away from the hug I wanted to receive from her. I saw her arms shift in reflex and she had to stop herself. The absence of hugs is one of the greatest losses of COVID. I knew from her words that she would do anything for me to help me through this. If I needed help, I only needed to ask. I was thankful for her and every gift of grace in that conversation. Because of COVID, there was a chance, a high chance, that school would begin online. As much as I didn't want to meet my 2nd graders on the computer, this situation could be beneficial for me. I could still teach even while recovering from procedures and treatments. I could make my own schedule. I trusted God had thought of everything.

# Chapter 16

## *Rollercoasters*

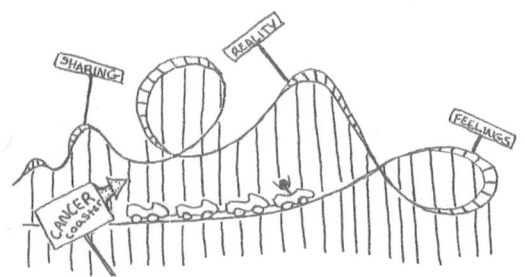

Thursday, July 30, 2020 arrived. It had only been 15 days since I learned I had to go through the steps of cancer treatment again, but it had been 8 years since my first experience with cancer.

My days were marked by doctors' appointments. They are the mile markers on my journey. Each appointment unlocks a new gate and directs me down the next road. I get the latest news, step onto a new path and spend a lot of time learning how to walk that path and understand the new dangers, potholes and terrain. After watching my feet for a while, carefully gauging my steps, I begin to feel comfortable enough to look ahead at the path, and eventually, I feel confident enough to look up at the scene around me and hear the animals and see the wild beauty for a while. I settle into the journey. I feel confident, like I can actually handle this journey. Then, a day like today arrives and I feel like I haven't even begun.

Each new doctor's visit is Siri announcing the next turn. Before smartphones, I meticulously recorded all the directions to my new destination on a piece of paper, including street names, landmarks, and clues I'd gone too far. I knew every turn before entering the car and referred often to my directions while driving. With the invention of the talking smartphone, I can enter the address, get in the car and press "Go." I simply drive and listen as Siri tells me, "In a quarter of a mile, turn left onto First Street." Then I turn. I'm not straining to read signs in an unfamiliar place. I'm not usually missing my turn. Sometimes when the road is particularly long, Siri will remind me to stay on this path, assuring me I am on track. I don't have to plan. Instead, I simply follow directions and adjust with each new turn, discover the speed limit, watch for pedestrians, stop at stop signs and lights, and follow the bend in the road. Once the warning comes, "In half a mile you will turn . . . ," I have to prepare to leave the road I am comfortable with and prepare myself for the unknowns of the new road. Unlike following Siri who guides me to new and exciting places I usually wish to go, these appointments guide me to new roads I never would have chosen. Each road is filled with difficulties I must learn to process before continuing on and I must learn how to describe these roads to others.

I met with my surgeon, Dr. M., today. I learned the next step. I learned which path I need to turn onto. I learned the new direction I must head towards. Today I learned more about my cancer, (both "my" and "cancer" feel wrong) and I learned what type of surgery is coming. I will probably need blood tests, I will probably be tested for COVID. I will probably schedule more appointments, more turns on the road.

In considering my choices, I discovered my greatest fear was having a bilateral mastectomy (removing both my breasts). I was afraid that was my best option. I was afraid of new boobs. The skin would be mine, but everything else would be removed, including my nipples. It surprises even me, but I'm attached to them (yes, figuratively and literally). As much as I've dreamed of having smaller boobs, I don't want to lose what I have and what I am familiar with.

Today I chose which surgery road I will take. Will I have a lumpectomy or a bilateral mastectomy? I chose the road that brought me the most peace. It wasn't until after I met with my surgeon that I finally felt the fullness of this peace and was fully prepared for the next step.

My surgeon was amazing! I thought I liked my surgeon from 2012, but Dr. M. was better. She didn't waste time. She began explaining every detail of my pathology report and what it meant. As Jason and I sat with our masks in her little room, she described my cancer as a goldfish rather than a dragon. It's still cancer and we want it gone, but it's easy to get rid of. We caught it before it became too vicious. She described how cancer has receptors that essentially feed on certain hormones and give the cancer fuel to grow. My cancer feeds on 2 of the 3 receptors: estrogen and progesterone. Therefore, a hormone blocker will be an essential part of my treatment. She reduced some of my fears of taking the blocker by claiming the side effects are minimal, like flushing. I'm still a little worried, but I was assured it is necessary. I can manage if I must.

We talked about my first cancer and how that was technically pre-cancer and she wouldn't have treated it the way they did. I had a feeling that it was very small, one time I saw that it was labeled stage o. It's difficult when your only choice is to trust doctors. Part of me wants to keep that information a secret. I unnecessarily went through the emotional and physical pain of cancer treatment for something labeled pre-cancer? It wasn't my fault. I knew nothing back then. I was shocked and could only follow directions. I could only trust.

I asked my surgeon if I should consider a bilateral mastectomy because the emotional roller coaster of this journey takes a toll on me. She patiently explained the whole procedure, where the incision would go, loss of the nipple, and the potential difficulties in stretching my radiated skin. I would need 2 surgeries, one to remove the breasts and another for reconstruction. The recovery would take 6 weeks as opposed to 2 weeks for a lumpectomy. I wouldn't need radiation if I had a mastectomy, but I would still have to take the hormone blockers.

She learned I would go smaller in breast size, which was good since the radiation damaged my skin and it wouldn't stretch like irradiated skin. She learned I do CrossFit and since exercising and remaining healthy are important to me, I probably wouldn't do well with the 6 week recovery. As she shared every detail, I told her, through my tears, I was worried about a mastectomy. She assured me there is no difference in life expectancy between the two surgeries. The only reason for a mastectomy would be for my emotional state. Based on her description, the surgery and recovery and loss of my own boobs might be more devastating emotionally than a lumpectomy and radiation.

We decided on the lumpectomy. I felt peace. Jason felt

peace. Dr. M. assured me this was the best choice. I am thankful I didn't listen to everyone's opinions. I am thankful I made the choice that was right for me. I feared a mastectomy and that alone meant I wasn't ready for it.

Dr. M. graciously scheduled my surgery for August 28th, just before my insurance switched to a new company. She took all my fears away with her knowledge, compassion and impeccable listening. She would have hugged me if not for COVID. I am grateful for her. If every doctor took notes and explained in detail all that was happening with our bodies and all that would happen, it would be much better. We would know why we are trusting them.

Before my appointment with Dr. M., I waited in the car while Hannah got some immunizations. I sat alone, filled with anxiety, so I listened to music and practiced breathing slowly to control my heart rate. It didn't work very well. After visiting with the doctor, all my anxiety fled from me like a scared cat. My anxiety covered me like an old, itchy wool blanket on the way in, and there was no trace of even a piece of woolen lint left on the way out.

I feel so much more present this time than I was 8 years ago. I see myself and others more clearly. I am actively accepting and interacting with my situation. Last time, in 2012, I sought to survive and simply tread water while everything happened *to* me. This time I am at least trying to swim. I am trying to control myself and my energy in the midst of what happens to me.

I was two different people. The first time I put my head down and walked into the storm as it beat against me and tried to push me back. I felt the beating of the wind and rain, but never looked up to see it. I stoically committed to take another step until the storm subsided.

During the second journey, I had my head up. I could see the storms coming from afar and I would gather my soul friends around me to gain strength. We held hands as I stepped through the storm. Each time I felt like quitting, their strength and encouragement would reach me like electricity passing through our bodies.

During both journeys, God gave me the ability to walk through the storm. The first time, He was my strength, teaching me I could trust Him and depend on Him. The second time He poured His strength and spirit into me through my soul friends, giving a face, voice and arms to the love and care He has for me.

Saturday, August 1, 2020, arrived. The first of August always marks the official end of summer for me in the sense that I begin to commit my thoughts and actions fully to preparing for a new school year. Summer isn't actually over in that the weather is warm and I will keep enjoying it until I no longer can, but it is over in that school has officially begun in my mind.

Even though I am at peace about surgery at the end of this month, cancer still hangs around. It is still the pestering monster: lingering, never quite leaving, refusing to let me forget. I texted back and forth with Carlie for an hour and a half last night. I shared my monster analogy with her, then we talked about our days. It feels so good to talk with a good listener who fully understands how to keep walking when life forces you to trudge through piles of shit while the hail and winds threaten to knock you down.

Carlie and I met when we were about eighteen months old. Our moms knew each other. We went to elementary school and middle school together until 8th grade. We regularly had sleepovers at each other's homes. We literally grew up together. In high school we stayed connected, even though we attended different schools. Our connection was established during the many years we grew and discovered the world together. We both went off to colleges in different parts of the Pacific Northwest. We had relationships, families, disappointments, and medical difficulties. After 25 years of living in different states and having different lives, we reconnected in December of 2019 when I was in her town for a science conference. We had dinner and drinks and told the story of our lives between high school and that moment. Our lives were very different, but we understood each other's seasons. We didn't have to be the same to be on the same page. Our two paths had little in common, but we found we were standing next to each other in this forest, looking at the mountains we'd traversed, the valleys we survived, and trails we conquered. Since Carlie and I have known each other almost our entire lives, we can easily see the true version of the other person. We can accept each other without any additional requirements.

Just 3 months after our reunion dinner, the COVID quarantine began. And 4 months after that, I was diagnosed with breast cancer. Carlie was there. She heard the news and called. She let me share all my fears and pain and she simply said she understood. She understood how difficult it is to walk when every step is a reminder of the terrifying path ahead. She understood how difficult it is to be strong for others and also share your weakness with them. From 400 miles away, she became a rock. Because our souls were connected by our childhood past and by pains and troubles we had overcome over the years, she was a comfort to me. The very thought of her and her own trials gave me hope and peace on my darkest days.

### *Truth*

*I am strong and I am weak*
*I am hopeful and I am discouraged*
*I am whole and I am broken*
*I am confident and I am lost*
*I am unbreakable and I am fragile*
*I am at peace and I am troubled*
*I am full and I am empty*
*I am determined and I am scared*
*I stand tall and I cannot stand*
*I am healthy and I am sick*
*I am too much and I am not enough*
*I am loved and I am alone*
*I keep moving and I stand still*
*I smile and I am sad*
*I am a capable, beautiful woman and I am not*

These are the dichotomy of truths that wave through me each moment of each day while cancer tries to make me not.

It is Sunday, August 2, 2020. I'm still having a difficult time being super productive. A part of me is storing up energy for school: that part enjoys writing, reading, exercising and watching TV. Another part of me feels there is some value to completing adult tasks like cleaning, and I am lazy or less of a person if I don't. It appears I need to work on how I think about this more than the actions themselves. I am bothered by messes, but I just can't find the energy and strength to fix them. I get overwhelmed. I need to find a system that fits how I am made and I need to learn to ask for help.

I spoke with my mom after questioning my motivation to accomplish adult things. Shortly after our conversation, I cleaned up the petunias. I created a shelf for the 10 books Jason is reading instead of three piles across the living room. I cleaned the refrigerator with Abby's help, I did some laundry, I harvested lettuce, and cooked over a dozen eggs to make a pile of hard-boiled eggs. I was very productive. By the end, my energy was waning and my back ached. I realized I am very capable of hard work. I haven't lost that. It's just that there are many days when I actually don't have the energy. I must learn to be nice to myself. There will come a time when I must work whether the energy is there or not. In the meantime, I will listen to my body and be kind to myself.

Last night, before brushing my teeth, I looked deeply into the eyes staring back at me from the mirror. Without warning, I started crying. I have donned my superhero clothes where I stand tall, smile, encourage others and operate rather normally, but inside, deep behind my mask is the ache and pain of reality. I'm still scared, I'm still tired, I'm still weary from continuous battling. My mask is firmly in place, but my eyes can't hide anything.

Right now, because of COVID-19 many people (mostly in other states, but some in Idaho) wear a mask over their nose and mouth in public. It helps prevent the spread of the disease. This mask hides the expressions on our mouths, but it accentuates the expression of our eyes. I can usually smile to hide what is deep inside me: pain, weariness, sadness. But with the mask covering my mouth, my eyes hold the truth I cannot disguise. I saw it in the mirror. My mask of positivity and hope is wonderful, but it cannot come close to disguising what is real and raw in my soul.

They say grief is a solitary emotion. Perhaps that is the reason for the mask. I want to remain alone in it.

This moment was followed by a few difficult days. I didn't feel well. I know the difference because I felt great before these days found me. It began with the sadness and pain deep in my eyes, not disguised by my smile. It moved to a slowness in my body and soul and included an upset stomach. I feel more recovered today, but am beginning to get anxious about the new school year while still trying to believe I'll do great.

Jason and I had a date on the porch with some drinks. After talking about school and changes, I coupled my second drink with a bold question. "How are you doing regarding me?"

Thankfully, he has his brother. He can speak freely to him, and Wes rarely says anything stupid. Matt, Kelly's husband, is an escape friend. He can hang out with him to forget. His protective claws have come out regarding me. It is important to him that people are safe and make good choices regarding COVID. Sometimes he worries about what my cancer is going to do between now and surgery.

I shared with him that he is doing everything right by me. He is present. I can count on him and he takes care of me. Besides feeding me (he does an incredible job of making dinner most nights), I told him I see the things he does to protect, care for, and love me. I know there are many moments in the day where he is searching for a way to make each step on my journey easier or smoother or just a little less painful.

I'm also aware that his journey is not the same as mine. Watching someone go through something difficult is a separate journey than going through it yourself. The watcher feels powerless and helpless. The person going through it has the easier job of walking while you painfully watch.

We had a good date. I can't remember every detail we talked about, but it was good. I'm glad he told me how he was feeling. I'm glad he has his brother. I'm glad we are stronger than we were 8 years ago and that this will just be another journey to walk together and learn from.

It was Sunday, August 9, 2020, and I was spiraling a bit. I was in my head, questioning everything I did, thought or said. I was feeling every feeling. I was feeling amazing and completely inadequate at the same time.

I knew I would feel better if I accomplished some things on my list, but my list was so long I didn't know where to start. I knew I was capable and strong, but I kept wanting to hide and waste time. I knew the crazy would start soon and

I could help it by working now, but I was afraid of losing peace. I was spinning. I couldn't see straight and I didn't know which direction to go. On this day, I had an almost impossible time finding my way.


On another day, I decided to let my spirit guide me rather than making a list to determine my direction. I took Shelby for a long walk. I have many choices on my walks. I can call someone, invite someone to walk with me, listen to a podcast, listen to music or walk in silence. I had an old friend on my mind so I decided to call her. She didn't answer. I left a message then took a moment to learn what my soul needed for the rest of my walk. I decided on music. Norah Jones' style sounded good so I chose a playlist on Spotify called "Norah Jones Radio." In addition to the titled artist I heard Carole King, Joni Mitchell, Sarah McLachlan, and Tracy Chapman. It was a great experience. The music lifted me, calmed me and strengthened me. I'm starting to renew my love affair with music again. Reading Alicia Keys' book and listening to how her songs describe her journey was the beginning of my renewed journey down this path. I found myself wanting to stay in my headphones long after my walk was finished.

It has been a number of years since I've sought out my own music. I've let everyone around me decide the score of my life. As I started taking up those reins again, I realized I was missing out. There is a soul connection with music that grounds one. When the words hit that same chord in my spirit, all of me comes alive. All of me feels seen and heard even if only by a stranger who may have sung this song 30 years ago. I know I am not alone when someone else's words narrate the feelings in my soul.

~

Each day I wake up, I have to deal with my feelings anew. It is Wednesday, August 12, 2020, and I'm anxious, fatigued and sad. In order to change my mood, I took Shelby for a walk. I decided not to try and call anyone or see anyone. If someone called or I bumped into someone that would be okay, but I wasn't going to initiate it. Instead, I listened to "Avett Brothers Radio" and cried. I cried off and on for most of the walk. Sometimes songs pushed tears out, sometimes my thoughts released them.

I'd sufficiently worn Shelby out and was taking her home when my mom texted she'd be ready to call and walk in 10 minutes. I decided to go for it. I told her I'd be ready, dropped Shelby off, then headed out alone for my 2nd walk, this time I would have my mom on the phone with me.

I wanted to share my darkness, but she was cheerful and talkative. I'm not sure what kind of response I wanted. I finally told her I'd had a walking cry or a crying walk. She listened to what I said and didn't really respond. What did I really want or need from her? I wanted to say more. I didn't want consoling or sympathy. I wanted to flesh it out. I wanted to share all the tough burdens, the list of to-dos. I wanted someone to be able, willing and strong enough to let me talk about all the shit and know I would still be okay. I just want to get it out of me and lay it at someone else's feet for a bit. I didn't want them to pick it up. I didn't want them to determine its worth or value, I just wanted to show it so we can both look at the pile and say, "that's a lot of shit." Then we can leave it. I want someone who knows it's crappy, they can genuinely ask, I can genuinely be honest with my answers, and we can know it is all crappy without needing to pick any of it up.

As I keep finding myself in these dark places alone, I wonder if I need to find a counselor. Their job is to listen to my shit. Their job is to hear me and dig deeper, to not judge, to really want to know the full truth. I wish with all my heart there was a person I could do that with, but it is rare. They get so distracted by their desire for me to be okay that they don't know how to let me be. I've come to accept that sometimes we are just not okay and sometimes we need people to simply see us and say, "I see you, I'm sorry."

Let's see if I can sort out some of my feelings. I'm anxious about school - can I really do this? I have to teach second graders online. I'm scared about surgery and recovery. I'm terrified about radiation. I'm worried what the hormone blocking pills will do. I'm weary of COVID and the changes it has caused - primarily separation from friends. I'm excited for Hannah's college journey. I'm hopeful Abby can find her way and be herself for these last 2 years of high school. I'm proud of my girls and their strength and character. I'm thankful for my family. I'm concerned Jason doesn't lean on enough support outside of me. I'm also content and at peace with my life in general. It seems I feel all the feelings.

I feel alone in my weakness. Everyone likes it when I'm strong. They can marvel and think I'm okay, but they don't know what to do with my weakness.

When I cry, Shelby picks up her ball, wags her tail and comes to me. She wants to bring me joy. Others stand and half look at me from afar, unsure if they want to know, unsure if I want to tell him. They see, but it feels like they avoid me. My girls see my tears and are good at hugging and sitting near me.

I have a friend who might listen to all of it, but she doesn't usually go too deeply into herself so it might be a bit much to go deep with me. I have another friend who might be willing to listen, but she often tells me to see a therapist. Even though therapy will be helpful, it isn't what I need to hear right now. Family will worry. I have another friend who might be there for me. We could even take turns sharing our shit, then looking at it on the ground, then walking away together. It would be okay to talk with a counselor, but I would rather talk with a friend. I would rather have a mutual relationship where we can both be real and honest and stand with one another than talk to a stranger.

# Chapter 17

## *Sharing Shit*

After all these thoughts and feelings on my need to share or not share, I attempted to share with Jason. I attempted to let him know that sometimes I want to share all the "shit" I feel, be heard, then be done. I just don't want to be the only one who knows about it - like it's a secret.

My words let loose a dam. It came out that he was worried. He wanted to help, but didn't know how. He felt like he was guessing on how to behave or help. He was very emotional. An outsider would have guessed he was angry, but I knew better. He was lost and hurt.

I heard him say a lot of things that may or may not be completely true. I tried to ask questions to understand more. He got more frustrated because he couldn't explain himself, and I often had to repeat to him what he said that I was asking for clarification on. He said I can't share things and expect him not to try and do something - to help fix it. If I share the shit, he can't help but try to fix something or pick it up and make it better.

What he couldn't hear was that I did need something. There was something he could do. I just needed a listener. I just needed someone who would dig deeper and hear me fully, see me fully. It makes it easier to pretend it's not happening when I don't talk about it. He couldn't understand that you can't fix shit or make it better. When someone lays shit at your feet, the last thing you should do is pick it up, and you definitely can't make it better or turn it back to its original state. You're supposed to look at it and say, "That stinks, that's horrible, let's leave it on the ground and go find something else to look at and smell."

He feels he can't do that. I feel I can't ask. He knows I need something, but he can't give me that. I don't know if anyone can. I don't know if it's fair to seek it.

Sometimes I fear I am my own confidant. I console and counsel myself. I dig deeper into my own feelings to find my own peace and hope and what I crave is to hear those words from someone other than myself. Is it time to speak with a counselor? Why do I need to pay someone to listen fully? Is there really no one in my life with the strength to handle all of me? Am I really too much? Do I need to become smaller and more manageable? Do I need to stop seeing and feeling everything?

In addition to the difficulty in saying, "I have cancer," I fear there may be another reason I am not eager to tell people. If I say it, if everyone knows, it becomes real. It becomes something big and heavy that I can't ignore because everyone will see it when they see me. They will give me their sympathy and I will break. They will be kind and caring and I will be forced to be honest with myself. I will be required to accept their words and sad eyes. I will be required to live in reality instead of pretending nothing has changed.

It is Saturday, August 15, 2020. It has been a month since my diagnosis. At this point, I have only told a few people the difficult truth of my second visit from breast cancer. I decided to post the news on Instagram. I had a "Colored Ribbons" Instagram account where I focused on things like breast cancer and MS, so it seemed appropriate and it was time. I was searching for a picture to attach to the news. I found the picture of my grandma Hazel and my girls standing in her garden in 2009. The tears instantly came. I miss her. She was my cheerleader. She died in 2014.

Later, when Jason and I were having coffee on the porch together, I felt the tears coming again as I remembered her picture. I just wanted to curl up in Jason's arms. So I did. I put myself near his chest, under his arm and cried. I know my tears scared and worried him while I wasn't talking, but I needed to simply cry.

I shared my revelation that my silence to others was, in part, because it was difficult, but also because keeping it silent kept it from becoming too real. Surgery isn't until August 28th. I would like to pretend I am normal until then.

He heard me. I shared my poem from early August about the opposing feelings. He understood that and could fully sympathize. He reminded me that vulnerability is strength. He knew I needed other people to talk to also. I explained the differences in my relationships. I shared my gratitude for all my different friends who meet me in different places. One friend is my rock. She can take anything. Another friend reminds me to be powerful. A faraway friend is everything, except nearby. I can be fully me and fully accepted.

We connected. We heard and understood each other. It was beautiful and good. I learned he can't handle all of me until he has dealt with himself, and he must reach out to friends to do that and become centered again.

I called Carlie later. My mood spiked to joy after talking with her. She listens fully. She shares honestly. I am beyond grateful we have reconnected. My trip to Seattle last winter opened the door - let us know we were safe and now we get to support each other from afar. We are very different people, but the events have connected us in a way that is precious. There are few words to fully describe the beauty of this relationship.

Carlie has experienced years of medical pain. She looks normal, but lives in pain. She understands. She knows how to let me be whatever I need to be and she never picks up the burden I attempt to lay down.

It took me another day, but I finally did it. I shared on Instagram that I have breast cancer. Once I created the post, I waited almost 5 minutes before I could finally push the "Share" button. I was scared of revealing myself. I was nervous about perception. I felt vulnerable sharing my problem. After I pressed "Share," I felt free. I let go and gave others permission to reach out to me and to share in the knowledge of my current journey. Part of me likes being private, but I realize it's not because I want to journey alone. It is because I'm afraid of what it will cost me to journey with others. How much more of myself will I be required to share? Can I be strong and vulnerable? Can I include everyone in the journey without sacrificing my own peace? All the responses were kind, filled with love, prayers, and support. Why was I afraid? Perhaps the real fear is that they only share words, that when I call on them to act on their words, they will likely fail to follow through. Even if that is the case, their "follow through" has nothing to do with me. It is a reflection of them.

I'm happy I shared. I enjoy hearing from people. I need to learn how to be more real and transparent. I need to learn how to trust myself. I need to learn how to trust others even if they might let me down.

∾

One of the difficulties of cancer is the many images that come with the word. People remember other loved ones, characters in movies and stories. Today, there are only a few people who haven't been touched by cancer in some form. When I say the word out loud following, "I have," I want to immediately tell you more. I want to tell you my story and my journey because I'm afraid of where your imagination may take you. I want you to know that much of the time I operate normally: do my job, exercise, be with my family. At this stage - pre-surgery, my obstacles are in my head and heart. The weight of the word, the unknown outcomes of the next few months, the pressure of the effects of this journey on my life all take turns pressing on me, weighing me down. I must use my energy to speak truth and encouragement to myself.

Right now, my body is fine. My mind and heart are battling for ground. They know the more ground they gain now, the more room my body will have to fight and heal when treatment begins.

Feel free to ask how I am. Don't be surprised if I feel good. I fight for that. I fight to see the beauty and the lovely truth. When you are winning a battle, you feel good and strong. I get to be there often. Once in a while the battle is difficult, I get weary and begin to lose ground. I've learned to reach out, share my load and I quickly gather strength to fight again. You'll probably catch me winning most of the time. If you catch me losing ground, thank you for standing with me and giving me strength to fight again.

∾

I worked at the school for about 4 hours preparing for the most unusual school year ever.

Many people knew about my cancer at school. They were kind, compassionate and willing to help. I felt buoyed by their caring. Previously, I feared it. I was afraid it would make me weak. Now it brings me joy.

I'm thankful for friends and caring people. Sometimes I'm afraid of people's kindness because I've received the fake version in the past and got burned. I'm scared of accepting their gift then feeling alone as they ask for it back.

My truest friends, those that my 12-year old self would consider best friends, are those who accept me fully just as I am. They don't expect me to be different and they aren't overwhelmed by my thoughts and words. They see me.

I was thinking about Carlie last night. I thought about her work, her pain, her laundry, her son, her painting and her struggles. I realized people often tell one another "our thoughts and prayers are with you." That phrase sounds ridiculous. How can a person's thoughts be helpful in a situation? Prayers are great and we know God works, but when we are in the mud, they are just words.

Yet, they are helpful. I feel strengthened when someone tells me they are remembering me. Why? I believe it is the encouragement that we are not alone. We aren't the only person who knows what is happening. Kind spirits are standing with us even though we can't see them. Even though we must walk our own path alone, we have a cheering section shouting out words of strength and encouragement. They are sitting in the stands using all their energy to give us that extra motivation, that extra strength to push us across the goal line to victory.

When I was in high school playing JV volleyball with

game times at 4:00 in the afternoon, I had no cheering section coming just to see me. Both my parents worked and couldn't afford to take time off. They were waiting for me to make varsity with 7 PM games, then they would watch.

Neither they nor I knew that my lack of cheering section drastically affected my ability to play. Without someone there watching just me, cheering for me to succeed, I had to find that motivation on my own and it was considerably more difficult. Once, a friend came to watch. I felt like a pro on the court that day.

I want you to know, when you send your thoughts and prayers, it means something. I know you are cheering me on, anticipating victory. Your thoughts and prayers are the crowd giving me that last piece of strength and energy I didn't know I had. Thank you!

～

I have surgery in 8 days. In 12 days, I begin a new school year teaching second graders online for the first time. One foot is trying to step into a new year while the other is preparing for a cancer journey. I almost have to forget about one to deal with the other. I need to figure out how to be efficient and organized. Spiraling through my list isn't working.

～

I found an app inspired by Marc Bracket and his book, *Permission to Feel*, called "The Mood Meter." I like using it to monitor my moods and take action to change them or keep them. During this real, scary and extreme season, it is actually inaccurate in its definitions and advice. There are four quadrants. The red and yellow are high energy, the green and blue are low energy. The red and blue are low pleasantness and the yellow and green are high pleasantness. Each quadrant answers a question of energy and pleasantness. Over the past few days, my mood has been red if I gauge it by the definition of the words in the red quadrant (high-energy, low pleasantness). I am feeling nervous or worried, but that category is high energy and other than the intense feelings I am nowhere near high energy. Also, advice given for shifting a worried mood is to think about positive outcomes or talk to a friend. A few times, I have inwardly laughed at the advice. I may be able to shift my mood for a moment, but because the cause is a very real, scary event and not my perception of an event, it is much more difficult to shift it.

It is Saturday, August 22, 2020. I've been avoiding writing this morning. According to the definition on my Mood Meter, I feel down: sad and like you have little energy. I don't know how sad I am. I definitely have little energy. I want to curl up on the couch and disappear into meaningless television. For the past 2 days, I've worked hard on school preparation, preparing to meet with families and thinking about the coming school year. Thursday, I felt drained. Friday was better. I felt accomplished. I got my work done and completed my list.

My mind is everywhere and nowhere this morning. It wonders about the first 2 weeks of school when I will teach and recover from surgery. It sees the overgrown garden and the household tasks. It sees the books and piles of unorganized life. I wonder what exercise I should do today. It sits on me. I vacillate between thoughts of productivity and complete numbness. This vacillation is the part I struggle with. I'm spiraling, running back and forth between all my thoughts. It is difficult to pin myself down.

The unknowns in the coming weeks are pressing in on me. Will I have energy to work on the first days of school since I will have just had surgery? Will I be able to do school when it starts, or will I be too weary? Will I be COVID free after meeting face-to-face with each parent? What will my surgery recovery look like? Can I really do this?

I know I can. I know I will take one moment, one day at a time. I know I will make this look easy to everyone else. I'm holding my breath. Reality is a lot right now. I can't look at it fully or I will be overwhelmed. I must conquer today. I must choose my actions in this moment and know I can make decisions for the next moment when it comes.

Two days until surgery. I am everything right now. I am tired from waking up at 4 AM the past 3 mornings. I am drained from speaking to 25 families over the course of 2 days. I am scared about how I will feel after the mag seed procedure today. This is where they insert a tiny magnet called a mag seed into the location of the cancer so the surgeon can find it. The surgeon uses a tool to find the mag seed, then removes the area around it. This procedure replaces the 2012 procedure of giving me an antennae. I am overwhelmed with getting ready for school to begin. I feel the weight of the next 3 days sitting on me like a tired elephant.

One day until surgery. In addition to feeling tired, drained, scared and overwhelmed, I feel the stress, worry and fear of the unknown of the COVID test and its results. I feel the tension as I try to calm my breathing in the car ride to the mag seed procedure. I feel the anxiety as I wait on the plastic chair for my COVID test, then wait again on a different plastic chair until they call my name. I feel the pressure as I walk to Breast Care Services, stopping by the bathroom first. I surprise myself by breaking down in tears while sitting on the toilet, quickly squelching them when someone walks in. While I wash my hands, I meet Jean, the interrupter of my tears. She is an older lady who has come in for a diagnostic ultrasound and can't find her way. I wait for her and we walk down together. I was struck by the strangeness that I have more experience in the breast services journey than these older women. They have no idea I, this 40-something woman, have spent more time here than they have.

First, I talked with the nurse about the procedure. She was very cheery, which in this instance brings just enough comfort when it usually would have been annoying. She directed me to change into the giant pink dress. I waited a bit more and watched them clean the bed and pillow I would be inhabiting soon. I kept breathing. I noticed they had no trouble breathing in their masks, which was so different than some of my parents and students who had difficulty with them just a few days before.

It was my turn. I removed my arm for Shannon, this

time no breast hanging out. I draped the gown over my chest and under my arm. I laid on the bed. She located the spot with the ultrasound just like last time during the biopsy. She rotated the bed for the doctor just like last time. I had a wedge thrust under my right side to put me at the correct angle and a warm blanket to calm me. I really love those heated blankets.

Dr. B. inserted a needle to numb the area which caused more pain than I planned. Then she inserted the magnet. They cleaned me up. Pat, the cheery nurse, dressed the hole they left behind. I crossed the hall for a mammogram to ensure they placed it in the correct spot. It was just about time to get a new bandage, get dressed and go home when the technician came back. They needed to do the procedure again. The magnet wasn't quite in the right place. They repeated the entire procedure, including the warm blanket and Pat's gentle fingers rubbing my lifted arm. If she had asked me, I would have told her I didn't need it, but I found it comforting anyway. I wonder if the three of them had any idea how scared I was.

After a second mammogram, it was finally time to get dressed and leave. When I got to the car I got a "good morning" text from my brother. I'm so thankful he does that. Then I cried.

I cried most of the way home. I sat in the 4Runner in the garage and cried. I exited the 4Runner to go into the house, but stopped at the nearest chair. I sat in the lawn chair in the garage and cried. I tried to go inside again. I paced the garage and cried. I tried one more time to go into the house, then had to go back into the garage and cry some more. Finally, I settled down enough. Kelly texted and asked how I was. I said "good and shitty." Good, because generally things are good, but shitty because the weight of this week sits on me like a lazy elephant.

She understood and said I was strong. I don't feel strong.

Meg texted too. I told her the truth. She is praying and caring. It's hard to be broken. Jason came to say "hi" in between the online classes he was teaching. I cried some more.

Somehow, I managed to get work done and meet with a parent. Hannah and I hunkered down with our over-whelming burdens and watched some funny movies. Three movies later, I was beginning to feel better.

Today Heavy Harold is next to me, not so heavy, but still there.

I am all over the place right now. I am pacing, energetic, but also lost and unsure of what to do with myself. I know I have pre-surgery tasks looming. I know I have a journey ahead of me. It could go smoothly. It could take me out. I am scared. I am tired. I am tired of trying to be okay.

I just talked to Carlie - I love her so much. I can trust her with the worst of myself. I need that. I hope I am giving her the same gift.

I realized I'm not scared of cancer, at least not right now.

I'm scared of not being whole. I'm scared of not recovering fully. I'm scared of losing control of my body.

Carlie, my faraway friend, told me about a geode painting she will create inspired by pain and difficulty, and under each is grief. With each new health problem, I grieve the loss of my health again. I fight to get it back only to lose again. When will I stop gaining it back? When will I stop winning?

This feels too difficult right now.

We discussed that it isn't strength that gets us through, but determination, perseverance, and stubbornness. I don't have strength, I just keep moving.

My heart feels empty and broken. It struggles to be calm or to go in one direction. I feel an emptiness inside me as I try to take in these next few days.

Surgery day. I'm not feeling anxious right now. I will be as time gets closer to the actual surgery. I'll try to be calm, but inside everything will be churning. Today, I vividly remember the last time I drove into surgery. I was terrified. It was my first surgery, and it was for cancer. I remember holding Jason's hand all the way in. I remember being quiet. That drive felt more like a journey to an execution than a surgery.

I think Jason is afraid of surgery and cancer and what they will do to me. Last night he couldn't look at me or he would cry. I'm afraid of not recovering, of losing more of my strength and ability. I fight so hard for the health I have. That is the battle I'm most afraid to lose.

Part of me is worried about next week.
  Part of me trusts it will be okay.
  Part of me knows I will figure it out.

# Chapter 18

## *Surgery: Take Two*

J ason dropped me off at Breast Care Services on Friday morning. He didn't get to join me like he did 8 years ago. We are in the middle of a pandemic and people must go alone to the terrifying hospital visits. Enough has changed in the last 8 years that this doesn't feel familiar enough to be easy.

I was supposed to go into the main entrance of the hospital, but I went to Breast Care Services instead. I'm not sure if I went to the wrong place because I misunderstood the directions, or because I remembered beginning my journey at Breast Care Services last time. They changed my appointments for today and I don't think everyone got the message because it seemed difficult for them to find my name on the correct list. I went to a waiting room for Medical Imaging. I was the second person to arrive there. A few people came in and were immediately taken to a different waiting room. A blonde lady read books to her 4-year old son and showed all the makings of a kind mother. He was super wiggly and was nowhere near as nervous as she. A much older, frail woman and her husband came in. She was in a wheelchair and had a special mask. Her hair was thinning and her body shook. They came and left while I waited. There was another older lady across the room in black pants and a black shirt with a pretty blue band across the chest who was there when I arrived and was still there when it was finally my turn.

The cheerful man in charge of the room wished me a good day. The top of his head was bald and he had a long, dark curly mullet. I walked down the hall with another man. His name might have been Roger. We took many turns and went through a few doors. I couldn't have given anyone directions through the white-walled maze. I changed into a hospital gown and laid on a hard bed intended for scans. They injected me with 2 lidocaine shots and 2 shots of radioactive dye that traveled to the lymph nodes associated with my breast. Dr. M. would later use a Geiger counter to find the node that carried the radioactive dye. I was finished, got dressed again, and then Roger took me to surgery. First, he took me to the wrong surgery area. The receptionist phoned Karen, who patiently walked me across the street to the correct place - The Surgery Center. It looked newer than the rest of the buildings with clean gray lines and plenty of snake plants resting behind each well-planned seating area. Should we celebrate or fear the fact that they built a separate "Surgery Center?" Did they build it because they wanted a nice place for surgeries or because there are so many surgeries, they required additional space?

Everyone I came in contact with asked me how I was doing. I would pause. I wasn't certain how to answer. I thought, "You all know I'm here for surgery, what do you expect my answer to be?" I assumed they didn't really care or they didn't really think about it, they were just making small talk. I replied with "good" or "fine" with a tone implying "under the circumstances ..."

I checked into the surgery center and exchanged my homemade blue flower mask for a blue hospital mask. They immediately directed me to my room where I changed into a long brown, green and tan checked gown with 5 white snaps down the top of each sleeve and long green bands to tie it together. Initially, I put it on backwards. The nice nurse looked at me like I was a bit crazy. I've been so used to wearing hospital gowns with the opening in the front, I didn't even consider this would be different.

Everyone was nice. I was nervous and scared. I didn't know what to do or say. I tried to do or say what I wanted, instead of what I thought I was supposed to do or say. I told the nurse I needed to use the bathroom. I asked for my phone. I asked her about her upcoming baby. I said "yes" to the lavender scent patch that would help to calm me. It shouldn't take so much effort to say what I want, but it did. It does. I live in such a way as to not impose myself on others. In the past, Jason has been with me and I could use him to communicate or ask him for things. This time, since I was alone, I had to speak for myself. As the minutes stretched out, I got more comfortable and confident about asking for what I needed or wanted.

Angelina, my nurse from Russia who moved here 14 years ago to be with her husband, took my vitals and got me settled. Amber, my nurse who was 29 weeks pregnant with her 2nd girl, gave me my IV and my pre-surgery medication. Dr. O. (I think) was my anesthesiologist. She repeated herself a few times as if she was reciting a script. She was sensitive to the fact that I probably responded strongly to medication and didn't give me too much. Her counterpart, James, would be with me in surgery. She would remain near in case she was needed.

Dr. M. came in and assured me she would remove both magnets they had inserted during the mag seed procedure, so my surgery became a double lumpectomy. In the end, she took a mass that was a little smaller than a ping-pong ball. She was optimistic she would try to make the two sides even. My breasts have always been different sizes. After my first lumpectomy, they were much different sizes. She was going to attempt to even them out. That sounded like a nice perk. Today, they are relatively the same size, but one resembles a pear and the other a pumpkin.

It was finally time for surgery. I used the restroom one more time. A man, I don't remember his name, wheeled me back to the surgery room. We were speeding through the halls and around corners like we were late or in a hospital bed race. He was an expert bed driver. He had once been a transport tech, so he knew his way around those corners with a big bed.

I remember turning into the surgery room. I heard laughing, which comforted me. I saw shadows of people and

3 large lights. The next moment, I woke up in a room that could have been the one I started in except the picture by the door was different. I was groggy and out of it for a while. I used the restroom again, then waited while moving in and out of sleep. It was over. I found out later they had been trying to call Jason, but they were calling my phone instead of his. Hannah, my oldest, was at a new student event at college. They were all anxiously waiting for the hospital's call, so he could come back and get me. He knew enough to call them when too much time had passed. He was on his way.

They seemed to ignore me toward the end. I don't know if it was because I was fine or because they thought Jason was ignoring their calls, and I was taking a bed they needed. I thought everything was fine. It may have been fine. I had just woken from surgery. I'm not sure I could completely trust all my senses.

I got dressed, taking my lavender scent with me. Angelina wheeled me out to the parking garage where Jason was waiting. I was moving slowly and carefully, but other than that, I felt comparably normal. Angelina gave me a vomit bag for the road, just in case. My only frustration after surgery was that my arms were numb and no one I told about it seemed to care.

I came home, changed my clothes and settled in on the couch. I boldly chose to watch what I wanted without asking permission or opinions. I finished "Three Muske- teers," sleeping through most of it. Later, I listened to Hannah's retelling of the college orientation brunch, the scarf ceremony and her new friend, Ashley. Then I proceeded to watch Toy Story 3 and Toy Story 4 before anyone else made a television request.

By the next morning, I had managed my pain with Tylenol and Ibuprofen. I hoped to keep it that way. I slept well. I was anxious to take a shower, change my bra and wash the pink, ancient styled one they gave me. I wiped most of the orange iodine off yesterday, but there was still some that escaped my cleaning.

Other than dull and achy pain, I felt pretty good. I felt like I was more out of it the last time I had surgery. It goes to show how much it helps to be healthy *before* these things happen. Because of CrossFit, we found an exercise regime that we could do as a family and that we could do for the rest of our lives. In addition to feeling better with this exercise and usually looking better, we strove to be fit, not just healthy. Imagine health is on a continuum. Place unhealthy on the left, healthy sits in the middle and fit is on the far right. If a person is fit, they must pass through healthy to become unhealthy when unexpected events invade their lives. I count on this continuum. I count on having a health cushion or a health savings account to give my body time to heal and recover before I become unhealthy.

I was surprised at how well I felt after surgery. I rested and didn't push too hard. I religiously took either Tylenol or Ibuprofen every 3 hours just to make sure the pain never got ahead of me. After the month long debilitating back pain in 2017, I was nervous about pain taking over. I was also nervous about the stronger medication they prescribed. After back surgery, I tried to stop taking the medication I had previously taken for a month, and went through horrible and scary withdrawals. No one told me the best way to stop taking it. No one warned me about what might happen to my body after I stopped.

On Sunday, I was a bit more tired and began the day in more pain than on Saturday. I believe the extra pain was due to the absence of anesthesia or medicine in my system. Any extra pain-killing medicine the hospital gave me was now fully gone.

I didn't have the energy to make food for myself, so I had to depend on others. I ate a banana. A little while later, Jason made me an egg. He was going to get wraps from Messenger, a local pizza place. At 2:00, I knew he had stopped to have a beer while he was out and wouldn't be home any time soon. I was hungry, but I lacked the strength and energy to make myself a meal. I ate some peanut butter. A little while later, I had more peanut butter. When Jason finally texted to tell me he was having a drink with his brother, I consciously didn't tell him how hungry I was because I knew how much he needed that time.

He wants to help me. He wants to make my load lighter; he wants to make my journey easier. I'm afraid if I ask too much of him, it will drain him. He wants me to be careful and ask for help, but if I ask for too much, I may become a burden. The balancing act is almost impossible to maintain. Sometimes I want him to reach out to other people and share what is going on, so he can have some relief from carrying this load alone. I didn't mention anything about my hunger or the time, because I knew this was a moment he needed to strengthen him and make himself feel whole.

I know sometimes he thinks I don't understand how hard this is for him. I do. I see. I see him and how he needs to control things and protect everyone. I see how lack of control eats away at him. I see him try to keep his intense emotions in check. I see him worry and hold his breath. I know. I see it and I take it into consideration when I share, don't share, act, or don't act. I control my needs as much as I can, hoping to keep him from being overwhelmed. I may be the one going through cancer, but I have something to do. I have treatments to complete, doctors to see, health to snatch and hold with all of my might. My loved ones are forced to watch. They watch me walk slower or walk in pain. They watch me become weary, but try to hide it. They feel their hands are tied and their mouths taped shut. They don't know what to do to help, they definitely don't know what to say. I understand.

I was relieved when I lasted 8 hours before I needed any pain medication on Sunday night. This simple achievement is a win. I didn't need any until I started moving around Monday morning. Less pain medication, less pain. It all brings me hope for healing.

Tuesday, September 1, 2020, was my first day of school. This year, the first day of school meant I put assignments and information out there for my students digitally. They did them at home, then I checked what they did. I prepared instruction videos for everything they needed to know. I created a schedule so they could work through the list. I stayed available to each student all day. It was a long day. I answered the same questions over and over. Things didn't always work out well. Parents weren't technologically savvy. It was a learning curve for everyone. Jason was worried about me. At the first sign of stress, he worries and wants to fix me or the situation. He can't remove any stress I may have. I still have to do my job and sometimes there will be stressful moments, especially in this unprecedented COVID year where all my little second graders are at home trying to learn in an environment they've never had to learn in before. I hear him and I understand I need to be careful, but I also need to do my job. I may just hide my stressful moments.

The surgeon's office called today. Dina said there were negative margins on the tissue, meaning they got all the cancer. Also, my lymph nodes were clear. This means there is no cancer in me right now at all. I should be celebrating more, but it's time to move to the next step.

On Thursday, September 3, 2020, just 6 days after surgery, I had my yearly MRI to monitor any changes MS might be making in my brain. I made sure my classes were ready to go, then I drove into town. This is definitely a benefit to teaching online. I can go to doctor's appointments without needing someone to take my place. Once I started driving, I realized it may have been too early for me to go out after surgery. It bothered my arm a little to use the steering wheel. While I was laying in the MRI machine listening to the moaning, grinding and beeping, I was aware that it felt different than all the other times I have had an MRI. My breast and armpit were throbbing. I didn't understand how a magnet would affect them. My arms started going numb like a thousand needles were poking them and my legs and back ached from emulating a sleeping statue.

Once I returned home, I ate something, went for a short walk, ate a little more, then got back to work guiding my second graders through their day. I was forced to recline on the couch because I quickly got a bad case of flushing and felt weak. Flushing is one of the awful side effects of my MS medication. Flushing feels like your face and chest are on fire from the inside out. It isn't a hot flash, it feels like the only solution is a fire extinguisher. After a few hours, the flushing began to subside. Just as I was finishing work for the day, I got a call from my neurologist's office, my MS doctor. I've already talked with them about my new insurance and I don't have an appointment until October. I had the foreboding sense this was not a benign call.

In a compassionate voice, the lady on the other end of the line informed me Dr. H. saw some new changes on my brain MRI. He wanted me to come in so we could talk about them and discuss a new treatment. I scheduled an appointment for Tuesday the 8th at 9:30 AM. I got special permission to bring Jason along. Since COVID was still very present, only patients were allowed to attend doctors' appointments. Knowing we would be discussing my MRI and future changes to my treatment, I wanted someone else with me. Considering the circumstances, they allowed it.

I hung up and laughed. This is getting a bit crazy. What will happen next? I shouldn't be surprised. Later on in the evening, looking at the messy kitchen and the list of things I can't do, I got irritated and annoyed. It wasn't really about the kitchen. Holding everything together was making me weary. Every once in a while, I simply wanted to quit, to lay down, to stop fighting for my health, to stop trying to be a good teacher, to stop trying to be a responsible adult, a good wife, and a present parent, but I honestly didn't know how to quit. I'm not made with the *quit* gene.

I had been living with MS for 5 ½ years when I answered the call for cancer number two. I might have continued the cancer journey without thinking about MS, except that it decided to move and take new ground. I was forced to think about both things. I was forced to wonder what I had done to cause a change. Whatever new development was happening in my brain was not manifesting in my body in any way I could measure. I didn't know what the new activity on the MRI was affecting. It could be the increased numbness I felt in my arms and legs. Perhaps the stress of the past 2 months weakened my immune system. Perhaps I didn't notice it manifesting physically because I have work-around connections in my brain that help me continue to function. I have a lot of tricks in place, a lot of connections. When one path is under construction or not working as well, my brain tries to find another. I wish I understood more about how MS works. I wish I knew what I could do to keep it at bay.

It's been a little over a week since surgery. I'm trying to catch and understand my emotions when I have them. At the same time I'm using a lot of tricks to avoid my emotions completely.

~

Hannah turned 19 on August 27th. My lumpectomy was on August 28th. The doctors didn't want me around people before surgery in order to reduce the risk of getting COVID. Since surgery was over, we were finally able to celebrate her birthday with family.

I was pacing-anxious about my in-laws' arrival. They are

the most loving people. I appreciate them, but sometimes communication isn't clear and it can be very tiring for me. Based on what they say to me, it feels like they sit around worrying about me and wondering about how I'm doing, but they rarely actually ask me questions. When they see me, they are watching for clues to answer their questions, rather than asking or listening. I felt all of that pressure yesterday when they were visiting. Everyone was talking. No one was talking to me. It was draining. I was ready for everyone to leave an hour before they actually decided to get up and go. I was ready to lay down. My boob and arm ached, and I needed to be still and to rest.

I kept hearing myself rehearsing, "I don't want you to worry." I realized I have no control over whether anyone worries or not. What I mean when I say that is, "When you find yourself worrying, talk to me and ask how I'm doing rather than wondering and worrying in silence." I can help if you talk to me.

I've observed there are two different kinds of worry. There is the kind that is cloaked in compassion and concern. A person is going through difficult times and you are thinking about them, praying for them and curious how they are doing. You check in with them. You ask them questions about how things are going. The other kind of worry is full of what-ifs and wonderings, but there is a wall keeping the person from checking in. They stand off to the side, their face shows concern and question, but they don't speak. I'm not prone to willingly talk about myself with no prompting. I don't enjoy the risk of talking about myself only to find you didn't really want to know. I will happily tell you all that is happening when you ask. The second group of worriers don't always ask. This creates a division between us. I don't speak up unless you ask me. I want to know you really want to hear all the things. You don't ask because you are worried about prying. It might be something we both need to work on.

I've heard a little from a few friends this week. I can tell they are afraid to bother me. When did checking on someone to see how they are faring become *bothering* them?

I'm frustrated with people's lack of communication. With the slew of social media choices, texting, and always the old stand by phone call as options to talk with one another, you would think we might be good at staying connected, but we aren't. People don't call or text because they are worried about bothering someone or interrupting their busy schedule. Today, people can check the caller ID and choose whether or not to answer. They can return the call any time, yet we don't want to bother anyone, so we don't call. Many people didn't contact me after my surgery because they wanted to "let me rest." They didn't know how I was feeling, they didn't want to bother me ... It's as if they thought I had an ancient phone and its old fashioned ring might wake me. I have an old model, an iPhone 8, but I can still turn it off when I take a nap. I can choose to let you leave a message if I'm not in the mood to talk. I can text and answer your question any time it is convenient for me. How is it a bother to let someone know you are thinking about them?

My wish is that people wouldn't make assumptions, but would be willing to reach out just so I know I haven't been forgotten. I know you are thinking of me, but talking to you can boost my spirits and turn a cloudy day to a partly cloudy day and sometimes even a sunny day, even if only for a moment.

Some people ask if there is anything they can do to help. I say there isn't. One reason for my answer is I know them and I know they already have a full plate and I think my burden would be too much. What I need most, are people who will let me be real and honest, broken or whole, strong or weak. I need people in my cheering section letting me be and not requiring me to make them feel better. Now that I write this, I realize I could begin answering their offers of help with, "You can be honest with me and listen to me fully as I share my story." I don't think that is the kind of help they are thinking of, but you never know unless you ask.

As Tuesday, and my appointment with my neurologist drew closer, I anticipated my anxiety would go up. The arrival of the moment when the unknown becomes known is difficult for me because I am forced to deal with reality, and I lose the ability to live in denial or to live in a fantasyland where none of these things are happening.

In the past 4 days, I've had more moments when the thought of quitting my job crosses my mind than I have had in the past 2 years. Each new thing piles on top of the others. It's just one more thing. I prepared myself for cancer, then surgery, radiation is probably next. I went through the stages of grief, mourning my losses, working towards acceptance. I was prepared for the journey. Now, I have to add a new MS treatment to this dirty laundry pile.

Just like memories of 2012 cancer cloud the reality of 2020 cancer and create more fear and dread than if I had never had cancer before, memories of 2015 MS and treatment make me fearful of a new treatment. For 5 ½ years I had it under control. I built a routine that sustained me each day. Now, everything that has been familiar and predictable will change. Whatever treatment I have will come with new side effects I have to incorporate into my life, and these side effects may never go away. I will be dealing with new treatment and side effects while recovering from surgery and enduring radiation treatment.

On top of the physical effects of this, something is happening inside my body that I can't control. For eight years, I've known I cannot control the presence of cancer. For five years, I've known I cannot control changes happening inside of me because of MS. Now MS is doing things I cannot see. Whatever showed up in the scan of my brain did not show up in my body. I can't explain it or see it. Its invisibility scares me and makes me feel like a marionette controlled by these diseases.

Back to quitting, I've thought, "I want to quit." Then immediately, I know I cannot. I'm not talking about quitting my job. I'm talking about quitting this fight. I want to quit working hard to be okay, showing up, monitoring my emotions and trying to improve them. I'm on the freeway or more likely a narrow winding mountain road with a steep drop off to the right. I can't see clearly what is ahead. The road is bumpy and rough. If, at any moment, I quit trying, fighting, or hoping, I will crash and it will take even longer to recover and get back on whichever road is before me.

. . .

It was just a little over a week since surgery. For 3 evenings in a row, I had managed to take a short nap. Two out of the past three mornings, I slept past 7 AM. This increased amount of sleep makes me wonder if I'm overdoing it. It's difficult to tell. The pain in my chest and arm is pretty constant unless I sit very still. I was accepting of its presence until yesterday, when I was ready for it to feel better. It's only been a week and a half since surgery, but the pain is now simply annoying and I'm tired of it and want it gone. It's interesting how the same pain is easy and bearable one day then overwhelming the next. The unbearability of this pain is not dependent on the pain scale, but on the number of days it has lasted. Poor Carlie, her pain never ends. She has dealt with head pain at a level eight on the pain scale for 4 years without relief. I cannot imagine this burden when I am ready to drop mine after such a short time.

I'm less emotionally stable these past couple of days. One moment I feel good and content, the next I am overwhelmed with tears. The tears release the overwhelming burden I carry and never put down. They are the sadness of losing something: part of my breast, freedom, days of exercise, wholeness. The tears are the weariness of continually trying to be okay when I'm not. They simply materialize. They wash down my face and don't apologize or try to stay in my eyes. They remind me for a moment that this journey is very difficult and sometimes it gains the upper hand. I am reminded of Glennon Doyle's words in *Untamed*, "Grief is a solitary emotion." I want to be alone when these tears come. I want to be free to release all the tough feelings. It will only take a few minutes, then I can put my armor on again and move forward.

Most people see me walking, winning, and being hopeful because this is what I choose for them to see. I also spend time feeling beat up, weak and discouraged. This journey is difficult. I want to make it look easy, but every second takes all of me. It takes all of me to get up in the morning, to do my job, and care for our home the best I can. It takes more than I have to ask for help. That task is the most difficult. I know what is on everyone's plate and I don't want to burden them by giving them something from my plate. I'm getting better each day, but it is like climbing a waterslide while wearing an eel suit.

I'm crying now. Being honest releases the concrete dam holding back the tears: tears that wash, that carry burdens away, that release pressure and tension which has built while I stood strong.

Today all of this feels more difficult. I want to lay down and rest, but I must keep walking this steep winding path. Sticks are scratching my legs, branches are slapping my face, but I must take another step because eventually I'll find the meadow, and I'll be able to run again.

It was nearing 8:00 in the evening on Tuesday, September 8, 2020, and I was thrilled to no longer take my Tecfidera pill for MS. Since March 2015, almost 5 ½ years ago, I have been taking 2 blue pills a day. One at 7 in the morning and one at 7 in the evening. I set an alarm on my phone so I wouldn't forget. It would go off in the middle of a movie or during a night out with friends. During school days the alarm would temporarily take me away from my task as I slipped my blue pill into my mouth before going on with my work.

I would try to remember to grab it when I thought about it and keep it in my pocket so I didn't have to leave the room when the alarm went off. I carried it in my pocket in the morning until the almond butter settled in my stomach to reduce the side effects. At night it might be in my pocket or my purse waiting for the gentle alarm. Every 12 hours I took a blue pill that reminded me I had MS. It reminded me I had a disease that could take any part of me it desired anytime it wanted. It reminded me I wasn't whole and had to take medicine every day to try and keep what I had. I attempted to not ask other people to retrieve my medicine for me because I didn't want them to carry any of that burden, but it didn't always work out, sometimes I needed their help. I would even try to take it sneakily so no one would notice. I was reminded every day, but I didn't need other people to have to carry that reminder too.

My MRI on September 3rd showed new activity under contrast in the left hemisphere of my brain. New lesions meant the medication I've been on wasn't working anymore. The purpose of MS medication is to keep the disease from progressing. You can't undo the effects of MS, you often can't repair the damage. You can only try to prevent new activity. It's like the effect of a landslide. Once the rocks and dirt and plants have tumbled down the mountain, you can't put them back. You can shore up the hill so it hopefully doesn't happen again, but you can't reverse the effects of the landslide. My neurologist would like to change my treatment plan to a once a month infusion of Tysabri. He is confident it is the right choice. It is more aggressive which is a good idea because my immune system is more active now than it will be in later years, he says. It has no measurable side effects and will do its work in the background while I continue this cancer journey. I'm a little worried about the infusion, but I'm also hopeful and optimistic. I'm thankful the pill is gone. No alarm went off this evening. It felt like I had been freed from a cave.

On Wednesday, I was still enjoying no pill days. The absence of that pill was a form of liberation. A fraction of me is concerned because I'm not taking any medication for MS right now, its like not doing anything to prevent another landslide, but my doctor said I will be fine.

I need to remember to take time to rest. It is very easy to work all day, but I'm still recovering from surgery. I had to read through my post-op information again yesterday to be sure I wasn't doing anything wrong. I'm doing most things correctly, but not always resting fully. The pain in my armpit is drastically reduced. My breast often feels like a needle is stabbing me right in the center under my nipple. When I get cold, my nipple hardens and pulls on my incision. Any movement of my arm flexes my pec and makes my boob ache. It isn't unbearable pain, just very annoying.

School has been taking a toll. I have felt the judgment and questioning coming through the computer hidden between each typed line from parents. I want to tell them all my qualifications. I want to tell them, before you compare me to your friend's kid's teacher or to your own experience with teachers 20 years ago, remember I know what I am doing and I have practiced and tested what is best. You may ask me questions. You may ask for help. This is an adjustment for all of us. This is new for all of us. Some parents wanted me to do more Zoom meetings with the kids. They thought it would be better if I was talking directly to their kids rather than talking to them through a video. Second graders on a Zoom call are spending more time looking at their own faces than anything else going on. One of my students would run around the house with his laptop, yelling. As much as the parents wanted me to, I wasn't going to be able to solve all their problems - no matter how much I tried. Usually, I get to teach the kids. The kids and I have a relationship and they understand what I require. Online school meant I had to teach the parents. They regularly tried to get me to adjust my teaching to meet their needs. Meeting the individual needs of 28 different families wasn't one of my top priorities.

In addition to my educational background, I just had a breast lumpectomy. I will be starting radiation for cancer soon, and I am beginning a new MS treatment. I will put your kids' needs high on my list, but I will put mine first. You will get the best I can give you, but not at the cost of my own health.

It's Thursday, September 10, 2020. It has almost been 2 weeks since surgery. My brain is going a hundred miles an hour this morning. I'm thinking about my students, what I need to do for school, all my emotions, the people around me, my future medical journey … I don't feel calm, but I also don't feel anxious. I can feel the storm rising in me and making me unsettled.

Last night, I realized I have a "use by" time. There comes a time in the evening when I simply need to lay down, rest my right side muscles, and let my body settle. I'm not expired at this time, just all used up.

. . .

I texted Carlie a bit last night and realized the only thing that pulls me out of my dark reality are joyful things. I need to seek out joy in my day. When I find it, it washes over me and makes me feel lighter. I am so intent on always being real and honest that I end up being super serious. I need to find joy and humor in my reality. I need to laugh at my honesty and pain. I don't know how, but I'd like to try.

# Chapter 19

## *Before and After*

I t is 2:00 PM. I am taking a break and finishing my drink. I consider texting or calling my dad, thinking he may want to know what's happening in my life. At the same time, I think if he cared, he'd call. I looked up the feelings I have about that in my mood meter. The word that matches my feelings is alienated - feeling like you have been made a stranger to others; left out and excluded. I have felt alienated from him since he moved out in 1990. I've worked to be included in his life. At every turn I feel disappointed - sad and "blue" because something did not happen the way I wanted it to. He rarely reaches out to me, and I don't feel like he notices when I reach out. I've made excuses for him.

I know he thinks of me and thinks of calling, then forgets. He gets busy and wrapped up in his day, but people make time for things that are important to them. If he valued me, he would want to know how I am doing. People I work with, who have known me for only a few years, reach out more often than my dad. The last time we spoke on the phone was July 15th, I'm guessing it was the day I told him I have cancer. I texted on August 28th to tell him how my surgery went. I attempted to call last Friday, the 4th. What am I supposed to do? Why am I trying to work so hard on this relationship seemingly by myself? Why does it still hurt? Why do I care? I am surrounded by people who love and care for me - why does this one person's actions affect me so much? It's in the title he carries and what it should mean. I need to get over the title. My real Daddy, my step dad (Lew), and my father-in-law are all more of a "dad" than he has ever been. The pain of a disconnect with my dad won't stop even when I know the truth.

It wasn't always like this. Before my parents divorced, my dad was a consistent part of my life. The first 13 years of my life consisted of predictability and security. I grew up in a yellow cinderblock one-story house on 21 acres. When my parents moved in, the house was in dire need of repair.

I've seen a picture of my grandma Hazel sitting in a dilapidated room with a handkerchief on her head holding a 6-week-old me in a large blanket. The look on her face betrays that I was inconsolably screaming during the renovation. When they finished remodeling, we had a little yellow kitchen, a cozy living room with a picture window and a fireplace. We had 2 bedrooms posted on either end of a short hallway. The one little bathroom marked the middle. After my brother was born in 1979, and it was no longer reasonable for us to share a room, my family finished the basement that had previously been a dirt floor and concrete walls, and created a little room at the bottom of the stairs for me. The rest of the basement was still concrete and unfinished, but my room was an oasis. I had a lavender carpet, one wallpapered wall with tiny lavender flowers, and my mom stenciled purple hearts on the border of my walls, just below the ceiling. We had a small porch off the front door and a large deck off the kitchen door on the side of the house. We could see for a half of a mile off that deck. We could see the school bus coming out that kitchen window. Of course, once we saw the bus, we knew we were late and wouldn't likely make it the quarter of a mile to the end of the driveway before the bus did.

We had a banana yellow '76 Toyota Corolla, a white 80s something Ford pickup truck, bicycles and motorcycles. The Corolla was our family and traveling car. We loaded our bags in a top-carrier and ventured to Disneyland when I was 10. We took the truck everywhere adventurous. The 4 of us fit in the front seat before the age of airbags. We didn't have the funds for big vacations, but I knew we would go camping for each summer holiday and a few other weekends in between. We loaded up the truck and camper every 3-day weekend and holiday from Memorial Day to Labor Day. We had a camper that lived in the barn next to the pile of hay all winter. When it was time to venture out, my dad backed the pickup truck under that camper, then lowered it and secured it so we could pack it up and prepare to leave. It hung a couple of feet over the back of the tailgate. I'm sure it wasn't safe, but my brother and I got to ride in the camper while my parents traveled in the cab of the truck. We ventured between the bed that sat above the cab to the table that rested where the bed of the truck would be. We played literal games at the table and made-up road games while looking out the window up beyond the bed. We laid on our stomachs on that bed with our feet hanging over the side. Our elbows rested on the mattress while we stared at the road. Our vantage point was the best. We hung a little over the cab of the truck so it felt like we were flying over the road. We watched the yellow lines fly by as my dad drove. We could see over the edge of each cliff as we drove up the windy mountain roads. We never once feared my dad wouldn't successfully make the turn. The sign resting in the back window of the camper said, "Are we having fun yet?" Always.

We usually camped with a group of people. They all had campers too so we circled them like Oregon Trail Wagons resting for an evening. The fire pit burned in the center. For many years, we hauled motorcycles with us to ride the back trails around our campsite. I loved my silver Honda 170. It purred like a kitten, but raced like a leopard. I loved racing down the old dirt runway at Horse Haven. The runway used to welcome planes, but it was run down and too bumpy to safely bring in a plane. I began at one end and raced straight ahead for over a half mile to the other end. I felt bold when I jumped my Honda inches off the ground. I would have told you I was feet in the air, but the pictures tell a different story.

My dad built a treehouse in the large willow tree at the edge of our yard. A swing hung from one branch, on the other side of the tree, the wooden ladder took us up to a multilevel treehouse. You could climb back down the ladder to leave or slide down the steep, metal blue slide. In the summer, we made a pretty impressive homemade water slide by placing our little plastic pool at the base of the slide and resting the garden hose at the top.

In the pasture, where the cows lived, nestled under two

more willow trees were two ponds. One pond was near the driveway and the other sat near the back of the pasture. In the heat of the summer, the lower one would often dry up. My brother spent a lot of time looking for frogs and playing in the mud. I may have joined him sometimes, but mostly, I just knew the ponds were there.

A popular prank was to run and holler, "The cows are out!" This one phrase guaranteed that everyone within earshot dropped everything and immediately ran outside to coax the cows back into the pasture. Once the target was outside, panting from exertion, they would turn to find the prankster laughing. I'm sure we pranked that the cows were out more often than they actually were.

I could depend on my dad leaving for work at a certain time and getting home at a certain time. My dad worked in Spokane Valley, which was a 45 minute drive from our country home. He worked for a family-owned surveying/engineering company. He arrived home, fed the cows, and then we ate at 6:00. My mom always made dinner. We ate meat from our own cows or from the deer my dad and brother hunted in the fall. We ate vegetables from our own garden that my mom cooked and canned. We grew our own potatoes and picked peaches and apples from local orchards. Going out to eat was uncommon. It was a very long trip to the nearest restaurant and more expensive than cooking the food we stored in our pantry and our freezer.

Every spring, we planted alfalfa in the fields surrounding our driveway and harvested it for our cows 3 or 4 times before the growing season ended. The quarter of a mile long driveway cut down the middle of 16 acres of alfalfa. My dad cut, baled and stacked the hay. We only owned a basic tractor, it resembled the common red tractor toy, but we borrowed my grandpa Ray's equipment: a baler, a swather and a bale wagon. I remember my dad starting that old red tractor with a crank. For its ancient age, it was still dependable to pull my grandpa's equipment and plow the snow in winter.

The barn, which sat at the other end of the driveway at the bottom of the hill, housed the hay we put up. My dad stacked it so there was a way to climb it like stairs. Even when the barn was full, he made sure we could climb the hay-stairs to the top. My brother and I often played in the hay barn for hours. The ultimate destination was a rope swing with a carved piece of wood at the bottom for us to sit on. The piece of wood was actually just a piece of wood, not much bigger around than an arm. It was flat on the top and round on the bottom. My dad carved a wedge in the middle for the rope to rest. He attached the rope to a pulley which hung from the rafters. We swung down from the hay for hours, only stopping when it was dark or our stomachs complained. In that barn, I was fearless and brave.

After the divorce, I wanted to escape my family. If the church was open, I was there. Not the church I grew up attending and sitting with my grandparents singing familiar songs and seeing familiar faces. I went to a different church, one where they only knew me, not my family. I volunteered to help with music. I showed up early and stayed late. I knew what to expect there. I knew how the people would treat me. My friends were there. The leaders were consistent and seemed to care. I took advantage of my driver's license and found every excuse to leave my house. I left for school an hour before I needed to in order to sit alone in the busy hallway reading my book. I found unnecessary odd jobs to do to fill the time. I was responsible and obedient. I got amazing grades and mostly did the right things, but I was lost. I was trying to find my way during a time when the road I was traveling was closed and there were no Google Maps to reroute me. My dad was busy discovering his new life. My mom was trying to pay bills and feed us. During this season, my dad was only present for small moments. I spent more time feeling disappointed because my hopes were left unfulfilled than feeling seen and loved.

The divorce created a before and after moment. Before the divorce, I could depend on my dad. He built hay-stairs, hunted each fall, took care of the cows and always came home at the same time. After the divorce, I couldn't reach him. I couldn't connect in the way I wanted. I wanted to very badly. During my 2012 cancer, he came to be with us during my surgery. It wasn't great, but he came. This time, he wasn't even calling to check in on me. I wasn't entirely sure what to do. I wanted to connect, but I didn't want to be the only one reaching out.

# Chapter 20

## *Radiation: Take Two*

It is Friday, September 11, 2020. I had an appointment with my radiation oncologist yesterday. I fulfilled as many teaching duties as I could during the morning since I had to leave around 1:00. They told me to get there early so I could fill out paperwork. I arrived at 1:30 for my 2:00 appointment, I had no paperwork, so I sat for a half an hour. I tried smiling and breathing slowly to calm myself. There is only a minuscule amount of peace that comes from having done this once before. I'm still nervous, I still don't want to be here. Misty took me back into another room and I waited another 15 minutes.

During the drive from home to MSTI (Mountain States Tumor Institute), I pulled from memories of 8 years ago to remember the location. I remember the route I took from Notus, down Holly Street by the college, past the 4-way stop by my old dorm. I drove down the road until I almost reached the Rec Center, turned right on Hawaii, and turned right into the parking lot. After moments of thinking, I remembered I took that route because I came from the freeway from Notus. If I took that route now, I would be going too far one way just to come back. I turned right on 12th Avenue then searched my visual memory and street signs until I found Hawaii. I took a left, then searched for the MSTI building. My memory expected it on the right, but since I came from the other side, I found it on the left. The sight of the sign was familiar and horrible. Eight years ago, this building was my regular daily stop for almost 2 months. I'm back. It was also horrible because it represented cancer. It didn't matter that they caught my cancer early and it was curable. I still have to walk around with that label. It is lonely. Since the beginning, this has been my journey alone. The first time, my family could not stop their responsibilities to hold my hand for my appointments. This time, because of COVID, they aren't even allowed.

I stepped into the building, past an old lady with thinning hair in a wheelchair. Her husband sat on the bench near her. Inside, the building looked older and colder than I remember it. It could be the 8 years that have passed, or it could be the signs reminding everyone to wear masks for COVID protection causing the chill. The barrier of backward chairs pushed against the counter, the spacing between chairs in the waiting room, and the bare book-shelves that used to hold pamphlets and books about cancer were designed to keep everyone from spreading germs. Everyone wore a mask and we accepted this as normal.

While I waited, a young twenty or thirty-year old man came in with his tube and chemo bag. A seventy-something thin woman in a white sweater and jeans stood silently while her husband checked her in. A petite, thinner woman near seventy walked confidently in her cute, gray-haired bob with her Dutch Bros coffee - I wanted to say something fun about her coffee, but I didn't know what. A 30-ish year old, overweight woman with a long white, purple and yellow sweater and yellow canvas shoes checked in. A couple of older gentlemen left after their treatments, making a pit stop in the restroom before driving home. A tired 60-ish woman with a low cut, V-neck, blue sleeveless blouse and scraggly chopped gray hair walked from her treatment to the restroom then exited the building. My apprehension is building as I watch and wait for my turn. I log my mood - troubled - it tells me to hold a smile for a minute. I try, thankful for the mask that hides how cheesy it looks.

I am finally called back, it's my turn. I stand on the scale, 60 kilos. Dang! I'm 132 pounds fully dressed with shoes on! The last time the scale came close to this number I was in 6th grade. I feel fit and strong. Misty, the young nurse with randomly wavy hair, a blue long-sleeved shirt and tan pants, takes me to my room and goes over my health history. I have to clarify that I have had 2 breast lumpec-tomies. She leaves. I wait. I try to make the unsettling feel-ings flee. I wonder what humor there is in my situation. The only thing I think, during this time of unrest and awakening, is cancer is not racist or sexist or feminist or any other -ist. It doesn't care if you're old or young, thin or fat, unhealthy or fit. It'll take whomever it wants. The reason to be healthy and fit is not to prevent cancer, but to have the strength to fight and heal from the treatment.

It's Saturday, September 12, 2020. I'm thinking about sympathy and empathy. Sympathy is when you see me from afar. You feel your own feelings. You are sorry for me, sad for me, in awe of me. You stand back and tell me your feelings. Empathy is holding my hand, standing with me and saying I understand. I understand this is hard. I understand this hurts. I understand you have no choice but to walk forward and that makes you tired. I am here. I see you. I do not imagine you are sick or weak. I do not put you on a pedestal of amazingness because I can't imagine your journey. Even though I am not in your shoes, I have felt difficult things and understand your pain and your strength in its midst. I am here. I see all of you.

Sympathy feels like you are watching me through a glass barrier like an animal in a zoo or an exhibit in a museum. Empathy feels like you are sitting by my side, holding me, holding my hand and letting me be whichever mess or version of myself I need to be. You don't expect anything from me, you aren't surprised by my togetherness. You aren't scared by my brokenness. You are okay with my ability to be broken and together at the same time or sometimes nothing at all.

I don't expect you to be able to do this, but I hope. I hope through the list of difficult things in my life you can see me. I hope you will sit with me and we will be together. Without your empathy, I am alone.

. . .

I have a dear friend who is a master of empathy and who I trust with the most vulnerable parts of me.

I had a social day today. I ran for the first time in over 2 weeks. I love having the freedom to move. I texted Kelly afterwards. She called and we walked and talked. When I got home, I called Carlie. My in-laws stopped by after taking Abby to her horse lesson. Later, we went to Matt and Kelly's for pizza and drinks. It was nice, but also tiring.

Today is Sunday. It is a particularly rough day. I feel tired and weary. I don't have the strength to fight away the sadness. Today, it consumes me. Today, it sits heavy on me. I know I'll feel better tomorrow, but today I don't have the strength to rise up. I watched the Raiders' game then escaped to the garage to catch up on a few shows and watch a movie alone.

I laid on the couch in the garage and cried. I gathered myself. Hannah came to see me, asked how I was and didn't believe me when I answered, "fine," while trying to hold in the tears. She hugged me. I found myself whimpering in her arms like a sad puppy while I still tried to keep some tears in. I felt bad I had gotten to a point where I was crying in my daughter's arms, laying my burden on her, but I was also comforted.

. . .

I have been extra emotional this week. I keep wanting to be left alone. I feel exposed, yet unseen. I'm weary of all these difficult things.

I had a really good experience when I went for my medical oncologist appointment with Dr. S. He heard me. He heard my concerns about side effects of medication. He explained why I need to take this medication. He made me laugh. He put me at ease. I was worried about the side effects of Tamoxifen. I shared each and every one of them, wondering what if I react harshly in about 5 different ways. He paused, then seriously said, "What if everything goes great and you have no reactions?" I laughed out loud. The "what if" scales fell right down to the tile floor.

I keep forgetting to breathe, I find myself holding my breath. I forget how much tension I am holding in my shoulders. It may be time to find a support group. I need to be able to let all the crap out. It is starting to weigh me down.

I think I'm in the avoiding stage right now. I see it because I don't want to write. If I write, too many thoughts and emotions come to the surface and then I have to deal with them or feel them. I feel paralyzed. I feel like I can sit and do nothing, sink into the couch like warm butter. Some of my immobilization is because I have 2 doctor's appointments today. One appointment is an end - a post-surgery checkup, and the other is a beginning - a CT simulation for radiation treatment. I've enjoyed this limbo time between procedures and treatments; I get to somewhat forget. Based on what I hear, these next steps shouldn't be too difficult, but my fear rises with potential surprises and unknowns.

I know I'll make it. I know I'll survive. I know it will be okay. I also know it is a fight, and sometimes the fight makes me weary.


First, I met with Jay, Dr. M's PA, for my post-surgery checkup. He said I'm good. Everything is healing normally. I told him about the fitness continuum. He hadn't heard of that idea. I learned this continuum from CrossFit. If I am fit, more than healthy according to the numbers doctors prescribe to health, then I must pass through healthy on the continuum to become unhealthy. I have more room and time to heal. I also told him how impressed I was with my incision. He said they try hard. I told him I appreciate that, it makes me feel seen when the surgeons care about the small details. Tears threatened to pour. Emotions wanted to come out.


After the appointment with the surgeon, I went home, had lunch, then left for my next appointment. I drove to the other side of town. It was time for my CT simulation. They lined up the lasers in the room and scanned my body just like last time. They use this scan to create a map they will use to guide and design my radiation treatment.

Before I went back into the room for my turn, I saw another teacher from Notus Elementary. I couldn't remember his first name in that moment. I don't think he recognized me. At first I thought I'd say, "Hi! good to see you!" Then I thought, "Dang! I don't want to see you HERE!" It turns out he was getting his first radiation treatment. How do you greet someone you haven't seen in 6 years, and tell them how pleased you are to see them, while telling them you are so sorry they got cancer? I didn't say anything at all.

I changed into the too-big-pinkish/maroon top. The snaps were 6 inches apart and I had to hold the top together so none of me would show while I walked to the waiting room. As soon as I arrived, it was time to begin. I sat in a chair and signed paperwork, then I sat on the edge of a board-like bed, removed my top and draped it over my chest and under my arms like a towel after a shower. I laid on the bed. The lady positioned me by sliding the sheet I laid on back and forth. My arms held two handles over my head. They would be asleep soon. I felt my hips shift and twist with each slide of the sheet, but I wasn't allowed to correct any movement or straighten my body. Surprisingly, my left arm began to sleep first, usually it is my right. Dr. S., my radiation oncologist, came in to draw on me with what resembled a Sharpie, so his assistant could add a special tape to the black lines he made for the simulation. I continued to lose sensation in my arm.

It was finally time for the scan. The bed raised up to fit into the plastic upright circle behind me. The bed moved forwards and backwards while the machine hummed. There were 15 bars of light above my head, 3 red, 3 light red, 3 orange, 3 yellow, and 3 green. They lit up from one side to the other. I imagined the lights meant I was almost finished. I never learned what the lights were for. The scanner rotated and took x-rays of my body so they can create the best map for my treatment. It will remain fascinating to me that in order to get rid of cancer I have to continually be exposed to things that cause cancer: x-rays, radiation.

I laid on the table, breast exposed, arms above my head. I no longer could feel my left arm, only the pain that resonated from the halted circulation. I was anxious to be finished, but had no idea how much longer the scanning would last. I didn't have music or a clock to mark the time, only humming and lights. I will never understand why someone doesn't place interesting things on the ceiling for those of us who must lay on our backs and wait.

The scanning and humming and numbing was finally over. The lady who helped Dr. S., who put tape on me, and who adjusted me to the right place used to live on the South Hill in Spokane and moved to the East End of Boise because crime was increasing, came back. She took more pictures of me to record my position, though, this time she covered my nipples. Last time I laid bare.

I received a new tattoo on my right side. They could use my other two tattoos from 8 years ago. Once it was over, it took a few minutes for the sensation of my arm to return. My favorite part of this procedure was when Dr. S. and the lady couldn't find my surgery incision below my nipple. It had only been 3 ½ weeks since surgery and already my scarring was minimal.

It has been a month since my surgery. I am in a weird place. I am tired. I am unmotivated, and I spend too much time annoyed with others. I'm afraid to stop and be too present because then I might feel my fears of radiation, infusion and Tamoxifen that squeeze me and steal my breath. I can pretend I'm normal and don't need intense treatments for a minute if I don't pause or look for too long. I'm tired of it all. I'm tired of fighting. I'm tired of looking for strength in the struggle. I'm tired of feeling everyone's concern. We're reaching the point when they forget about my journey and move on with their lives while I am still very much in the trenches.

### *Don't*

> *Don't look too closely*
> *You might see fear*
> *It dances behind my eyes and fades my smile*

*Don't listen too closely*
> *You might hear my sadness*
> *It hides in my throat and coats my words*

*Don't sit too closely*
> *You might feel my vulnerability*
> *It pours from my skin in trembling waves*

*Don't come too closely*
> *I might fall to pieces*
> *I am held together with thread made of flower petals*
*becoming dry with age*
> *It smells nice, looks nice, but is fragile and fading*

. . .

*The only thing that keeps the petal thread in place are my tears of grief and loss that add needed moisture to the drying petals so they can hold me just a moment longer*

*Don't worry too much*
*I gain no strength from that*
*I only know not to share my burden since you are near breaking too*

*Don't look at me with too much compassion*
*I might unravel*
*Seeing your tenderness shatters my protective shell*

*Don't ignore me too often*
*I might fade into the background*
*Being fully seen and heard gives me hope and strength*

### *One Moment*

*One moment I am strong and victorious.*
*The next I am weak and conquered.*

*One moment I know where to go.*
*The next I am lost in a maze of choices.*

*One moment I am at peace.*
*The next I am frozen in fear.*

. . .

*One moment I smile and laugh.*
　　*The next I cry.*


*One moment I have hope.*
　　*The next I feel despair.*


*One moment all is well.*
　　*The next, all is lost.*


*One moment I can do this.*
　　*The next I simply want to quit.*


*One moment I want to be near you.*
　　*The next I need to be alone.*


*One moment I am whole.*
　　*The next I am broken.*


*One moment I am present.*
　　*The next I am eager to escape.*


*One moment I feel everything.*
　　*The next, I feel nothing.*

. . .

*One moment and then the next.*

∼

I am very tired this morning. It's Tuesday, September 29th. My eyes are trying to fall closed and I am moving slowly, sloth-like. The only real cancer event that has occurred was surgery a month ago. I've prepared for radiation, but that hasn't started yet. I've been waiting for the next thing, trying to heal, trying to process what is ahead.

I walked with Meg two days ago. We talked about all the things. Eventually, we talked about me and how I am in limbo: avoiding, knowing this stage won't last long. The tears and sobs escaped when I spoke out loud how afraid I am of these coming treatments. I know they may be fine, but my past experience fills me with fear. I know I will keep moving, I know it will be okay, but the fear is real. It rests on me like an awkward weight, it whispers doubts and trouble in my ear, it sits behind my eyes reminding me of visions of the past. It grips my heart and surprises me with its spontaneous squeeze when I think all is at peace. It moves in and through and around me like a mist searching for a home.

When I shared my fear with Meg, when I said the words out loud, I felt all of it. I felt every sensation and desired only to wrap and release all the feelings in a neat package and send them far away. Weeping brings relief, but sadly, it's temporary. I'm thankful for my visit with Meg. I'm thankful to have another person I can be fully honest with, fully real with. I'm thankful for genuineness.

∼

My fear permeates me. I feel a deep need to help my little second graders and give them tools to succeed and thrive. I am weary and desire to lay and do nothing while life swirls around me, stealing my energy, using time, carving down my edges and moving and filling me however it pleases.

To conclude each *Unlocking Us* podcast, Brené Brown asks her guests a series of rapid fire questions. This one came to mind while I was walking: "You are called to be brave, but your fear is real, it is stuck in your throat, what do you do?"

My answer: Keep moving.

My fear of the future does not change the fact that I must enter into it.

Another day has arrived. I am tired again. My body feels slow, like it moves through air made of molasses. My many thoughts are traveling through my brain, but never landing on or completing one. I am distracted by my list of tasks and by my fear of treatments coming. A part of me knows I will walk through these treatments with more ease than last time. I will take one step and then another. I will bear each side effect and discomfort as I bear a newly formed bruise - I know it is there, but my feet continue. But another part of me is terrified and doesn't want to do any of this. I don't want to feel pain and discomfort. I don't want anything to steal the joyful, peaceful, contented parts of my life.

I find myself trying to hurry the process so I can gain the strength back I lost during surgery, but I know I must be patient. I know I must trust the process and be kind and gentle as I gain again what was lost. I must be faithful to keep taking care of myself, even if I don't see the effects I want soon enough.

～

More on fear:

Most of the time, fear is a breath resting in the background of my mind. Every once in a while, it rises up and takes my breath away. It surprises me and consumes me. I know everything will be fine and even if it is not, I'll walk through it like I always do. I'll take one day at a time, one moment at a time.

The fear comes from the unknown, the *what ifs*.

Fear is not helpful. It is not useful. Jesus said, "Do not be afraid." Fear steals moments of peace and joy. Fear wastes time. How do I keep it away?

"Do not fear, for I am with you."

"In all things, in prayer and supplication bring your fears to God."

I combat fear by leaning on my Daddy. I combat fear, not just by walking, but by trusting, by handing my fear over and knowing my Daddy cares about me and will take care of me. I have nothing to fear - I only have to hope.

. . .

Fear takes away my breath
    Hope fills my lungs


Fear freezes my steps
    Hope warms my path


Fear steals my joy
    Hope brings peace

On Thursday, October 1, 2020, I had the dry run for radiation. This day is the 8 year anniversary of my first cancer diagnosis. This day marks the beginning of Breast Cancer Awareness Month. This day is when all children begin to think "Halloween." On this day, my second radiation treatment journey begins.

I go into MSTI as if I am receiving treatment. They do everything they would normally do except they take pictures, x-rays, instead of giving treatment. I lay on the table in my jeans with my hands gripping the bars overhead. My shirt is draped over my left breast for some semblance of modesty while my right breast is exposed for all. At one point I could see its shadow on the metal rectangle which sported the confusing name of "cassette."

The technicians were the same ladies I had in 2012. Seeing their familiar faces and hearing they recognized me was comforting. It made a tremendous difference to recognize and be recognized. I was relaxed. I knew the routine. I questioned them about how the treatment worked, the first time I just let it happen. I remember the large arm. I remember the green lasers that make a cross on my skin. I remember the plastic fingers that click into place inside the machine that whirr. The familiarity of it was peaceful. My arm was beginning to fall asleep, but it never reached the deep, numbing sleep like last time. I was thankful. I was prepared for the pain, but glad it never came.

Radiation treatment will turn out to be 4 weeks long. They told me I would have 3 weeks of treatment. I believe when they said 3 weeks, they meant about 21 days. When you include weekends it becomes 4 weeks. My first treatment will be October 5th, and my last treatment will be October 30th.

I wonder how much of my crazy emotions this past weekend were due to the beginning of radiation. I keep thinking I'm okay, but my subconscious may have other ideas.

It's Monday, October 5, 2020. Today is my first radiation treatment. I cannot get out of this funk. Each morning, I wake up feeling broken and down. I'm having a difficult time getting good sleep. I feel beat up. It's harder to find hope and joy and peace. It doesn't matter how many times I trust and rest in God, I feel the fear in the back of my throat. It tries to choke me. It tries to push me down. It tries to make me freeze. I know I can do all this. I can move forward. I can be victorious. I can survive, but at what cost? What will I lose? Maybe there is something I can gain - a story, strength, determination, peace. It just feels too hard right now.

I've completed 2 days of radiation. I think I was anxious about treatment even though I had done it before, even though it should be easier this time. I was trying to make it "no big deal" in my mind, while I felt everyone around me surrounding me with compassion and love. My mom, my brother, Norma and Carlie have been ever present. They send me kind texts that make me smile and feel like "warm hugs" during moments when I am simply walking, trying to take another step and not let any additional weight I carry slow me down. They probably feel useless hundreds of miles away on their phones, but their thoughts reach me and wrap themselves around me, assuring me I am not alone. They remember. They remember this day, this moment might be tougher than others. Their simple words bring enough comfort to make any person strong and brave, to assure any person they are loved and seen.

*I know you feel useless and helpless, distanced from me during this time. You are not.*

*I know you wish there was more you could do to alleviate my load. You cannot.*

*You feel far away, weak and insignificant. You are not.*

. . .

*What you don't know is I feel every thought.*
    *It lessens my load and assures me I am not alone.*


*What you don't know is your simple message makes me feel seen in a way that brings me Hulk-like strength.*


*What you don't know is your listening ear that truly hears and your heart that truly listens washes peace over my soul.*


*Thank you for seeing me.*
    *Thank you for remembering me.*
    *Thank you for hearing me.*
    *Thank you for answering the nudge to reach out.*


*Knowing I do not take this journey alone is more than enough to buoy me forward into the scary and unknown.*

Okay, so how is radiation going? It's easy. I drive to MSTI at 2:10. I change. I wait. I lie on the board-like bed with my arms over my head, my breast exposed and a crisscross of green light beams marking my position. This time they elevate the bed 4 feet in the air, so the giant machine with the arm can move around me. They leave. It ticks, hums, beeps and rotates for a few minutes. They come. I leave. I change again. I drive home. The whole process takes a little more than an hour. It is simple.

The first day, I immediately felt the heat in my breast. It

throbbed and ached like someone was pressing on a deep bruise. I rested in the recliner, disappointed I could already feel the effects. Soon I was dozing. I may have dozed because of radiation, but it was more likely sleep overtook me because it had eluded me all weekend. I had been consumed with all the thoughts while trying not to be consumed at the same time. I couldn't run from them anymore.

My mom remembers every day I have treatment and sends me a text. My brother remembers and says good morning. Carlie remembers and asks how I am. My family sees me leave and return every day. I see it in their eyes - the longing to help. They didn't see this part last time. They didn't see all I accomplished in a day, then walked out the door for treatment. They don't know what to say, but they smile and wish for the best anyway.

So far, it isn't too bad. My breast immediately swelled after the first treatment. I felt heat and slight pain. I know it is different, but it isn't unbearable and taxing yet. Perhaps it won't be. I have 19 days to go. This feels doable.

I am feeling better each day. It is Thursday, October 8, 2020. The pain hasn't increased in my boob. It is bigger and redder. My nipple is very red and swollen, but other than that things are about the same as the first day.

I'm finally sleeping. I fell asleep before 10 last night and slept until after 7. My weight is a number that whispers possible health.

Teaching in this manner requires a lot of time, and sometimes I don't feel efficient. I need to work on organization and focus on the most important things first.

∾

It's Friday. Part of me wants to submit my resumé of health issues to everyone so they know the cards I carry. Part of me doesn't. My question is why? Why do I want people to know this is my second journey with breast cancer? Why does it matter? Am I looking for sympathy? It may be more likely I am looking for admiration. Look at what you have been through - you are so strong . . . Am I seeking that? Do I want people to see me diligently walk forward in life, succeed, then shock them with the list of reasons I have every right to not succeed? Can I just live and walk and not seek that prize?

Am I too aware of every emotion and physical sensation? Should a part of me be numb and just exist without analyzing everything? Can I just exist? Is it possible I analyze because that is just how I am built? Does my analysis help me connect with others? Does it help me encourage others?

Perhaps I want others to know they can survive, they can thrive. Each time the trial comes I keep walking. I keep striving to be the best version of myself. Perhaps I want my actions to encourage and strengthen others. Perhaps it's really just about me.

Maybe this is why I prefer to hide when things are especially difficult. When the tears come and the pain and fear overtake me, I don't want you to see. I want you to watch when I feel strong again, when I have overcome.

It is a fight. It is a battle. I'm daily trying to preserve what I can of myself. I'm trying not to lose ground to emotional and physical thieves. Waging that silent battle against them is exhausting. I fight the hardest when people are watching, then I go and sit alone and grieve and rest in order to gather strength to resume the battle.

I don't fight cancer or MS, the medication and treatments do that. I fight the loss of peace and strength. I fight to keep my joy. I fight to keep my energy. I fight for balance and hope.

Realistically, this is a battle I fight daily - whether or not I have an added health problem. The difference is I need to be more diligent, yield my weapons more often and be more watchful. It takes longer to gain lost ground when there are enemies attacking from all sides.


It's Saturday. It is a tough day. I can't pinpoint one reason any more than I can pinpoint the rate of a hummingbirds' wings. I feel down. I feel tired. I feel sad. It would be easy to hide in a corner and cry. I would love to be alone so I could freely do that.

People keep misunderstanding me and misinterpreting me. That is exhausting. I keep wanting to plead with them to truly see me and truly hear me instead of assuming and running. It feels unfair that I fully know and understand others, but I rarely feel the same in return. I feel very alone. I know I need to take a long walk. I'm not sure who to bring with me, besides Shelby: a podcast - which one? My mom? Carlie? Just myself? I'm not sure what I need to fill and strengthen me - other than being seen and heard.


I'm weary. I suppose the week wore me out. I stayed positive and present. Today I am spent.

.  .  .

I took a long walk. It helped a little. My mom asked how I was and I answered with silent tears. I spent most of the day lying in the recliner or on the couch watching episodes tick by. I slept for one of them and felt tired for the rest.

I felt a bit better when I woke up, but now I'm crying again. I don't exactly know why except, perhaps, my burden is simply heavy. I am simply tired. I've been trying to keep it together for so long, put on a good face, do what is in front of me without complaining, so that I am now fully depleted. I feel invisible. Every word, every tone is misinterpreted.

When Sunday, October 11th arrived, I felt a bit better, but definitely still small and weak.

It's another Monday. I was okay when I woke up. Then suddenly, I felt down. I'm ready to curl up in my cocoon and wait for everything to be over. I feel like I'm not enough for everyone around me. I feel like I take too much and give back too little. I want to hide. I don't want anyone to see me. I want to be sad by myself. I want to be by myself. At the same moment I want to be seen, but not too closely. If they peer too closely, I'm afraid someone will see my weakness and take advantage of it.

The weight is so heavy. It makes me small. It makes me tired. In reality, all that is happening doesn't seem so bad when you make a list on paper, but what it does to my insides is debilitating. I'm losing the battle for peace. I'm losing the battle for balance. I am either falling apart or pretending to be together: neither are healthy places.

My mom and Lew are coming Thursday. I'm looking forward to it, but at the same time I'm afraid to be seen. I battle between putting up a strong front to make everyone believe I'm okay and falling apart and not caring what anyone thinks.

Radiation isn't so bad. Why am I struggling? Surgery went well. I have much to be grateful for, and I am: so thankful, but I am also so tired and broken.

I spent the day trying to be alone and invisible - it didn't work. I kept switching rooms and trying to get some peace and to limit distractions. It didn't work. Everyone kept following me.

On Tuesday, October 13th, I woke up too early. It's frustrating when I wake up early and can't go back to sleep. I don't like it when my mind insists on beginning its work while my body feels fatigued and sluggish, screaming for a bit more sleep. I've been awake for over 3 hours, drank 3 large cups of coffee, played my games and read my book. My eyes are heavy. I could take a nap like an exhausted puppy. I'm warm and itchy. My mouth is heavy and cottony. It is so difficult to remain in a healthy place.

I don't need that alone time as badly today as I did yesterday. I just need a nap.

# Chapter 21

## *Internal Battle*

Thursday, October 15th arrived. It was officially time for my new MS treatment. The day was tiring. Fortunately, I slept until 5:30 AM. That was an improvement from 3:30 and 4:00 the other days. I drank my coffee and took two Tylenol and two Benadryl to prepare for my first infusion. The Tylenol and Benadryl are intended to keep my body from reacting to or rejecting the new medication. I drank as much water as I could manage. I asked Jason if he would drive me to my appointment because I was afraid I'd fall asleep in the car after the lack of sleep/Benadryl combination. On the way to my first Tysabri infusion, he said I was brave because he would be freaking out. I explained the "freak-out" comes weeks before the main event. I think about it, worry about it and dread it when I add it to the calendar. As the day draws nearer, I make peace with it, find my way through and take the next step.

I carried my 15 pound backpack, full of all the potential things I might want to do during this three hour infusion, into the room. I had already passed by the room once and didn't know it. I walked past it until the only doors left were the ones leading outside. I turned back and quickly found the small room. I was the first to arrive. The nurse, Casey, was waiting in one of the chairs for me. I settled into that same chair when she got up, nervous and as ready as one preparing to step off a cliff can feel. Abby (another patient) came in soon after me. Casey got her infusion started quickly then came back to me. She tried finding a vein in the crook of my left elbow. It didn't work. It only caused pain. She tried my hand, missed the vein and deposited saline under my skin. She tried the crook of my elbow again. I felt pain shoot down the side of my thumb. She was too close to a nerve. At this time, I was dizzy. Casey put cold cloths on my head and neck and pulled the chair out so I could recline more. She brought me a blanket and gave me time to recover before she tried again. In the meantime, Yvonne and her service dog, Tesla, came in. Paige came in shortly after Yvonne. Casey started them both on their medication before she returned to me. This time, she found a vein in the crook of my right elbow. The needle went in. The infusion drip began. I settled in for 2 hours of medication. I didn't feel any adverse effects once everything finally began.

When you are essentially strapped to a chair for hours, you don't have many options for how you pass the time. There was no television. I could read a book, take a nap or visit with the other people receiving their infusions. Paige and Yvonne have dealt with MS for more years than me. Yvonne has had more surgeries than she can remember. Paige's husband is dying, and her daughter struggles mentally, resulting in attempted suicides and a feeling of lack of connection. After the last suicide attempt, Paige got a tattoo on her forearm that her daughter designed of a battle between the head and the heart, accompanied by her daughter's favorite flowers. Her daughter feels connected now. Her mother's simple act connected them in a way no words could. Her church friends and family shun her for getting a tattoo. They don't understand that her daughter's life is more important than following archaic rules about marking the skin. They don't understand that it's about love.

Both Paige and Yvonne have a more difficult time with their MS than I do. They both have hard things in their lives that weigh heavier than mine. They don't seek pity. In fact, they talk about them like describing a new pair of shoes. I get that. I get the ease of describing horrible things like the weather. For me, it makes it easy to share and be honest. We aren't sharing horror stories, just true stories.

Later, I met Jen who is only 6 months into her treatment and diagnosis, and she is still very scared. Sophie is 10 months in, a very young mom and full of positivity. Skee came and spent most of the time on her phone. Marilynn arrived later with her own blanket. Most of these ladies came and went as I waited out my slow drip of medication. I use the phrase "treatment and diagnosis" because when you are diagnosed with MS, treatment begins. There is a shock that comes with the diagnosis. This shock has no time to subside before treatment begins. These young women learned a few months ago they had MS because some traumatic event happened to their body. Their arms or legs stopped working or they lost their vision or they just found out something was wrong. They received their lifetime diagnosis, then began a treatment where a needle is inserted into your body and they infuse medicine directly into your veins. So treatment and diagnosis is one unit.

Each person who walked through that Tysabri door had MS. Each had a discovery story where their body no longer worked correctly that led to an MRI that led to a diagnosis. Each person gets regular MRIs to measure the progress of the disease. Paige's MRI lasts 3 hours because MS has traversed her brain and spine. Each person knows they have no real power over this disease. It can do whatever it wants whenever it wants. They simply keep moving, keep taking the treatments, keep hoping, and counting each blessing.

Because each of us walks through the door with this common reality, we already share an intimacy beyond what I have with people I've known for years. We are already in the trenches together. Regardless of where we are in our journey, we know. We know the fear, the pain, the determination. We understand. Because of this shared knowing, we can just talk. We can be real. We can understand the most basic of sentences that everyone else is confused by. We understand the silence. We understand the fear behind the eyes. This moment, this moment I was terrified of, opened my eyes. I need to participate in support groups to surround myself with people who understand on a higher level than those without MS or cancer ever can. A support group isn't necessarily there to encourage and help. They are there to let you know they get it. You are not alone. You have comrades who know!

I arrived in the Tysabri room at 9:45. I left at 12:30. Even though I never fell asleep, it helped to have Jason drive because I was not alone. I was not alone in the journey. Even though I was capable of driving myself, I was not left alone in the car to think and worry and wonder. I was not alone.

Caretakers, insist on driving your loved ones to their treatments, so they aren't alone on the journey. It doesn't matter how capable they are. They shouldn't be alone.

When it was finally over, I was just as drained as I was that morning. I made lunch when I got home. I called Kelly. My mom and Lew arrived a little after 5:00. They took a detour by accidentally getting on the freeway and heading towards Notus, so it took a bit longer for them to get here. They wondered how the treatment made me feel. Other than sore arms where the needle went in, I felt no effects of the medication.

My mom hugged me and refused to let go. She was holding onto me to see if I was real, to make up for the missed hugs, to send her love and support through my skin, to say she is here for me, to send her strength to my bones, to fill me, to fuel me. I sank into her arms, but I also held back. I wasn't ready to lay down my armor just yet. I moved slowly through the evening, hearing conversations, but not participating. My body was weary and tired and worn out. I sat in the shadows of the evening, hoping I was enough, but also not caring if I wasn't. I wanted them to reach out to each other and love each other. I would be available later.


Saturday sneaks in at the end of a long week. I keep waking up before I want to. I don't think it's the early hour or the number of hours of sleep that is a problem. It's that I constantly feel tired. I'm using all my forehead muscles to prop my eyes open. I'm still going through the motions of the day, but slowly and carefully.

I have a headache this morning because I had too much to drink yesterday. My mom made a drink with grapefruit vodka, lime and soda water. I enjoyed it, it tasted good, so I had another. About half way through the second drink, I felt the effects of the alcohol and knew I had made a poor decision. I don't know if I'm out of practice or just more sensitive to it. I definitely am not able to drink as much right now. There is nothing wrong with that. I'm thankful I know how to listen to my body.

My mom and I went for a short walk. It was warmer than expected. We didn't talk very much. I wasn't sure why. We usually talk nonstop while we walk, perhaps it was the absence of the phone.

I asked her how she was, expecting a fully honest answer. She said, "Fantastic!" Her answer surprised me. She was happy to be here and to see me. Every time she hugs me, she clings. I still haven't fully sunk into her arms. I'm still trying to hold myself together. I don't have a lot of practice letting go and allowing others to hold me together.

The sinking into someone else and releasing all I'm holding in usually comes when the dam breaks and I no longer have a choice.

I know people want to see me and know how I am, but sometimes it can feel like I'm an exhibit. People are watching my every move, judging if I am okay or not, measuring my behavior against past behavior, determining if I am successfully handling this - hoping that I am, while searching for signs of weakness. If there wasn't pity in their eyes when they find the chinks in my armor, I might lay aside my armor more often, but I don't like seeing their eyes. So I sit up, walk, hold my eyes open with each muscle in my forehead, hoping they will forget I am broken, all while wanting them to be fully aware of all my broken parts. It's an odd conversation in my head. It's an odd set of emotions battling for attention. It is, yet, another reason I need to be alone - to be real with myself when I don't feel like I can be real with others.

∼

### The Banning of Fine

This word has been over-used and under-defined. It has become the sign of pretend connection and politeness:

"How are you"

"Fine, how are you?"

No one is fine. Fine means I don't really want you to know how I am. Whatever is happening with me I will keep to myself. I'm choosing to put up my "fine" wall so you can tell your friends all is well. I don't feel safe telling you the truth or I simply don't want to. No one is fine. Answering with fine is a choice we make to pretend everything is in order, for the sake of everyone watching, including ourselves.

I have banned this word from my vocabulary in response to how I am. There are dozens of other words I can use: content, calm, peaceful, happy, tired, blessed, thankful, hopeful ... All these words are more honest and tell the other person I care enough to truly answer their question rather than regurgitate a habitual word that has no other meaning than, "I don't really want to be honest with you."

Because of this ban, it may take me more than a half a second to answer your question, but I will answer it honestly with a thoughtful word that truly describes how I am. If you don't want to know the truth, don't ask, just say "Hi," and be on your way. We should practice only asking questions we truly want the answers to.

I am no longer fine, I am forever hopeful.

It takes a bit more work to remain in a positive place, to keep moving, to smile, to function than it normally does. A large part of my desire to be alone stems from being free to feel whatever weakness and suckiness I am feeling without smiling for others or trying to remain aware and alert of those around me.

Yesterday, I had my moment of tears in the closet. The sobs came. I was too weak and dejected to remain standing, so I sat on the floor in the closet crying - waiting for the flood to end, so I could begin to repair the dam and survive another day, attempting to be whole when I only felt broken.

~

I left the recliner to meet our new neighbors: Phaedra, Iosif (yo-sif), and their son Aaron. They are welcomingly nice. After standing in the sun for a couple of minutes, I discovered that was the medicine I needed: sunshine. I gathered my shoes, changed my clothes and went for a walk. My mom and I walked almost 4 miles. By the time we got back, I had the ability to function again.

~

My mom keeps giving me long hugs. I want to know what she sees. What does she fear? What does she think?

~

When I look at myself, I see a constant contradiction. I want to know and understand everything. I also want to avoid everything. I want to be seen and known and heard, and I want to be left alone. I want to be recognized for my amazingness, and I don't feel amazing at all.

~

I told my girls how proud I am that they are who they are. They are responsible, resourceful, kind, fun, and intelligent. They are young women who someone can depend on. My heart swells when I truly see them. At the same time, it is so overwhelming to see them, to watch them grow and move onto new stages of their lives. Our lives are blessed to have these young women to participate in this life with us.

My mom clung to me and cried every time she hugged me. In the past, she played a song for me that said, "I'll love you through it." In her hug, is she passing strength to me? Is she holding on to give herself strength? Is she sinking into my arms because this burden and weight is heavy? When I am tangible, she has a bit more control, I won't just disappear. Is she afraid? Does she wish she could take this away and ease the trial? From my perspective, I keep going. I feel, I walk, I endure, I find peace, I conserve energy, I protect myself. She is forced to watch. She is helpless. She can't make it easier. She is powerless except in her ability to be there when I am ready to talk or cry.

Those that must watch need to know their power and their encouragement is in their presence. Allowing me to continue, allowing me to pretend today is normal, allowing me to be strong or weak or whatever I need. I don't need to be coddled or babied. I don't need your pity or even your sympathy. I need you to know this is complicated, and even when I'm crying on the floor in the closet, I am still choosing strength and perseverance. I am still going to get up as soon as my tears are spent and go back to life. I will do what needs to be done, rest when I'm tired, but attempt to be present for my life even if it is difficult and taxing. I even have the ability to encourage you and give you hope regardless of where my own hope meter is.

I like being cared for. I like it when people make me food, clean up the kitchen, vacuum the floor and do laundry. I like it when people take the trash out when it is full. I like it when people see what can be done and don't simply leave it for the next person. Those small tasks make me feel loved. I feel seen and not ignored. I feel appreciated and not taken for granted.

During this trip, my mom and Lew stayed in a hotel. They usually stay here and take one of the girls' rooms. I actually enjoyed that they stayed at a hotel. I didn't have to be "on" all the time. The only thing I didn't like was that we had less time. We didn't have those early morning minutes to drink our coffee together or the late nights when we just couldn't stop talking.

There comes a moment when the tiredness one feels prevents any kind of productive behavior, yet no amount of sleep or rest will alleviate the fatigue. I am there. It is Tuesday, October 20, 2020. I keep waking up too early. My gas tank or my battery or whatever energy source I have fades out long before my "to do" list, and I must resign myself to a chair and wait for the end of the day. The uncontrollable tears came again yesterday. They sneak up on me. They take the stage. I feel the weight of every difficult thing in every part of my day.

Yesterday was the first day in a while that I went to radiation and didn't listen to a podcast on the journey. The weight was heavier. The reality of my trip, the reality of the destructive nature of my treatment rode in the car with me. We didn't have a conversation, but he whispered fear and despair in my ear. My weariness took away my ability to fight for joy and peace, and I had to sit with it.

Listening to a podcast or talking to a friend on my journey requires my brain to focus on those words. It doesn't allow it to focus on my reality. I get to escape to history or hope and simply be transported to treatment rather than journey through the sludge to treatment like walking to my death. It isn't death, but that is the only difference. I distract my brain with interesting and beautiful things in order to keep the dark truth away until it is absolutely necessary. It is the same reason I make small talk with the technicians. If I only think about treatment while it is happening, it is much more palatable than thinking about it on the journey there and home.

I am saddened when I look in the mirror and see the destruction they have done to me. I'm not as sad as I was last time, but still sad. My left breast is soft and small. It hangs like a 43 year old woman's breast who has had 2 children should hang. My right breast is puffy and pink. They radiate the area near my nipple so my nipple is permanently dark pink and protruding. The breast is starting to swell around it and make a sort of moat between it and the areola. It is more than twice the size of the other one. The areola is 4 times the size of the left and resembles the color of angry cheeks on a cartoon. There is an indent at the bottom, between my nipple and my ribs. It is obvious they removed a chunk and now there is empty space. It resembles land-forms where volcanoes have blown or sink holes were created. It is uneven and bumpy. I see it. I feel it. I know after this is over the swelling will go down and I may not look so deformed, but then again, I may.

With age comes the acceptance of an old body that is tired of being firm, tired of moving smoothly, tired. Surgeries reconstruct us into forms like the melting of a candle or imperfect pottery. Scars mark moments when trials were at their worst. They leave behind evidence of a time we would have preferred to avoid, but instead survived.

I look at the changes in my body and am sad. At the same time, I am empowered. I retain battle scars. Evidence I have fought. Evidence I have survived, if not won - again and again. Those with no marks are soft. Those with no wounds have not seen battle, but nor have they seen triumph. They have not learned to overcome. My scars and imperfections are a badge. They remind me I am strong, I am resilient, I can endure.

It's Wednesday, October 21, 2020. Here I am again, tired of being tired. I wish I had more useful hours in the day when I could think and function. It feels like I have a running timer and I have to hurry and get my work done before the timer runs out. I never succeed, so the next day is full of more tasks than the day before. One thing that helps is sleep. When I get more sleep, my battery doesn't die out quite so quickly. Yet, sleep continues to elude me.

Fredrick Backman's book, *Anxious People*, has made me reflect on myself and my relationships. I cried over the good "dad" relationships in the story and my lack of this type of relationship. I felt all the feelings that come with simultaneously loving and being tired of your spouse. I felt the draw of doing anything to give your child more and dreaming they become more than you have become. I felt the speed of life between babies, career and old age where you are in danger of waiting to die. I felt the emptiness of pain and loss and the fullness of hope. Backman is an incredible author.

I sit here crying - feeling all the feelings because that is what I am good at. I teeter between being a strong, tough, silent warrior and being real, raw and honest about the fear and pain. Will everyone remember I am strong even if I tell them I am weak? Will everyone be in awe of what I endure even if I cry in the closet? Perhaps it is because of my weakness and tears that I become strong and unbreakable. Perhaps I shouldn't care what others think and just walk in my own shoes.

The other day, on the phone, I got brave enough to ask my mom what she sees in me, what her long hugs were. It turns out I knew. I'm not sure if I needed to hear it, if I needed to talk about deep things or maybe I just wanted this moment.

She said her hugs were making up for the 10 months we hadn't seen each other, the canceled visits and all the times she couldn't hug me over the phone. She clung for her - to soak me up to fill time in the past and future. She clung for me - to give me whatever she could in strength and love and hope. Sadly, I had to hold back a bit in those hugs. I tried to sink into them, but the family's watchful eyes helped me build a wall and I was afraid if I sank in I would lose all my dams and fall apart in her arms, unable to put myself back together. Even as I write this, the tears flow like a spring rain. The dams break when I just think about sinking into someone's arms. I'm sure she would have loved it if I let go and let her hold some of the burden, but the journey back to strength would have been too much for me.

Perhaps if she held on longer, perhaps if she looked in my eyes, perhaps if she asked, "How are you?" in the tone that says I really want to know. Perhaps, even then, I would protect myself from melting like a snowman in spring. Perhaps the only reason I am mixing tears with my coffee now is because I am alone and am not concerned about the scene I portray. She said she sees a strong woman. She wonders if she could handle these things as well as I do. I'm not surprised to hear that part, I hear it often. I usually don't feel strong, just determined and stubborn. I don't have it in me to quit.

My mom is fast and busy. I am slow and contemplative. When she comes, she wants to go and do all the things in order to keep me busy. I am content to sit and talk and feel and reflect. I want to see and know the depths of the ocean. She prefers to stay busy on the next wave. Perhaps, next time, I can remember this and require her to spend some time in the depths with me.

∾

I have been reflecting on depression. The past few days were especially difficult for me. I looked up the definition of depression. It says sad, unhappy, without hope. I'm never truly depressed because I'm never without hope. A more accurate word is spent or weary. I am physically and emotionally tired of fighting for joy. So, that is what I felt this week: spent and weary.

I had a difficult time keeping my eyes open. I had a difficult time finding energy to work. It was difficult to do more than lay in the recliner, but I did.

I thought about this weariness and sadness this week and remembered again the real fight is to stay out of the dark pit. There is a pit of depression. It is full of despair, hopelessness and the heaviest, bluest sadness. Once one is in the pit, there is no easy ladder or rope to climb out. There are tiny ledges and rocks one must cling to in order to escape. The best defense is to not fall into the pit. When I feel myself getting too close to the edge I have to force myself to do something that brings me joy and makes me feel good. That act creates distance between me and the edge. It buys me time. It creates a buffer. I am safe for a bit. When I see the edge again, I choose another joyful activity. Regardless of how joyful the activity is, I never fully land where the pit is out of view. It threatens me, but I am safely away so I can spend a few moments in peace before I fight to move away from it again.

The battle is for my mind and heart. The battle that makes me weary is to gain enough ground so I feel I am a safe distance from slipping into the pit and needing more energy than I have to pull myself out again.

My breast hurts more. The radiation is right at my nipple area. It is red and on fire. The area under my armpit hurts because my arm is constantly rubbing on it. I only have 6 days left. I am thankful for that.

The most difficult thing a person can do is to unapologetically be one's self. Some people are raised in a world where they are fully accepted. Their strengths and weaknesses aren't judged, they are known. I envy those people.

I have fought for many years to accept myself - flaws and all. I have worked for just as many years to know myself. In every situation, I wonder if I am behaving correctly. Am I listening fully? Am I speaking the correct words? Does my face show openness? Did I wear the right clothes? It takes an almost insurmountable effort and a lot of work to walk into the day with no doubts, choosing to be fully myself. Honestly, I often don't know who "myself" is.

I surmise that most of my doubt comes from growing up in a church that judged and put value on appearances and behavior, and in being in close proximity to parts of my family that did the same. There was acceptable and unacceptable. There was definitely good and bad, and there still is.

I want to shake off the filter that worries what others think. I want to wear my own coat, my own hat and walk with confidence. I want to be brave enough to speak truth. I want to be secure enough to share my faults without feeling I must fix them. I want to discard the shame of my past or my personality and don confidence and ease. I want to know and be myself. I want to be known and seen for myself and not for some facade I portray.

～

I would love to quit. I would love to not do anything on my list, but I'm not built that way. I'll get it done, then perhaps I'll sleep.

I am still exhausted and weary. It doesn't matter if I wake up at 3 AM or 5 AM, I move slowly and have a difficult time finding energy. Each week, I lose 5 ½ hours of working time because of my trips to radiation treatment. It taxes me and makes completing my job to the level I desire difficult. That is what it comes down to - the level I desire. I have a vision. I have a standard I want to meet. Because I seek continual improvement, I rarely meet that standard. I would like to learn how to prioritize, how to be amazing, yet efficient. It is not an excuse that I am weak, tired, battling cancer, receiving treatments and living with MS. It is not an excuse that everything I do is difficult. It is not an excuse that my energy runs out faster than everyone else's. I still expect and seek greatness for myself.

My breast hurts. I tried to use the numbing lotion over the weekend and my skin became irritated, red and itchy. My nipple is red. My breast no longer has a tan line; I'm burnt all over. The place where my arm rubs my side is agitated and bright pink. I only have 5 days of treatment left, but it feels like they may be long days. It feels like someone is constantly pinching my nipple and it feels like tiny needles take turns poking the rest of my breast. Anything tight hurts, yet I can't go completely without support because too much movement hurts also. The mental battle decreases slightly as the physical battle increases with pain and weariness.

. . .

I will say it again. I am tired. It is Wednesday, October 28, 2020. My eyes are heavy and threatening to close, yet I wake at 5:30. My breast aches and burns. My nipple feels like it is being pinched. I'm aware that to everyone else I have cancer and am going through stuff. To me, it is just my life. I am enduring and hoping to thrive. I can't envision not fully doing my job or ignoring my family or quitting exercising. I just keep moving. I move with a weight on my shoulders and weariness in my bones, but I must keep going.

I'm reading *Becoming* by Michelle Obama. Her life rarely resembles mine. She went to two Ivy league schools, got a law degree, lives in Chicago, is a mighty powerful woman, a good mother and volunteers and loves to be enveloped in people. Even though our daily lives look very different, I can connect and understand her daily struggles.

I feel inspired to take advantage of each moment and opportunity. I want to learn how to believe in myself - that I am good enough to win a Presidential Award and write a book and be a leader. I want to believe in my amazingness and stop comparing myself to what appears to be others' amazingness.

This is a mindset I am not good at yet. I am good at standing in the shadows. I am good at being the foundation someone else stands upon. I am good at dimming myself to let others shine more. I am not good at turning up my own light. I don't plan on trying to change my essence, but I need to give myself more credit, see fully my own light even if I dim it so others shine brighter. I want to embrace and use each gift I have while still caring for myself. I won't run myself ragged, but I need to make space for my dreams. I need to place them at a higher priority in my life or they will never come to pass. I need to make real deadlines that I keep.

I just realized something, something I've known down deep, but I found words for it. When I read books or listen to podcasts or even watch television, I internalize the message. I apply it to myself. I ask how this information fits into me. It causes me to constantly be learning and growing. The magic is that a story read in January will tell me something different from the same story read again in December. It isn't the story itself that moves and shapes me. It is my interaction with it, my state of mind going into it, my relationship with it, my needs and desires in the moment.

I'm still so tired. I feel drained today. My head hurts, my eyes only want to close. I would love to take today off, but I won't. I will push through and rest later.

It's Friday, October 30, 2020. There are continual battles going on within me. I desire to be seen, considered and known, yet I want to be invisible, part of the furniture and left alone. I desire to be a person who accomplishes great things and moves mountains, yet I love a quiet existence of simple pleasures. I desire to share my reality and my truth, yet I also just want everyone to believe all is well. I desire to be amazing and good at my job and other endeavors, yet I spend much of my time doubting I am good enough.

Reading Michelle Obama's *Becoming* inspired me, but I'm not exactly sure what that looks like. I feel the movement and prodding in my soul. I want to step out and reach fully for my dreams, yet I fight with my small reserve of energy.

# Chapter 22

## *Nothing Will Be the Same*

I t's Saturday, November 7, 2020. Radiation treatment has ended, and I've reached the most difficult stretch. The worst part is I didn't anticipate it. In 2012, radiation treatment ended with an infection and too much pain. I thought I would end this treatment session more gracefully.

Treatment is over, doctors' appointments are months apart now. Technically, by all logical accounts, I am cancer free right now. Despite that fact, right now, I have the most pain. The piercing pain of needles and pinching continues. The pain makes me weary and unmotivated and it doesn't seem to be decreasing.

My breast is purple, darkest near and under my nipple. My nipple looks like someone sticking their fat tongue out through a round mouth. My areola is swollen and looks like melted wax. I don't remember how long it takes for this part to get better. I'm tired of not feeling well. I'm weary of being hopeful and fighting for peace. I would like to lie down and quit and wait for it to get better. Ironically, laying down and waiting will make the healing take longer. Moving, functioning, hoping, and trying are things I must keep doing in order to heal, in order to stay mentally healthy. The battle is discouraging and exhausting. Saturdays tend to suck. I feel tired, sad and depleted. Tears flow freely and I have little strength to fight today.

I want to remember it takes a week after my last radiation treatment to begin to heal. It is Tuesday, November 10th. It has been a week and a day. In the beginning my breast started to swell and it turned pink. After another week of treatment, it turned red. At its worst, it turned purple. Now, as it is beginning to heal, it is becoming brown, like a tan after a bad sunburn, but not as healthy. I have darker brown scabbed covered areas and a few spots of fresh pink skin where the scabs have fallen off.

I wake up each morning groggy and in pain. I am often found holding or gently scratching, but not really scratching my breast in an attempt to ease the pain and pinching and needle pricking. My efforts make no difference, but I do them anyway.

Another week and a day has passed. Each day of the past week, I felt a little better. My skin began to peel. The destroyed, damaged brown skin shriveled up and allowed me to peel it away from the healthy pink skin. Only the section they boosted (extra treatment for the last 4 days) is really discolored. I still have pain, but it comes mostly when I apply pressure instead of all the time. I am exercising and walking more again. I'm hoping to get rid of the extra pounds I put on while I wasn't feeling well and was devouring leftover Halloween candy like it might become extinct. I feel like talking to people again and cleaning things again.

For a little while, I made it through the day doing the least amount of work. I have to think about starting Tamoxifen soon. I'm scared. I'm scared of how this medication will affect my hormones, my weight and my emotions. Thankfully, if my body doesn't handle it well, I can stop. I still have choices. They aren't the best choices, but I still have them.

It's Friday, November 20th. I am a rock on the outside, not easily broken or damaged. On the inside, I am a hurricane of doubt, uncertainty and pain. I am an over-ripe peach that feels everything. I am weary, lost and exist with the hope that I am okay. I am on the teeter-totter between desiring to quit and fighting to be victorious.

.  .  .

Monday, November 23, 2020

"Nothing will ever be quite the same again." - from *Zoya*, a novel by Danielle Steel

These words are spoken after a son who is in the military is killed by his comrades. The family knows their lives will never be the same without him. There are problems in the country and their whole existence will never be the same.

These words are echoed for us today. Nothing will ever be the same again after this Coronavirus pandemic, after online school, after a selfish dictator-like president refuses to leave office, after experiencing breast cancer and treatment for a second time, ... There are many milestone moments in our lives when we say this phrase. Sometimes it's joyful: after a marriage, a birth, a graduation, or a job promotion. Sometimes it's so sad your body aches.

What do you do in those moments? You understood and could predict your life until ... "nothing will ever be quite the same again." How do you move forward when you just want to grieve? How do you find joy and hope when you only want to quit and cry? When you see thousands of people keep moving forward after their lives have been altered, you can't help but be in awe. The blow they took should have knocked them out, yet they stand. They are so beat they should throw in the towel, yet they swing again. The human spirit is resilient. It is powerful. It shifts quickly from grief to action. We seem to know sitting in our grief will be more painful, so we begin walking again. We never fully leave the grief behind, but it is behind us, a fading spot like the remnants of a city you leave in your rearview mirror.

Everyone experiences this grief at some point. Entire

countries experience this. Families experience this. Individuals experience this. And we keep moving. We can take comfort in knowing many before have reached this same bridge and have successfully crossed to the other side. They look back and remember, but can only truly move forward.

The day before my birthday, I struggled with sadness tugging on me while I fought with determination and hope. It could be hormones. It could be the absence of seeing my friends, shopping leisurely through a store for Christmas gifts, and having typical holiday traditions. On Friday, December 4th, 2020, I turned 44. My body seems to be healed enough to start the cancer medication. I'm not 100%, but I'm as ready as I'll ever be. I wore a regular bra, I have less pain, and I don't need to lotion my heat-damaged skin. I am still afraid of what the medication will do to me, but I will take it and figure it out as I go.

It has been a month since I finished radiation treatment. I am healing well from surgery and radiation. I've stopped using the lotion. I can wear regular bras. I still have pain, but it is less. I have to start taking Tamoxifen today, the cancer medication. I'm scared. I'm scared about the havoc it can do to my body. I'm scared about weight gain, emotional roller coasters and general changes in how I feel. There is a chance I won't notice any changes, but I am still terrified. It also reduces blood cells that fight disease, so I'll be getting a double dose of immunity depletion during a worldwide pandemic: one from Tamoxifen and the other from Tysabri, my MS infusion.

~

I took my first Tamoxifen pill tonight. Before I actually took it, I was overcome with fear about what it *could* do to me. I held the small, white pill in my hand and tearfully went to Jason in his recliner. I finally got the words out between my overwhelming emotions, "Would you pray? I am terrified about what this medication might do to me". He silently prayed, and I ingested the first pill. That night I may have felt some flushing and weirdness. It may have been in my head. It has been 3 days since then, and I have had no measurable side effects. In fact, I may have reduced my weight. I'm thankful I haven't noticed anything.

~

It's Thursday, December 17, 2020. I just calculated this bout of breast cancer stole 4 months from me. I spent the first month preparing my heart and mind for the battle ahead. This was interrupted by surgery. I spent the second month recovering from surgery and preparing my heart and mind for radiation. I spent the third month juggling a job and radiation treatment. The fourth month was spent recovering from radiation and psyching myself up to begin another medication, Tamoxifen, which I will take for the next 5 years. Thankfully, there are no measurable side effects from that medication right now. I am starting to increase my exercise again and plan to get rid of some of the fluffiness I gained.

Nothing about cancer is easy, but looking back, it wasn't

too bad. There were no surprises this time. I feel relatively normal right now and can move forward to more health. Eight years ago was also a 4 month journey, but I remember having more difficulties. I barely kept my head above water. This time I floated with the current.

In 2012, I depended on God to help and guide me. I depended on my outpouring of thoughts, fears and prayers in my journal each morning to give me the strength to trudge through the mud of each day. I walked like I had blinders on. I could literally only take one step at a time. I gathered strength and energy like a squirrel gathering his nuts on the cusp of winter. I stored what I needed for each day, each moment, then stepped into it. I didn't have the language to describe my fear and anxiety. I didn't have people who I thought were strong enough to hold any of those emotions with me. They may have been strong enough, but I didn't know how to share those emotions. I didn't know what it looked like to trust someone else with those emotions. So, I wrote and walked on.

In 2020, I was blessed with beautiful friendships. Regarding friendships, my two journeys were completely different. During my first cancer journey, I didn't really have any good friends I could lean on, which is why I depended so wholly on God and had to write my worries and prayers every day. It wasn't until I read over the part of my journey to relearn the details of surgery in both 2012 and 2020 that I realized in 2012 I didn't have any close friends. I had plenty of friends: people to do things with, people to visit with while our kids played, people that I adored and enjoyed being with, but at the time they were not what I have come to understand as a "soul friend." During my second journey, I was surrounded by friends. I also gained a language for my feelings I didn't have before.

I first heard the phrase, soul friend, in Spanish: *alma gemela*. It translates as "soul twin." Recently, I read about a soul friend, *anam cara,* in Julianne Stanz's book, *Braving the Thin Places*. She discusses the Celtic origins of the term. I also read about a soul friend in Susan Cain's *Bittersweet*. These authors reminded me that a soul friend is someone who lets you be exactly who you are. They help you write your story. You can't be too much for them. You are deeply connected.

I am grateful for the soul friend friendships and the other relationships that sustained me during the 2020 cancer journey. I'm thankful for every call my mom took wondering if I would be happy or crying. I'm thankful Lew was my consistent rock. I'm thankful for coworkers who cared and neighbors who reached out. I'm thankful for family who felt the weight of this journey and simply showed up.

During Christmas, I didn't feel well. My face felt thick, I had flushing in my face, my neck creaked like an old deck, my arms and legs kept falling asleep, my back ached, my head felt foggy and I was simply tired. How much of this was a result of Tamoxifen?

People keep looking at me thinking I'm strong or amazing. I don't feel strong. I feel persistent, diligent and stubborn. The fact that I am still standing has nothing to do with strength. The strong fall every day. It has to do with smart fighting. I seek out hope in the dark corners. I find true words that give light like blessed, content, calm, and grateful. I find joy in the simple pleasures of my daughters' smiles, or completing a puzzle, or a visit with a friend.

These are not strong things, they are smart things, survival things. These are minute by minute choices that bring me up when all I really want to do is go down. I *feel* like eating all the bad food, laying around, watching television and quitting. But I won't. I know doing what I "feel" like won't help. I must do what will help.

Today is the last day of 2020. It is another day like all the rest, but with the turning of the calendar comes a fresh hope. A hope that this pandemic will end, a hope we can see friends and family again, a hope we can find some pieces of life as we knew it.

This past year was packed with grief over lost things and hidden blessings. We lost the ability to go to work and teach in our classrooms. We gained a flexible schedule and less exhaustion. Hannah lost 2 months of her senior year, a normal graduation ceremony and a graduation party. Instead she experienced her graduation in the car with her best friend. They laughed at the ridiculousness together.

We lost a trip to Ireland. Instead, we will take both girls and go to Scotland and Ireland when we are free to travel again.

We lost regular outings with friends. We drew closer as a family. We lost the ability to simply run to the store. We gained the ease of online shopping. We lost visits with family. We relished the preciousness of that time when we did get it.

We still went to the Oregon Coast. We still went paddle boarding and swimming. We just did them slightly differently than before.

In the middle of summer, Cancer snuck in, threatening

to steal more than COVID did. I had to walk myself through the emotional and physical journey. Five months later, it is almost all behind me. Because of COVID, I worked from home during treatments and didn't miss much school. I took 2 sick days during those five months.

I'm practicing new teaching strategies I hope to continue in the future. I don't have to deal with naughty kids. I don't have to wake up at 4 am to get my workout in before school starts.

I'm ready to return to life, to drinks with friends, to visiting family, to going to a store, but I will be patient and try to continue to find blessings in the dark. This new reality can't go on forever. I feel like I'm waiting to begin again. I need to remember to take advantage of what I do have and what I can do.

As the calendar turns and a new day and a new year come at once, I pray I don't forget or lose what I've gained. I pray what we have lost will soon be restored. I pray people will care about people. It breaks my heart to see the cruelty of people to one another.

Welcome new year! Welcome hope and promise of something new!

~

I am under no delusions that new years are magical and everything gets a fresh start and old pains disappear. It is another day. Its significance comes because on this particular day, it is also a new month and a new year. It feels like a new beginning when so many things start fresh.

.  .  .

Difficult things don't care what the date on the calendar is. They don't care if it is supposed to be a new beginning or not. I will always remember March 13, 2020, as the last normal day. Everything before that was business as usual. Everything after that has been different: sometimes more difficult, sometimes a bit better.

I read the story of the Phoenix in Elizabeth Lesser's book, *Broken Open*, this morning. The Phoenix arises anew from its own pain and difficulties. It is a new bird because it experienced death of self, death of old ways and habits, still itself, but more so - changed.

For me, rising anew and death to self comes in two processes. In part, I am constantly dying and rising anew. Moment by moment I try to throw off habits that are undesirable and become new - changed. Also, this process is happening in a long drawn out sense that takes months and years. Sometimes the big tragedies come and force a large change. They require a new beginning if one desires anything more than mere survival. Even amongst these larger moments, the changes come again and again. Perhaps, this is, in part, what Paul meant when he said he dies to himself every day. There is a death of the parts of us we don't desire so the new can grow. To those who allow it, the Phoenix Process happens repeatedly and there never comes a time when one has fully arrived with nothing left to die to.


It is Saturday, January 16, 2021. It has been 6 months since my diagnosis. I am not the same person I was 10 years ago, 5 years ago, 1 year ago, or even yesterday. I do not have the same stamina and energy as any of those versions of me. I need to stop and learn again what I can and can't do. I need to look only at myself and no one else. I need to accept my abilities and not apologize for my lack of other abilities. I need to be wise and efficient. I need to breathe, take a step back, be nice to myself and celebrate what I can do. I can work smarter. I can say no. I can take care of myself. I can plan ahead to make each day easier and less exhausting.

It's been so long since I've had to regulate my energy, I had forgotten how. Plus, everything was difficult, so I wasn't prepared for how I had to change. There is a long list of things I can no longer do. I often grieve those things, but it is time to know and celebrate what I can do.

I slept off and on most of the day. I worked a little. I wrote a little. I feel better today, but I'm still a little broken. I've learned that it's in the broken places where the light shines through, so it's time to find the light and to selfishly put myself first.

~

Similar to the division of my life between pre-divorced parents and post-divorced parents, is my view on health from 2012 to 2020. During this period of time, a switch was flipped in my entire being about what it means to be healthy. The switch didn't come as suddenly as the news of divorce, but the difference was just as distinct, the equivalent of night and day.

I don't know how I would have answered, "What is health?" in 2012. I might have submitted it is a feeling, a sense of well-being, good numbers at the doctor, lack of medication. According to my journals, my view of it included checking "no" on the list of possible ailments listed on the paperwork at every doctor's visit. When I was diagnosed with cancer, I was more consumed with a loss of health based on the number of times I checked "no" on the form in the doctor's office than on how I felt and how healthy I actually was. I believed if I rested a lot I would get better. I believed if I moved easily and slowly, my body would heal. I believed waiting and resting would ultimately give me the freedom to move and be myself once again. I was wrong. Today, I still carry stiffness and pain from that season.

When I was sent for a biopsy in 2018, my first concern was the loss of my health. If I had another cancer diagnosis, I would have surgery and some form of treatment that summer. I wouldn't be able to go for long walks, go stand-up paddle boarding with my friends, play tennis, or go swimming in the pool with my daughter. I felt grief like a young child. I didn't want to lose the ability to enjoy my summer and to rejuvenate myself. The loss of health meant the inability to do things I enjoyed. I was blessed when none of these worries came to fruition.

When Wednesday, July 15, 2020, arrived and cancer 2.0 was here to stay, the fear of losing my health was akin to my fear of haunted houses. I dreaded the unknown. I was scared of what might loom around the corners. I was in the best shape of my life: physically, emotionally, spiritually, and socially. I was terrified of losing what I had gained. Surgery would slow me down. I may not be able to exercise the same. Radiation would wear me out. I may gain weight from the sheer exhaustion. COVID still permeated our world, keeping out people I needed near me during this time. It has been almost 2 years since that diagnosis, and my fears were valid. My progress was pushed back. I did gain weight. I did lose muscle tone. My relationships did change. But, did I lose my health? I am not a doctor or any other health professional. What I share here is what I have learned about health, mostly my own.

Multiple Sclerosis and CrossFit forced me to look at my health differently. MS is that unpredictable neighbor. One day he is kind and generous calling to tell you your garage is open, the next he is getting his mail in his underwear. He takes care of his yard, but has too many lawn ornaments and decorates with too many colors of lights all year. He brings you the best food you have ever tasted. He is generous with his time, tools and assistance, but sometimes he has 20 cars out front and talks too loudly while you are trying to drink your coffee in peace. The problem is, you don't know from day to day which neighbor you are getting. You might get the generous neighbor or you might have to listen to him throw a party. There is no predictability. MS is always there like the neighbor. Most of the time, it sits in the background, not asserting itself, letting time pass. Every once in a while, it gets an inkling to walk around in its underwear and disrupt your life. It throws parties and interrupts the peace you have established. There is no warning, and unfortunately, these moments damage the neighborhood so badly there is no recovery. The word has gotten out. You are changed.

MS forced me to listen to my body. If I feel tired, I have to stop and rest. If I feel hot, I have to find a way to cool my body or I will wilt and slow to a halt. If my brain begins to feel mushy, it is time to pause. In any of these instances, if I push through and ignore my body, I can have a relapse. I can lose mobility in my face and arm again. I can have something worse happen. Putting my body through stress can harm me permanently. I can't go back. I can't fix it. I can't undo what has been done, just like the neighbor who ruins the neighborhood's reputation. MS made me pay attention. It made me say "no." It also taught me how to say "yes." I say yes to activities that bring me joy. I say yes to time with loved ones. I say yes to anything that fills my soul and buoys my spirit.

The medication I took to keep relapses of MS at bay wreaked havoc on my body. The flushing took away my ability to think and focus. The stomach pain sent me to my bed, doubled over. The solution was diet. Once I omitted dairy and gluten from my diet, the stomach pain went away and the flushing wasn't so debilitating. The healthier I eat, the better I feel. Eating too much gluten actually makes me feel sluggish. It increases the effects of MS on my body. It makes it difficult to speak and focus. If I eat poorly, I feel poorly.

Because of the arrival of MS in my life, my family found CrossFit. We learned functional movements. We learned we love lifting weights and moving our bodies. We learned we could feel strong, energetic and amazing when we moved regularly. If we sowed energy into our day, we received more energy. From 2015 to 2020, I exercised regularly. I did traditional CrossFit workouts. I ran. I walked. I lifted weights to get stronger. I lifted weights to get leaner. I played tennis, swam and SUP-boarded because I could, because it was fun, and because it was a healthy activity.

When I was journeying through cancer treatments, I didn't stop exercising, but I did rest more. I didn't stop walking, but sometimes I walked slower. I didn't stop lifting, but I lifted lighter weights. Once radiation was complete and I started Tamoxifen, the estrogen blocking hormone, I gained an immediate 5 pounds on top of the weight I put on during radiation. By the beginning of December, just 5 months from my diagnosis, I had gained 10 pounds. Was I still healthy? Today, it is two months short of two years since my diagnosis. Honestly, it is the first time since then I feel like I'm on a trajectory towards the health I was once intimate with. I am moving more, eating less, and feeling more whole than I have felt in over a year. I don't believe I ever truly lost my health. I sat on the continuum between healthy and fit. It was common for me to say, I'm looking good considering ... I'm 45, taking medication that makes me gain weight, healing from cancer .... I am daily stepping closer to the fit I once was. Today, I am relatively healthy.

So what do I deem is healthy? I've always had good numbers. My blood pressure sits around 110/70. My weight stays in the average range. My resting heart rate is in the low 50s. I can function on my own. I can take care of myself. I'm more active than sedentary. If my blood pressure jumps up to 121/85, I might tell the nurse it's a bit high - *for me*. The nurse will look at me like I'm nuts. You see, those numbers are high - *for me*. They aren't high according to the doctors and nurses and the average American. But it is high blood pressure for me. My normal is my normal. When my numbers are off, I don't feel well. There is a weight I feel best at too. The doctors never tell me I am overweight, but I know where I feel best. I know when I feel comfortable in my skin.

Health means I can do whichever activity I want. I can exercise, I can ride my bike, walk, run, play tennis, volleyball, basketball, swim, SUP-board. I can play games with my students. I can sit on the floor. I can get up off of a chair. I can easily do my job. I can wear my clothes, instead of my clothes wearing me. I feel whole. I have trusted people whom I can tell if I feel joyful or sad. I have people who love me, who check in on me. I have a community that cares about me. I never lost my health during cancer 2.0. I had moments when I didn't have this entire list of criteria. I knew what was missing. I gave myself grace and I stepped towards that criteria again.

Health means paying attention to your body. It means knowing what your body needs. It means being kind to yourself. It means loving yourself. It means making one healthy choice at a time that brings you closer to that version of yourself you are most comfortable with. It means loving yourself with the same care and intensity you love others.

I am counting the days until I no longer need to take Tamoxifen. I'm planning a celebration when the time comes. I will celebrate the end of Tamoxifen. I will celebrate being free of cancer. I will celebrate the health I have and the road I traveled. I will celebrate the people who journeyed with me. All of that celebrating will coincide with my 49th birthday.

Over the past few years, I have spent time feeling strong and victorious and sick and depleted. Most days are good, but really bad days sneak up on me. I call them "down" days. The word describes my feelings and the fact that I will be down on the couch for the majority of the day. My body feels spent on these days. My emotions sit on the edge. The slightest breeze pushes me to sobs. I prefer to be alone and invisible, but I've learned to be down even when surrounded by people. My body wants to take a day off and I must let it.

I'm still teaching. I teach 5th grade now which is a better fit for me than 2nd grade. The students take less energy and I love the more challenging content. I can be honest with them and we talk a lot about emotions. My school moved to 4 day school weeks after COVID which has made it possible for me to continue teaching. Because I have an extra day to rest, I can continue to do my job and do it well. I can move at the pace that fits the health I have for that day. Students take care of the small tasks around the room, which they love, so I can focus on teaching.

I've changed my MS medication again. Now, I get an infusion that takes 8 hours of my day once every 6 months. I feel less side effects from the medication. I'm tolerating it well and I do enjoy only having to think about it twice a year.

I finally found a counselor in 2022. I was scared to put myself in such a vulnerable situation with an essential stranger. I was blessed to find one on the first try. She has made a tremendous difference in my life, my confidence, and my personal growth. It has helped to have someone hear all the things, validate me, and advise me when I need to try something different.

I still work hard for the health I have. I am grateful for each gift. I am grateful for my family and the strength we enjoy together. I am blessed. Even on my worst days, I feel blessed.

# Epilogue

Thank you for sticking with me on this journey. Sometimes I succeeded in moving forward. Once in a while I even moved upward. Then, there were those moments I seemed to move in circles, tracing back along my same fears over and over until a slight nudge would move me out of the muddy loop. That was my journey. It was messy and beautiful and even though I would have preferred to skip it, I see how it formed me.

I would love to say this journey has made me more accepting of bad news. I would love to say I no longer panic, worry, become fearful or hide from my loved ones. I don't know that. The next time a diagnosis comes my way, I will probably still be scared of what it will do to me and take from me, but since I've already endured so much, I know I will be able to endure this new thing as well. I still won't want to endure it because it's so much better to live without health problems.

Today, I am blessed to be 48 years old. If no phone call arrives before December of 2025, I will have survived 5 years without a major health diagnosis. Each year, actually each day, is a victory. Since I've already had cancer twice, the chances of me getting it again are very high. I will do my best to keep it at bay, but I am under no delusions that I will live cancer free for the next 40 years. It is not a cliché when I say I am grateful for each day and fully live in the present moment.

I know all too well how suddenly a phone call can completely change the trajectory of your life. I prioritize the health I can control. I exercise the best I can without depleting myself. I listen to my body. I rest when I'm tired. I reach out to friends. I lean on family. When things aren't going the way I would like (energy, weight), I try to give myself grace. I tell myself it's okay, you are doing what you can. When the dishes look like the buildings of a metropolitan city, but I'm too tired to take them down, I tell myself it's okay to let them be. There is no need to wear myself out.

I'm learning how to prioritize my needs. Becoming a mom often corresponds to putting oneself last. I've learned this does not make me a good mom. I must care for myself and complete my tasks, so I am strong and healthy for those around me.

I'm better at being honest about how I'm doing. I don't hide as often. I'm still a rock, but I also allow my soft spots to be seen. I've learned my loved ones and friends appreciate my honesty and vulnerability. I'm getting better at letting them see that part of me, but sometimes I still hide.

The primary things I learned during this journey were that I need people around me. I need to ask for help. I need to give myself grace for the things I'm unable to do or am no longer good at doing. I need to accept all the feelings and thoughts even if I don't like them. I need to remember these times are seasons and they will eventually end.

. . .

On January 2, 2013, I began a new routine. I woke up at 4 AM, yes AM. I made coffee. While it was brewing, I got ready, then I sat down, read a little and wrote a little. At 5:00, I got out the computer and began to write. Following Anne Lamott's advice, I just wrote. I wrote for an hour. I let the words flow out of me.

*"Perhaps an hour a day will one day give me a completed book. Perhaps this discipline will turn into a fulfillment of my dreams. A book will surface one day. One day I'll revise and edit what I've written. Today I will just write. I have no goals or deadlines. I'm getting it out so I can do something with it later."*

I wrote those words in my journal on January 3, 2013. On May 9, 2022, Mother's Day, I finished the book I started on January 2, 2013. I worked diligently: one word, one line, one page at a time for 9 years. Since 2022, I have been editing, sharing and trying to find a path to put this book in the hands of anyone who might be blessed by it.

I'm grateful I didn't quit my journey. I'm grateful you have included me on your own.

# Acknowledgments

I am grateful for all my dear friends who read this book in the very beginning: Kari, Amy, Meg, and Heather. Thank you for taking the time to read my first draft and for giving me feedback. You helped me know I needed to reorganize it and guided me on what I should keep and what wasn't necessary. This final version is only possible because you were honest with me. You were the first people I was most vulnerable with and you honored that privilege.

I'm grateful for everyone who told me they can't wait to read the book. Your words filled me with hope and moved me to keep going.

I also appreciate the input and help from the experts: Rob Bell, Bob Goff, and Jane Friedman. Your wisdom guided my steps, directed me in the organization of my story, and showed me the steps I needed to take to finish this project.

I'm grateful to the authors that have helped me grow as a person and inspired me to tell my story by being brave enough to tell their own: Anne Lamott, Cheryl Strayed, Brené Brown, Glennon Doyle, Marc Brackett, Alicia Keys, Michelle Obama, Kate Bowler, Jedidiah Jenkins, Suleika Jaouad, and Clare Pooley. I read your books. Your words left a permanent mark on me and my life. I encourage others to seek out your books.

I'm grateful for my friend Carlie, who upon hearing about my second cancer diagnosis painted a painting inspired by my story called, *More Than Her Share* (Carlie Williams Art). It is her moving work of art that inspired the title for this book.

I'm grateful to Sarah for jumping at the chance to read my book upon meeting me. Her edits and input were honest and helpful. I appreciate your bravery in being brutally honest all the time. The journey through this was more beautiful with you. I will always be grateful and in awe of our relationship.

I'm grateful for both of my daughters. Hannah helped me market and promote myself and my book. She acted as my agent before I had one. She is also the final designer of the beautiful cover. Abigail created a drawing for each chapter. She listened as I read the book, and she let my words inspire a work of art. I'm so grateful she took the time to listen to me read my story. The edits we made refined the story to its most beautiful parts. You have both been consistent and amazing supporters as I lived this story and wrote it for others.

I'm grateful to my husband for supporting me through this long process. He always believed I would accomplish this. I'm also grateful for how he has been my rock and safe place through all my difficult journeys. I truly could not have completed this project without you.

# About the Author

Janelle LaRae is a teacher and emerging author. She teaches elementary school and inspires students to be the best versions of themselves. She has been writing for many years. She uses honesty and vulnerability in her writing to describe how she has overcome cancer, Multiple Sclerosis, and other difficulties of life.

She received a Bachelor's in Elementary Education from Northwest Nazarene University in 1999 and a Master's of Science in Science Education from Montana State University in 2017.

She understands how life rarely goes as planned and is adept at finding a way through those difficulties. She has lived in southwest Idaho with her husband since 1996. She enjoys spending time with her 2 amazing daughters. She does everything in her power to stay active. Exercise and health are priorities in her day and she won't miss an opportunity for some stand-up paddle boarding. Since 2007, her family has been vacationing in Newport, Oregon where she runs on the beach and surfs the waves as long as they aren't too big and the sharks stay clear.

www.ingramcontent.com/pod-product-compliance
Lightning Source LLC
Chambersburg PA
CBHW070906130626
46555CB00001B/27